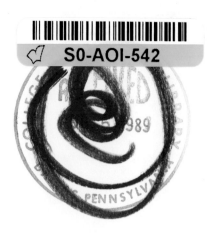

HUMANISTIC
HEALTH
CARE

health

administration

press

Edited by
Gerald P. Turner
and Joseph Mapa

⌐ T ¢ A

HUMANISTIC HEALTH CARE

Issues for Caregivers

HEALTH ADMINISTRATION PRESS
Ann Arbor, Michigan 1988

The editors are grateful to the authors and publishers for their contributions to this book. Because of the variety of sources, references were not
changed to a consistent style, but follow the citation style of the journal in
which they first appeared.

Library of Congress Cataloging-in-Publication Data

Humanistic health care: issues for caregivers/edited by Gerald P. Turner,
Joseph Mapa.
    p.   cm.
    Includes index.
    ISBN 0-910701-36-9
    1. Medical personnel and patient. 2. Helping behavior. 3. Humanistic
psychology. I. Turner, Gerald P., 1930– . II. Mapa, Joseph, 1950– .
    [DNLM: 1. Delivery of Health Care. 2. Ethics, Medical. 3. Helping Be-
havior. 4. Humanism. 5. Professional-Patient Relations. W 84.1 H9177]
R727.3.H86 1988
610.69'6—dc 19
DNLM/DLC   for Library of Congress   88-24580   CIP

Health Administration Press
A Division of the Foundation of the
   American College of Healthcare Executives
1021 East Huron Street
Ann Arbor, Michigan 48104-9990
(313) 764-1380

This book is dedicated to:

Clare, Robin, Marc, Daryl, Neil, Lisa, and Brian

Gerald P. Turner

My dearest parents, Kalman and Manja

Joseph Mapa

Table of Contents

Preface

"In the sufferer, let me see only the human being."

Maimonides

THE PURPOSE OF THIS BOOK is to focus attention on and sensitize the reader to the importance of providing health care in a humanistic way. The term "humanistic" refers to the supportive and compassionate behavior of the caregiver in providing care to the patient. It recognizes that illness is often a traumatic experience and that patients and their families are apprehensive and dependent. It also implies that medical science and humane care must go hand-in-hand in meeting the total needs of the patient.

By addressing key issues and perspectives, we hope that all health professionals become more reflective about the way they provide care to patients. This is particularly critical in today's health care field. The range and complexity of technological growth, medical progress, changing delivery systems, financial and competitive pressures, make it increasingly difficult to focus on the emotional and empathetic needs of patients.

The literature on humanism in health care is vast. Although Daniel Callahan has observed that "most of that writing has by now the quality of rhetorical placebos, strong on exhortation and moral uplift, but short on insight," there are some excellent contributions from the literature of various health disciplines that have added substantively to the concept and practice of humanistic health care. This book is a collection of articles selected from this literature; all of them have significant common elements and universal applications of value to all health professionals.

PART

I

Empathetic Care—
A Philosophical Framework

Introduction to Part I

IN 1927, FRANCIS PEABODY made one of the most useful and durable philosophical statements about humanistic care. "One of the essential qualities of the clinician is interest in humanity, for the secret of the care of the patient is in caring for the patient." Peabody's challenge is contemporary: to sustain humane values in the practice of health care. With this challenge as a background, we present "The Practice of Empathy as a Prerequisite for Informed Consent," by James E. Rosenberg and Bernard Towers, in which they analyze the vital role of empathy in the relationship between caregiver and patient.

Rosenberg and Towers suggest that the traditional medical model of patient care, which takes a purely biological approach to diagnosis and treatment, is insufficient in addressing the patient's total needs. Instead, this approach must be broadened to take account of the patient's psychological and social needs. The key to humanistic patient care, the authors conclude, is the caregivers' ability to empathize with others, their appreciation of the value of empathy in communication, and their effective use of empathy as part of the interpersonal process.

1

The Practice of Empathy as a Prerequisite for Informed Consent

James E. Rosenberg • Bernard Towers

INTRODUCTION

THE MEDICAL LITERATURE is replete with concern that the patient-physician relationship has deteriorated in recent years. The concern is nothing new. Peabody in 1927 called it the "most common criticism made at present" against the new generation of physicians ([32], p. 877). Indeed, younger physicians have long been characterized as wanting in sensitivity and interpersonal skills compared to their (idealized) elders ([14], p. 171). In general, the physician has not sought to understand the personal meaning of the patient's illness experience.

One consequence has been a lack of consensus between patient and physician as to what constitutes proper therapy. Prior to World War II, medical paternalism (or better, parentalism) clearly dominated the clinical decision-making process ([33], p. 243). There has since been increasing recognition of the patient's right to self-determination. As a result, contrasting models of patient autonomy and medical parentalism have been erected as opposing frameworks in which clinical decisions are to be made. Both models have their particular shortcomings, and both skirt the

Theoretical Medicine 7 (1986) 181–194. Copyright © 1986 by D. Reidel Publishing Company. Reprinted by permission.

Mr. Rosenberg's work on this article was partially supported by a 1985 Summer Fellowship from NIMH administered by the Department of Psychiatry and Biobehavioral Sciences at UCLA. We are also grateful to Mr. Russell Newstadt for his translations and transliterations from the Greek.

issue of consensus (literally a 'feeling together') by investing either the patient or the physician with clinical decision-making power over the other ([33], p. 247).

The patient seeks relief from illness, which constitutes a disruption in psychosocial functioning. The physician responds with a disease-or biologically-oriented approach to diagnosis and treatment [4, 12, 14, 15]. The chasm separating the needs of the patient and the ends of the physician often precludes the possibility of meaningful consensus between them. Furthermore, the physician's overriding desire to heal may lead to witting or unwitting manipulation of patient decisions so that they conform with the physician's judgments rather than with the patient's self-perceived needs.

THE TRADITIONAL BIOMEDICAL MODEL

The current defect in the patient-physician relationship seems to stem from a misapplication of the reductionist paradigm of nineteenth-century natural science to clinical medicine [3, 13, 14, 15]. The natural scientist has traditionally sought to suspend all feelings, attitudes, and other presumed sources of potential bias in the observation of external phenomena ([13], p. 50). Thus, in the traditional biomedical model, the physician does not attend to the patient *qua* person [3, 12, 14, 15], but rather, attempts to conceptually isolate both the disease process from the patient, and his or her personhood from the professional medical persona ([3], p. 11).

The patient perceives a deviation from normal biologic functioning—a disease process—only as it manifests itself as a disruption of personhood. He or she does not experience a hormone-imbalance or an electrolyte-imbalance or an immune-complex injury. Rather, the patient experiences perhaps some pain or discomfort, some weakness or lassitude leading to inability to work, or some other symptom that disrupts normal psychosocial functioning. This applies equally so to the medically sophisticated patient, including physicians who become patients. Everyone brings the dis-comfort or dis-ease (i.e. the illness experience) to the first consultation. However, the consulting physician, if educated solely in the traditional biomedical mode, is likely to be inherently more interested in things (such as laboratory data) than in the patient-as-person. The I-Thou of the personal encounter gives way to the I-It relation which Buber suggests has affected modern living in so many different areas [8].

Modern physicians thus do not, in general, validate the psychosocial as they do the biologic. In fact they tend to see the pursuit of such a comprehensive understanding of the patient as an intrusion into and as a defection from their role as scientist ([14], p. 170). The extraordinary successes enjoyed by biomedical science and technology in elucidating and treating many forms of disease has served to reinforcce what is currently regarded as the "correct" biomedical approach ([14], p. 170). This paradigm of medicine, despite its being one-sided and inadequate, has become virtually unshakable dogma [2, 14, 15]. Its very faults are currently underscored by opposing folk dogmas that emphasize personhood and eschew scientific method ([15], p. 543).

The biomedical model is in fact a supremely useful approach to disease as such. It must not be neglected in the more acceptable, more comprehensive paradigm of medicine we advocate, one that recognizes equally the biologic and the psychosocial, and their reciprocal influences upon each other [14, 15].

Illness is apprehended through the patient-physician relationship. At present, the ideal clinician is depicted as being warm towards and 'appreciative' of the patient's feelings and concerns, and yet detached and emotionally neutral [1, 7, 10]. In natural science, emotional neutrality is thought of being best achieved by mechanical devices ([13], p. 50). Fanciful predictions that someday a mechanical computer will represent the ultimate clinician emphasizes an unfortunate parallel between reductionist science and medicine. The patient-physician relationship must be instead reforged in such a way that misplaced concerns for *sympathetic objectivity* are replaced by the pursuit of an *empathic understanding* of the patient's personhood and how it has been impinged upon in illness. (For the distinction between sympathy and empathy see below.)

Blumgart ([7], p. 452) exemplifies well the parentalistic disease-oriented approach that must be superseded:

> . . . (The physician should use) the listening technic, which enables the patient to relate his experiences in terms of his own values and concerns. It frequently enables the physician to understand more clearly the meaning of the illness to the patient and help in an understanding of the patient as a person.

That sounds fairly innocuous. However, he also advocates that, in using this technique, the physician adopts a position of "compassionate detachment" to avoid what he fears as a "loss of objectivity and perspective . . ." ([7], p. 451). This is the attitude of the observer—the traditional natural scientist—who supposedly stands on a privileged platform outside of the phenomena to be studied.

Blumgart's notions of patient-physician interaction are clearly parentalistic. The physician does not relate to the patient as one person to another, but rather collects 'data' from the patient's behavioral expressions for analysis and response within the physician's own perspective. The physician is satisfied merely to observe the *signs* of the patient's illness, rather than to comprehend its experiential *content*. Cassell makes this point with reference to the affective element of the illness experience ([12], p. 643):

> Injuries to the integrity of the person may be expressed by sadness, anger, loneliness, depression, grief, unhappiness, melancholy, rage, withdrawal, or yearning. We acknowledge the person's right to have and express such feelings. But we often forget that the affect is merely the outward expression of the injury, not the injury itself.

The physician, then, does not seek to venture from his personal perspective into that of the patient. Instead, the physician formulates sympathetic judgments *about* the patient as a substitute for the sharing of experiences between them.

Bertman and Krant provide a segment of Siegfried Sassoon's poem "Does It Matter?" that sharply illustrates the impotence of such *sympathy* ([6], p. 640):

> Does it matter?—losing your leg? . . .
> For People will always be kind,
> And you need not show that you mind
> When the others come in after hunting
> To gobble their muffins and eggs.
> Does it matter?—losing your sight . . .
> There's such splendid work for the blind;
> And people will always be kind . . .

A 'sympathetic appreciation' of the patient's illness experience satisfies the physician more than it benefits the patient.

A MORE COMPREHENSIVE APPROACH

Truly effective medical practice requires that the physician interact with the patient on both an observer-to-subject basis and a person-to-person basis. The goal should be to achieve a comprehensive understanding (both cognitive and affective) of the patient's problems. This requires that the physician use both personhood and past experience to construct a state of mind that can mirror what the patient has communicated of himself or herself. The good clinician strives to apprehend the "illness as lived" ([3], p. 17) as a foundation for a truly scientific and comprehensive understanding of the patient's experience of both illness and recovery from illness.

Engel presents a 'biopsychosocial' model of medicine in which the biologic basis of disease and its manifestation in the patient as illness are given equal weight [14, 15]. It is an alternative scientific paradigm that utilizes general systems theory in place of classical reductionism. Engel's model furthermore emphasizes, within a more comprehensive framework, the reciprocal influence of personhood on biologic function and biologic function on personhood. Dysfunction in one can well lead to dysfunction in the other. In order to be an effective healer the physician must be able to understand both types of dysfunction.

EMPATHY AND SYMPATHY

The physician apprehends the personal meaning of the patient's illness experience only through *empathy*, the successful use of which leads to an *empathic understanding*. The notions of empathy and sympathy are frequently confused. They can be distinguished in both the *quality* and *object* of the experiential content. Both the empathizer and the sympathizer draw inferences and form judgments on the basis of the subject's combined verbal and nonverbal behavioral expressions. The sympathizer may experience cognitive and affective elements (experiential quality) that are either similar or dissimilar to those experienced by the subject of the sympathy. For instance, a patient (let us call her Mrs. Rorty) describes her horror at having learned of her husband's illicit affair. The sympathetic physician may react with similar horror, or perhaps with pity, dismay, etc. The object of the sympathizer's experience is the subject with whom one is sympathic, and not the object of the subject's experience. Mrs. Rorty's horror is or was directed towards her husband's infidelity. Her physician's sympathy is directed towards Mrs. Rorty, not towards her husband. However, with empathy, in contrast with sympathy, the experiential quality and object of the empathizer's reaction mirror those of the subject. The physician's empathic response to Mrs. Rorty's experience is a sharing of horror in respect of her experience of her husband's infidelity.

The sympathetic physician, in contradistinction to the empathic physician, is relatively uninvolved, and forms judgments on the basis of personal reactions to the 'data' supplied by the patient. No attempt is made to form judgments on the basis of a sharing of the patient's perspective of the illness experience.

The real differences between empathy and sympathy (which many modern dictionaries give as synonyms) are suggested by their origins in ancient Greek. The noun form *empátheia* occurs in Galen as *empátheia tēs sarkēs* ('affection of the flesh') [26]. Aristotle, Plutarch, and Alciphron use the adjectival form *empathēs* ('in a state of emotion') [26]. The particle *en* or *em* translates as 'inside', 'into', 'on', or 'within' [26], whereas the *syn* or *sym* of *sympátheia* translates as 'with', 'together', or 'along side' [28]. The word *patheia* means 'feeling', 'emotion', or 'affect' [27].

According to Violet Page [24], writing under the pseudonym of 'Vernon Lee' [25], the German *Einfühlung* ('feeling into') was derived from the verb *sich in etwas einfühlen* ('to feel oneself into something'). Its literary heritage spans at least as far back as German Romanticism [23]. *Einfühl-*

ung apparently was introduced in aesthetics by Rudolf Hermann Lotze and Friedrich Vischer [23], most notably in Lotze's *Mikrokosmus* [21].

Theodor Lipps in 1897 and Wilhelm Wundt in 1903 were the first to use *Einfühlung* in the psychologic literature [24]. Hunsdahl gives a detailed account of the usage of *Einfühlung* during 1900 to 1925, including its development in the works of Lipps [19]. Aesthetics, in Lipps' view, is a type of applied psychology in that it involves elucidation of the personal, subjective way in which one contemplates an aesthetic object ([19], p. 182): "Nothing can be the object of aesthetical consideration without being considered, i.e. perceived, intimately mastered, 'apperceived'" ([19], p. 183). Lipps discusses the essential role of *Einfühlung* in understanding the mental state or, for our purposes, the psychosocial make-up, of a fellow human being ([19], p. 184):

> Nobody doubts the fact that we cannot sensuously ascertain anything about a man whom we see, as the manifestations of his senses and his visible and audible expressions. But these sensuous manifestations are not the "man", they are not the strange personality with his psychological equipment, his ideas, his feelings, his will, etc. All the same, to us, the man is linked to these manifestations . . . This connection is created through Einfühlung.

This is a translation of an excerpt from *Ästhetik: Systematische Philosophie*, written in 1908 ([19], p. 181), as quoted by Lipps. It clearly suggests the importance of grounding one's understanding of another individual in experience. The psychologist Edward Titchener, a student of Wundt [18], translated *Einfühlung* into English as 'empathy' [22].

Interestingly, psychoanalysis, a field often derided by the biomedical establishment as unscientific, has debated for years as to whether the use of empathy is therapeutically sound or whether it is too vague and subjective, representing a breach of neutrality ([5], p. 111). Empathy is essential to Freud's approach to understand the patient [30]. The psychoanalyst listens to the analysand ". . . in a state of *evenly suspended attention* . . . to catch the drift of the patient's unconscious with his own unconscious" [17].

The technique used by one of us (BT) in somatopsychotherapy with patients suffering from organic disease makes use of this insight. The patient is encouraged to relax and enter into a "waking dream state" in which sensory experiences and conversations occur without preplanning or control. Everything that happens in the dream is recorded by the therapist. The patient draws on the roots of all his or her stored "wisdom of the body" [11] in order to understand more clearly a) the nature and origins of the im-balance(s) or dis-ease(s) that are troublesome, b) the benefits that can result from the various medical or surgical regimens that are proposed or are in process, and c) the ability of the body finally to recuperate and to restore itself to good function, if such an outcome is feasible. While the patient is describing the images and events of the waking dream the therapist acts merely to encourage (if necessary) further pursuit of the somatopsychic unknown, and then to discuss the possible meanings of the symbols if they are not (as they usually are) immediately clear to the patient.

In a one hour encounter of this kind, especially when a patient is under threat of coping with a potentially serious illness, a vast amount of understanding can be achieved by both patient and physician. It is based on the dialogue and dialectic of the I-Thou relationship, in which neither one asumes a dominant, controlling posture.

AN ELUCIDATION OF THE EMPATHIC PROCESS

Discussions of empathy in the medical literature tend to be simplistic and unclear, and they capture nothing of the processes involved. Buie offers a clear functional account of empathy [9], which has been adapted here for use in the context of clinical medicine.

Empathic understanding is the result of a complex inferential process ([9], p. 293). The patient presents the physician with a set of verbal and non-verbal behavioral 'cues'. At the unconscious, pre-conscious, and conscious levels, the physician compares these cues to his or her own cognitive and affective 'internal referents', that is, to elements of an internal repertoire of past experiences and knowledge ([9], p. 293). Those elements that are associated with the expression of the same cues by the physician are inferred to be alike or similar to the patient's currently operating internal referents. Usually only the results of the completed inferences, but not the process itself, are available to the physician's conscious awareness ([9], p. 294). If the physician chooses in turn to communicate that understanding back to the patient through behavioral cues, such an action is distinct from the empathic process itself ([9], p. 299), which aims primarily at comprehending or understanding ([35], p. 5). Other investigators, most notably Truax and Carkhuff [36], do not make this distinction.

Buie describes four types of internal referents ([9], p. 294). *Conceptual referents* represent the cognitive component of the empathic process, and are of two types, *specific* and *general*. Specific conceptual referents are elements of the physician's understanding of the patient's and his or her own psychosocial make-up. General conceptual referents are elements of psychosocial understanding derived from the "creative symbolism of myth, art, and religion" ([9], p. 294).

The affective component of empathic understanding is based upon the other three referent types. The physician's various sorts of remembrances constitute *self-experience referents* ([9], p. 295). They have both cognitive and affective content, but their emotional intensities are markedly attenuated compared to the original experiences.

Patients frequently communicate behavioral cues for which the physician cannot readily find either homologous or analogous referents. The physician may face, for example, a cultural or socio-economic barrier to empathic understanding because the patient's experience as described is unlike anything that the physician has ever experienced [16]. The physician should then employ *imaginative imitation referents* whereby one constructs, from the raw data of personal life history, impressions of new experiences that are inferred to be in agreement with the patient's cues ([9], p. 296). Obviously, the physician is limited here by personal creativity and resourcefulness.

Communication of strong emotion by the patient may trigger a similar strong affective response in the physician—one which may greatly exceed the emotional intensity of a self-experience referent ([9], p. 297). Inferences drawn from these *resonance referents* do not *per se* provide the physician with much insight into the patient's illness experience. However, they are essential to the task of reconstructing the experiential context within which the patient's strong emotion has arisen. Inferences via conceptual, self-experienced and imaginative imitation referents are guided in part by the consistency of the experience inferred with the strong emotion that accompanies it.

Even intense resonance will not be disabling for the physician who appreciates its role in a larger cognitive understanding of the patient. The physician who is overwhelmed by a patient's affect is not being truly empathic, and the term 'loss of emotional separateness' is merely a metaphor for being overwhelmed. On the other hand, maintaining an emotional distance from one's patient for fear of resonance necessarily removes the physician from the entire empathic process ([9], p. 297).

It is important to recognize that, since the empathic process is by nature inferential, there are limitations to how fully and accurately the patient's illness experiences can be comprehended ([9], p. 301). Primary sources of error are the completeness and genuineness of the behavioral cues, the uncertainty inherent in drawing inferences, and the physician's store and use of personal referents, including the "capacity for and comfort with resonating with varieties of strong emotions" ([9], p. 303).

In view of these limitations, the physician must take care to verify empathic impressions. This should include comparing such impressions against one's general scientific knowledge of psychosocial phenomena for consistency, and sharing one's conclusions with the patient. The patient's reactions to these impressions also will likely be corroborative or invalidating ([9], p. 304).

Another danger of "empathic understanding" is that to which all psychotherapists are subject, and of which some patients are understandably afraid. That is that the therapist will come to understand the patient more clearly than the patient understands himself/herself. If knowledge is power then empathic physicians could turn out to be more manipulative and parentalistic than ignorant and uncaring ones. But any good therapist knows that he or she cannot or should not try to impose an interpretation on a patient, but instead must wait for realisation to spring from within. What is being sought in therapy is that which is *true*. Truth is unique to every person's experience, and can only be known ultimately by the individual.

The physician does not need empathy, or any other special faculty, simply to *understand* what a patient means. The callous, uninterested physician understands as well as anyone the patient's statement, "My leg has throbbed for seven days." Empathic *comprehension* is more than that. It allows the physician to advance from an understanding of sentence meaning to a comprehension of what it would be like to have a throbbing leg for seven days. The sympathetic physician understands and feels with the patient's description; the empathic physician truly understands the experience so described.

A succinct and accurate definition of empathy is: "The power of projecting one's personality into (and so fully comprehending) the object of contemplation" [31]. The notion of projection here is of course purely metaphoric, just as is the psychologic notion of merging, which has similarly been used to explain empathy ([9], p. 285).

We may be led to suppose that a genuine understanding of *any* object, whether it be Van Gogh's "The Sower", hepatocyte ultrastructure, or a patient's personhood, depends on the use of empathy. Empathic understanding does apply to aesthetic objects, to the psychosocial make-up of fellow human beings, and perhaps to some other kinds of entities as well. It applies to an object X wherever a substitution of "What is it to be X?" with "What would it be like to be X?" leads to greater comprehension of X.

Other objects, such as those of natural science, are normally understood through application of the contemplator's conceptual scheme and perhaps some derivative thereof. The natural scientist approaches a group of phenomena by applying to it a theory, constructed within his or her conceptual scheme. Neither the logical consequences of that theory nor the experiments that it encompasses involve the imaginative construction of experience of empathic understanding (except sometimes in the research setting). Frameworks for making sense of these sorts of natural phenomena, such as scientific theories, would not be publicly useful if they involved empathy, the fruits of which are relative to the individual empathizer.

Empathic understanding of an aesthetic object must furthermore be distinguished from empathic understanding of another person. Both involve an imaginative construction of experience in the empathizer based upon some inferences drawn about the object or subject of empathy. Empathy towards an object gives that object significance by imbuing it with a personal meaning for the empathizer, who experiences the object by comprehending what the experience would be if one were in fact that object. This is the notion of becoming 'lost' in a painting, a symphony, etc. By contrast, empathizing with another person does not involve giving the described experience a new personal meaning of one's own, but rather, it involves "mirroring" the meaning of the experience for the subject in one's own mind with the least possible adulteration. The empathizer 'creates' experience in a non-human object, but strives to uncover it in another person.

IMPLICATIONS FOR INFORMED CONSENT

Patients have complained for 2,000 years that physicians do not attempt to comprehend the personal meaning of the illness for the patient ([2], p. 437). It is surely time to adopt a new, more comprehensive paradigm of medicine that includes an empathic psychosocial understanding of the patient's illness experience. This new framework of patient care has important implications for informed consent in medicine.

Kimball aptly states the notion of informed consent as it should ideally obtain in the patient-physician relationship ([20], p. 871):

> . . . informed consent should represent not just the requisite signature of the patient on a piece of paper, but rather the mutual agreement of patient and physician to follow a course of action in terms of an illness that makes not only appropriate medical sense in terms of the biological considerations, but social and psychological sense in terms of the intrinsic responsibilities, goals, and other values of the individual.

As stated earlier, within the traditional biomedical paradigm of medicine, consensus between patient and physician is not achieved because they enter the relationship with different agendas, namely, psychosocial for the patient and biologic for the physician [4, 12, 14, 15]. Models of clinical decision-making give priority to one agenda over the other, or at best advocate a compromise between them. The goals of the patient and the physician ought instead to be coincident. Thus, a comprehensive 'biopsychosocial' approach to patient care does not lead to a restructuring of the physician's disease treatment plan to suit the patient's psychosocial needs. Instead it leads to an integrated treatment plan that aims at healing both body and personhood. Compromises are made in therapy that maximize the return to proper functioning of the whole patient.

When conscientiously pursued, this approach is inconsistent with physician manipulation of patient decisions. Medicine is guided above all else by the principle of beneficence, namely, to help the patient ([33], p. 244). Once the physician apprehends the impact of the illness on the patient's personhood, and the patient understands the physician's concerns over the biologic problems, the course of 'biopsychosocial' therapy that best suits the patient's needs becomes clear to both. Any other plan of treatment would not as adequately serve the patient's best interests, and would therefore not be the most helpful. In fact, the physician's ignorance of or indifference to a patient's illness experience predisposes the patient to unnecessary or increased suffering ([12], p. 641), which violates the basic medical-ethical principle "Do no harm."

Physicians tend to manipulate or coerce their patients because they work within a biomedical paradigm of medicine that recognizes only cessation or amelioration of disease (a biologic entity) as a treatment goal. Likewise, philosophic models for clinical decision-making, most notably those of patient autonomy and medical paternalism (parentalism), are formulated within this same defective framework. The patient autonomy model does not, for example, recognize that the impact of serious acute illness compromises the patient's judgment as to what might be the best form of treatment [33, 34]. The parentalistic physician views the patient as little more than the carrier of disease ([33], p. 245).

Moral philosophers of medicine apply to the patient-physician relationship rules and conditions that need to be drastically revised, as described above. The term 'patient autonomy' is simply a label for personhood couched in the idiom of biomedical ethics. Thomasma writes that "Autonomy ought not be taken as a starting point or a right in medicine. Rather it should be seen as the goal of treatment" ([34], p. 4). This is certainly correct. It is equivalent to stating that the physician must not assume intact personhood initially in the patient, but rather must help the patient achieve it through the relief of illness.

We are also told that the patient's overriding desire for relief from illness prompts him or her to tolerate "cure at the expense of normal freedom and routine" ([33], p. 245), that is, at the expense of normal psychosocial needs. However, the patient ultimately defines the illness experience as an impingement or limitation upon personhood—a deviation from normal psychosocial functioning [4, 12, 14, 15]. Thus, in the traditional patient-physician relationship, the patient accepts further compromises in that for which he or she seeks therapy. Patient and physician alike tend incorrectly to assume that restoration of normal biologic function, even at the expense of the patient *qua* person, will indirectly result in a return to normal psychosocial function as well. The term 'patient' here seems to refer to the acutely ill person who tolerates stress on personhood for a relatively brief time interval. The chronic patient, on the other hand, is intimately involved in clinical decisions, so that therapy for disease ought to complement rather than to compromise his or her psychosocial needs ([29], p. 542). In the 'biopsychosocial' paradigm, the patient and the physician would not be placed in such contrary positions.

Genuine consensus or true "informed consent" will be realized only if this more comprehensive approach to patient care supplants the traditional biomedical model. Otherwise, moral, legal, and other artificial constraints will continue to be applied in vain to a patient-physician relationship which is fundamentally flawed. The key to understanding and appropriate action is the proper use of empathy. This is a skill with a cognitive purpose. It should form an integral part of all clinical teaching and practice.

REFERENCES

1. Aring, C. D.: 1958, 'Sympathy and Empathy', *Journal of the American Medical Association 167*, 448–452.
2. Altschule, M. D.: 1984, 'The Doctor-Patient Relationship Through the Ages', *Alabama Journal of Medical Sciences 21*, 435–439.
3. Baron, R. J.: 1981, 'Bridging Clinical Distance: An Empathic Rediscovery of the Known', *Journal of Medicine and Philosophy 6*, 5–23.
4. Barondess, J. A.: 1983, 'The Clinical Transaction: Themes and Descants', *Perspectives in Biology and Medicine 27*, 25–38.
5. Berger, D. M.: 1984, 'On the way to Empathic Understanding', *American Journal of Psychotherapy 38*, 111–120.
6. Bertman, S., Krant, M. J.: 1977, 'To Know of Suffering and the Teaching of Empathy', *Social Science and Medicine 11*, 639–644.
7. Blumgart, H. L.: 1964, 'Caring for the Patient', *New England Journal of Medicine 270*, 449–456.
8. Buber, M.: 1958, *I-Thou* (2nd Ed., trans. by Ronald Gregor Smith), Charles Scribner.
9. Buie, D. H.: 1981, 'Empathy: Its Nature and Limitations', *Journal of the American Psychoanalytic Association 29*, 281–307.
10. Bulger, R. J.: 1982, 'Service as a Professional Sacrament', *Archives of Internal Medicine 142*, 2289–2292.
11. Cannon, W. B.: 1932, 1963, *The Wisdom of the Body*, Norton, Inc. N.Y.
12. Cassell, E. J.: 1982, 'The Nature of Suffering and the Goals of Medicine', *New England Journal of Medicine 306*, 639–645.
13. Dorpat, T. L.: 1977, 'On Neutrality', *International Journal of Psychoanalytic Psychotherapy 6*, 39–64.
14. Engel, G. L.: 1978, 'The Biopsychosocial Model and the Education of Health Professionals', *Annals New York Academy of Sciences 310*, 169–181.
15. Engel, G. L.: 1980, 'The Clinical Application of the Biopsychosocial Model', *American Journal of Psychiatry 137*, 535–544.
16. Fabrega, H.: 1975, 'The Need for an Ethnomedical Science, *Science 189*, 969–975.
17. Freud, S.: 1923, *The Standard Edition of the Complete Psychological Works of Sigmund Freud*, 18, Hogarth Press, London, p. 239.

18. Harris, W. H., Levey, J. S. (eds.): 1975, *The New Columbia Encyclopedia*, Columbia University Press, New York, p. 2754.
19. Hunsdahl, J. B.: 1967, 'Concerning Einfühlung (Empathy): A Concept Analysis of Its Origin and Early Development', *Journal of the History of the Behavioral Sciences 3*, 180–191.
20. Kimball, C. P.: 1977, 'The Ethics of Personal Medicine', *Medical Clinics of North America 61*, 866–877.
21. Lee, V., Anstruther-Thomson, C.: 1912, *Beauty & Ugliness and Other Studies in Psychological Aesthetics*, John Lane, London, p. 17.
22. Ibid., p. 20.
23. Ibid., p. 46.
24. Lee, V.: 1913, *The Beautiful: An Introduction to Psychological Aesthetics*, Cambridge University Press, London, p. 66.
25. Legg, L. G. W.: 1949, *The Dictionary of National Biography*, 1931–1940 (Supplement), Oxford University Press, London, p. 668.
26. Liddell, H. G., Scott, R.: 1978, *A Greek-English Lexicon*, Revised by Stuart Jones, Ninth Edition, Clarendon Press, Oxford, p. 542.
27. Ibid., p. 1285.
28. Ibid., p. 1680.
29. Lidz, C. W., et al.: 1983, 'Barriers to Informed Consent', *Annals of Internal Medicine 99*, 539–543.
30. Olinick, S. L.: 1977, 'Empathy', in B. B. Wolman (ed.), *International Encyclopedia of Psychiatry, Psychology, Psychoanalysis & Neurology 4*, Aesculapius Publishers, New York, 314.
31. Sykes, J. B. (ed.): 1976, *The Concise Oxford Dictionary of Current English*, Sixth Edition, Clarendon Press Oxford, 338.
32. Peabody, F. W.: 1927, 'The Care of the Patient', *Journal of the American Medical Association 88*, 877–882.
33. Thomasma, D. C.: 1983, 'Beyond Medical Paternalism and Patient Autonomy: A Model of Physician Conscience for the Physician-Patient Relationship', *Annals of Internal Medicine 98*, 243–248.
34. Thomasma, D. C.: 1983, 'Limitations of the Autonomy Model for the Doctor-Patient Relationship', *The Pharos 46*, 2–5.
35. Towers, B.: 1982, 'On the Practice of Teilhardian Principles: The Role of Empathy in Transdisciplinary Studies', *Teilhard Revue and Journal of Creative Evolution 17*, 3–31.
36. Truax, C. B., Carkhuff, R. R.: 1967, *Toward Effective Counseling and Psychotherapy: Training and Practice*, Aldine Publishing Company, Chicago, p. 46.

PART

II

The Patient's Perspective

Introduction to Part II

THE FOCUS OF HUMANISTIC CARE is meeting the psychological and social needs of patients. It is therefore essential that health professionals understand the nature and psychological impact of illness and disability. The readings in this section provide this insight and touch upon many different aspects of how patients experience illness.

"Psychological Aspects of Disease," by Z. J. Lipowski, discusses the key concepts of the psychology of illness. Lipowski suggests that, to understand the varied reactions to illness such as fear and anxiety, the caregiver must take into account the patient's personality, previous experience, and life situation.

Within this general framework, Eric Cassell's article, "The Nature of Suffering and the Goals of Medicine," examines the nature and causes of suffering and gives the reader an appreciation for its complexity. Drawing upon his own experience as a clinician, Cassell explains that suffering is ultimately a personal matter which includes physical pain but is by no means limited to it. Suffering is affected by many factors including the caregiver's relationship to the patient, which can become a source of suffering in itself.

The experience of hospitalization adds another dimension to the experience of being ill, according to Daisy Tagliacozzo and Hans Mauksch in "The Patient's View of the Patient's Role." The authors analyze the effect of institutional dynamics on patients' attitudes and reactions. The discussion is based on a major study which examined the relationships among caregivers and between caregivers and patients in terms of role expectations, staff interactions, and authority lines.

2

Psychosocial Aspects of Disease

Z. J. Lipowski

THERE IS CURRENTLY MUCH DISCUSSION and controversy about the place of behavioral sciences in the teaching and practice of medicine (1, 2). It is generally acknowledged that the psychological and social aspects of every patient's illness need to be evaluated and should influence the total medical management. Terms such as "comprehensive medicine" and "psychosomatic medicine" have been coined and various postulates and slogans formulated in an attempt to promote the approach to the patient as a person, a psychobiological unit dependent on and interacting with a given social environment. Despite much proselytyzing, however, this holistic approach does not seem to have made much headway. It appears to be preached rather than practiced. Psychosomatic medicine has bogged down due to its obsessive preoccupation with hypothesized psychogenicity of a few disorders misnamed "psychosomatic." Although the role of psychosocial stress as a causal factor in human diseases remains an important area of investigation, the experience and behavior of persons already suffering from a physical illness have aroused relatively little scientific interest. Yet it is this very area of medicine to which behavioral scientists may contribute practically useful observations, hypotheses, and guidelines for action. The development of psychiatric consultation services in the general hospitals (3–5) during the last 2 decades has given some students of human behavior an opportunity to study reactions to somatic disease, hospitalization, to diagnostic and therapeutic procedures, and so forth. We have had to try to understand how the patient

Reprinted from *Annals of Internal Medicine* 71, no. 6 (December 1969): 1197–1206, with permission, The American College of Physicians.

experiences his illness regardless of its cause, how he copes or fails to cope with it, how the family interaction is affected by and in turn affects the sick member, how the doctor-patient relationship evolves and gives rise to conflicts, and a host of other pertinent issues. A conceptualization is needed of this whole area, which is as equally relevant to medical practice as it is to the study of human behavior.

The subjective experience and the related observable behavior—that is, communications and actions—of the physically ill and disabled are emphasized. Viewed from a purely biological angle, disease is an abstract concept devoid of psychological and social connotation. A broader concept of disease is implied in a definition in a recently published medical dictionary (6): It is the "sum total of the reactions, physical and mental, made by a person to a noxious agent entering his body from without or arising within. . . ." In this definition disease is viewed as a state having no separate existence from a patient, a person. And a person is not only a biological organism, but encompasses the realm of feeling and of symbolic activities in thought and language. Furthermore, he is a member of a social group with which he interacts. A concept of disease is incomplete unless it takes cognizance of these facts. How a person experiences the pathological process, what it means to him, and how this meaning influences his behavior and interaction with others are all integral components of disease viewed as a *total human response*.

In this discussion experience and behavior of the sick person are the primary data. What an individual experiences is directly known only to him, and we may learn about it by obtaining his introspective reports. Behavior, both verbal and nonverbal, can be perceived and described by an outside observer who can make inferences about unobservable psychic processes. Any person will experience and respond to a given episode of somatic disease or injury in a unique manner determined by many variables. No single set of generalizations can account for all the individual nuances of experience and behavior of a sick person. Yet generalizations are necessary and practically useful as a framework for the clinical study of the individual case. One must make a clear distinction between *description* of relevant psychosocial phenomena and *generalizations* that we make about them. The latter include explanatory hypotheses about determinants of observed psychological processes. To explain why a person responds psychologically to a given disease process or injury one must consider the following four classes of variables:

1. The patient's personality and relevant aspects of his life history.

2. The patient's current social and economic situation.

3. Characteristics of the patient's non-human environment.

4. The nature and characteristics of the pathological process, injury,

or physical disability, or all of these, as they are *perceived and evaluated by the patient.*

The resulting psychological response includes three dimensions: *the intrapsychic* (experiential), the *behavioral,* and the *social* (interpersonal). These factors refer to what the patient perceives, feels, and thinks; to his actions and communications; and to his interactions with others, especially his family and the medical professionals.

THE MEANING OF ILLNESS

The key unifying psychological concept in this discussion is that of *meaning.* It refers to the personal, subjective significance of the total information received by the patient which is related to his illness. In other words, this concept includes evaluations and beliefs that the patient evolves regarding his illness and its likely consequences for him and those close to him. The process of evaluation resulting in meaning begins with the first perception of a pathological process or injury and continues unabated throughout the course of illness and its sequelae. It is a cognitive process but not necessarily rational nor conscious. The meaning is the core of the person's psychological response to his disease. It is of crucial importance for his emotional and behavioral response. The meaning to the patient of his symptoms, lesion, diagnostic label, loss of function, doctor's statements, and so forth, is determined by multiple factors, internal and external. Any attempt to understand why the patient feels and acts in a particular manner must include an inquiry into his subjective interpretation of what is happening to him—into his personal meaning of events related to his illness. It is useful to distinguish four broad categories of subjective meaning of symptoms, disability, and so on, for the patient. They are: *threat, loss, gain* (relief), and *insignificance.*

Threat

Threat implies anticipation of a personally dangerous event whose occurrence would cause suffering, physical or mental. Such anticipation may be brought about by perception of any bodily change if this is interpreted as signifying harm. Such interpretation is in turn influenced by specific susceptibility conditioned by previous life experience. Thus, some individuals will react with alarm to harmless palpitations or any somatic perception which is new to them. Anticipation of danger, whether realistic or not, is usually accompanied by anxiety of some degree of intensity. Anxiety has physiological concomitants, such as tachycardia or hyperventilation, which may lead to symptoms. The latter are often interpreted by the patient as precursors of an ominous event, such as a heart attack, and thus threat is increased and anxiety intensified—a good example of a positive feedback or vicious cycle. Anxiety in turn tends to set off cognitive and behavioral responses aimed at avoidance, minimization, or warding of the anticipated danger and thus elimination of the unpleasant experience of anxiety itself. The strategies used by individuals to reduce anxiety are numerous and range through unconsciously operating defense mechanisms, such as denial of danger, to the intake of sedatives or alcohol, to compulsive overwork, sexual activity, and so on.

Loss

In this context loss refers not just to body parts and functions actually lost but also to deprivations of personally significant needs and values. The latter are related chiefly to self-esteem, security, and satisfaction. Any disease may involve partial or total deprivation of sources of pleasure and self-esteem derived from eating; from physical, sexual, or intellectual activities; esthetic qualities of the body, and so forth. Furthermore, loss of some of these functions or qualities may lead to disturbed interpersonal relationships resulting in further actual or feared losses. The emotional response to real or anticipated loss, whether concrete or symbolic, takes the form of a grief reaction. The latter may at times assume a psychopathological form, such as a depressive syndrome, self-destructive behavior, hostility, paranoid reaction, or even elation.

Gain

The concept of gain refers to a subjective meaning of disease which results in relief of a sense of guilt, if disease means deserved punishment; satisfaction of dependent needs overt or unconscious; ability to control others by using one's illness to arouse their guilt and thus ensure compliance with one's wishes; avoidance of social stresses; and abatement of inner conflicts. Thus, conflicts and anxiety related to sexual activity, competitive striving, and social responsibilities may be temporarily or permanently abated as a result of disease or injury. For example, a young person struggling against sexual impulses may be relieved when development of epilepsy allows him to rationalize avoidance of contacts with the opposite sex. That any meaning of illness may be partly or totally outside the patient's awareness, and his *overt* attitude may be at variance with the unconscious one must be stressed. A person may deplore in good faith the fact that he is ill, and yet his behavior may suggest relief rather than loss. On the whole, when subjective gains derived from illness, disability, and so forth, outweigh the losses the patient is likely to cling to his sickness and develop an emotional disturbance when recovery occurs. This sequel has been observed, for example, when cardiac surgery for chronic valvular disease resulted in physiological improvement but psychological disorder. Whenever an illness has lasted for a long time there is a possibility that the patient may have derived from it gains that could not be removed with impunity. A thorough psychological evaluation before radical remedial intervention in such cases is mandatory.

Insignificance

Insignificance means relative lack of personal importance attached to one's symptoms or illness. This may be the result of ignorance or indifference. Early symptoms of a neoplasm, for example, may be disregarded by the patient if they do not signify a threat to him.

DETERMINANTS OF PSYCHOLOGICAL REACTION

Personality and Life History

The patient's personality type influences what meaning the given illness has for him (7). In general, physical disease constitutes psychological stress that tends to evoke the patient's characteristic ways of dealing with stresses of life in general. Such habitual coping techniques are a major aspect of personality style. The latter tends to come out more clearly under stress. Thus, an obsessional individual who habitually tries to explain and order events as a way of mastering them will tend to apply this strategy even more pointedly when he becomes physically ill. He must know what is going on and why and insists on detailed explanations and instructions so as to maintain a measure of security. He cannot tolerate uncertainty about his diagnosis, prognosis, reasons for treatment, and so on. It is helpful to offer such a patient what he seeks in order to have his cooperation and trust.

An hysterical individual, volatile and exaggerating, tends to become more so when ill. This may lead to misdiagnosis of "hysteria" in a person, usually a woman, who presents her symptoms in a flamboyant, attention-seeking manner. A suspicious, mistrustful, or frankly paranoid person is likely to show these traits in bold relief during physical illness. He is liable to blame others for his illness, or its course, or both. If something goes wrong, it is the doctor whom he is likely to accuse of incompetence or ill will. Such patients respond best to a scrupulously open, honest approach and avoidance of vagueness and evasion.

A person's life history—his past experience in general and with illness in particular—influences reaction to disease. Childhood experiences with the latter and the response to it by the significant adults may establish an enduring tendency to react to physical illness with fear, shame, guilt, or willing acceptance.

Current Social Situation

The quality of the patient's interpersonal relationships at the time of onset of illness and during it tends to have a profound effect on his experiencing illness and coping with it. When disease occurs in a setting of serious interpersonal conflict or of loss of a loved person, its impact tends to be greater, its course more stormy, and its recovery protracted. The response of the family and other meaningful people to the patient's illness or disability, to his communications of distress, and to his inability to perform the usual social roles may spell the difference between optimal recovery or psychological invalidism.

Non-Human Environment

The physical milieu in which the sick person lives is an important, although neglected subject. The esthetic quality of his surroundings influences the patient's mood and thus his ability to cope with illness. Factors such as the quantity and quality of the sensory input in hospitals, for example, in intensive care units—may lead to or increase cognitive disorganization (8).

The Pathological Process

The nature, site, and extent of the lesion; duration and rate of progression of pathology; and the kind, degree, and reversibility of the loss of function are biological variables that attain psychological significance only if they give rise to perceptions, thoughts, and feelings. The meaning for the patient of any of these variables depends in part on his specific susceptibility, which may be formulated as a general law: *The greater the value and psychodynamic significance the body part or function affected by disease has for the patient, the more intense the psychological reaction is likely to be.*

A given organ or biological function has especial subjective significance for its possessor when it: [1] constitutes a source of pleasure, pride, or self esteem; [2] helps him maintain satisfying human relationships; [3] reduces his intrapsychic conflicts; and [4] enhances his sense of personal identity and stability of the body image and of desirable social roles. Any disease or injury that jeopardizes or destroys these personal values will have far-reaching psychological consequences. Commonly seen clinical examples follow.

Individuals who set a high value on their physical prowess and activity are liable to break down psychologically in response to even minor injury or illness. Little (9) calls such a person "athletic personality." In a study of male acute neurotics he found that in 72.5% of "athletic" subjects a neurotic syndrome, mostly anxiety or depression, followed an injury or physical illness almost immediately. The physical trauma was usually relatively mild, and it appeared that specific psychological vulnerability was the crucial factor. These patients showed a good premorbid adjustment, but once the neurosis had set in many of them became chronically disabled. Persons who value their physical appearance highly are prone to develop serious psychopathological reactions to mutilation and deformity. A middle-aged female patient of mine illustrates this. She developed blepharitis that was slow to respond to treatment. She became increasingly more anxious and agitated and finally manifested a depressive psychosis with suicidal trends. Since childhood this patient had been complimented on the beauty of her eyes and came to regard them as her greatest asset, an esthetic value that attracted people to her. When disease marred the appearance of her eyelids she broke down despite reassurance that her condition was curable.

Impairment of intellectual functions by cerebral disease, reversible or not, readily disrupts the adjustment of an obsessional individual for whom intellectual activity is the mainspring of pride and security. A man whose source of self-esteem is sexual performance will react intensely to impotence due to spinal injury or diabetes, for example. Hysterectomy or hormonally induced masculinization in a woman may revive latent conflicts over sexual role and identity and lead to psychopathology. Persons whose normal adaptive patterns involve stress on cleanliness and orderliness tend to develop agitated depression after construction of a colostomy. Such patients have expressed their feelings in terms such as "I have been transformed into an animal" (10). Many male colostomy patients reported feelings of having become feminized, weak, and fragile (11).

There are many such examples of the crucial role of an individual's specific vulnerability as a determinant of his psychological response to somatic symptoms, disease, and disability. Different organs and functions may have different value and psychological significance for different perons. These values have often little to do with biological factors related to survival. Injury to the nose or amputation of a breast may have greater psychological impact on a person than, for example, hepatic disease directly threatening his life. The unique life history of the person, his conscious and unconscious conflicts and fears, as well as sociocultural factors determine which particular organ or function is invested with special meaning and importance. The unconscious aspects of such meaning should be stressed. Their influence is outside the person's awareness and thus unavailable for his critical scrutiny. The unconscious meaning is liable to be distorted by his desires, conflicts, and fantasies. Thus, any aspect of disease may arouse unconscious wishes for passive dependence on others, for suffering, or death. The more such impulses are unacceptable to the patient's conscience, the more intense the inner conflict and its emotional concomitants: anxiety, depression, sense of guilt. Such conflicts and emotions influence the patient's conscious attitude towards his illness as well as his behavior. In general, *the more the meaning of disease and its symptoms is influenced by unconscious factors, the more irrational, idiosyncratic, and unpredictable is the patient's overt response likely to be.* Severe anxiety, depression, massive denial of illness, disregard of medical advice, and delay or excessive haste in seeking help are familiar examples of illness behavior influenced by irrational factors.

In summary, even though objective aspects of disease are all-important, the patient's subjective appraisal of them, conscious and unconscious, exerts a crucial influence on his illness behavior.

The relative importance of the variables touched upon here will vary from case to case and must be evaluated in each patient.

Psychological Response to Disease

We may turn now to the description of the psychological response proper, in both its subjective and observable aspects. For the sake of clarity, the psychological reaction to disease will be described to include three aspects: the *intrapsychic* (experiential), which refers to what the patient perceives, feels, and thinks—that is, to perceptual, emotional, and cognitive components of his total subjective response to his illness; the *behavioral* aspect—that is, how the patient communicates with others and acts regarding his illness; and the *social* aspect, which concerns his interactions with others.

The Intrapsychic (Experiential) Aspect

Disease and the suffering that it usually causes are universal components of human existence. An illness is primarily a personal experience affecting a person's view of his body and world, values and goals. To describe these changes one needs to pay attention to the patient's communications and supplement them with empathy. The latter is made easier by our personal experiences of illness. Novelists (12, 13), writers of autobiographical accounts of illness (14), and some existentialist thinkers

(15) help us appreciate the human experience aspect of various diseases. Every episode of illness is a unique experience, but certain common trends may be found. Thus, one often notes a narrowing of interests, egocentricity, increased attention to bodily perceptions and functions, irritability, and increased dependence on others (16). The diseased part clamors for attention and is sometimes experienced as alien. The pathological process itself may be viewed as an invasion by malevolent outside forces. Proust expressed it well: ". . . the body imprisons the spirit in a fortress; soon the fortress is assailed at all points and in the end the spirit has to surrender" (17).

A more scientific but also atomistic descriptive approach views the experience of illness in terms of its *perceptual, cognitive,* and *emotional* components. The meaning of illness discussed previously is primarily the outcome of cognitive processes (thinking), although perception and emotion can be detached from it only artificially. An almost universal cognitive attempt at gaining some degree of mastery over the disease is to try to explain its origin and mechanisms. The commonest modes of explanation are to blame oneself or another person or nonhuman agent for having brought on the disease (18). Such beliefs range from scientifically sound ones to the most irrational and even delusional (19). In any case, they tend to satisfy the patient's need to understand what is happening to him and thus reduce ambiguity, uncertainty, and anxiety.

Perceptual aspects are of prime importance for the understanding of symptoms. Psychological response to every disease begins with the *perception of a bodily change.* On occasion such response is initiated by *a doctor's statement* that a pathological process exists, even though the patient has no related somatic perception (for example, in hypertension). The quality, intensity, and spatiotemporal features of the perception are important. A sudden attack of vertigo or severe chest pain will force an appraisal of what is happening with greater urgency than a painless lump or transient bowel dysfunction. Characteristics of the perceiving individual play a part. It has been proposed that people habitually augment or reduce what they perceive. This personality trait has been called perceptual reactance (20). An augmenter will tend to overreact to somatic perception (for example, pain), complain, and seek help more readily. A reducer finds it easier to disregard or deny the likely significance of his symptoms since they bother him less.

How bodily perceptions are evaluated by the patient—a cognitive aspect—is influenced by his personality, knowledge, cultural background, current emotional state, and other factors. This area has been studied for two practical reasons: to find out why some persons delay seeking medical consultation for serious disease such as cancer; and why others rush to a doctor with any somatic complaint. Gold (21) found that of 100 patients with cancer of the breast 64 came to the doctor so late that only palliative treatment was possible. This tendency is usually explained as indicative of the excessive use of the psychological defense mechanism of *denial* of signals of danger—a personality trait. Depression and severe anxiety related to the symptoms or to other factors may also lead to delay in seeking help.

Sociocultural factors influence appraisal of symptoms and disease. Attitudes in the patient's social milieu toward certain conditions as well as prevalent beliefs about cause, prognosis, and efficacy of treatment tend to influence the response to illness. Diseases such as syphilis, epilepsy, or leprosy usually carry the connotation of social stigma. Cancer is dreaded at all levels of American society, and about 60% of adults queried in a poll stated that they would conceal from others that they had cancer (22).

The *emotional* component of the subjective response to illness may range from the "normal" that is, realistic, anxiety or grief to the whole spectrum of emotions pathological by virtue of their intensity and inappropriateness to the actual danger or less. When discussing emotions, one must consider that the patient may or may not be aware of them as well as be willing and able to communicate them. At one end of the spectrum one may encounter apparent lack of appropriate emotional response to disease—apathy, indifference, or even paradoxical euphoria. At the other extreme one finds severe anxiety or depression, anger, shame, and so forth. Pathological emotions may present as components of identifiable psychiatric syndromes, neurotic or psychotic. It is recognized that physical illness constitutes psychological stress for most persons and may be a causal factor in the development of any type of functional psychiatric illness.

The Behavioral Aspect

The behavioral aspect concerns the patient's communications and actions related to his illness. What the patient communicates, how he does it, to whom, and when, is a problem of considerable importance for the delivery of medical care. Of course, communication is not a one-way process but is modified by the responses of the recipients. In the case of illness, the communication of the patient's complaints will influence and be influenced by the response of the doctor, patient's family, or other listeners.

Zola (23, 24) draws attention to the effect of sociocultural factors on the manner in which patients communicate their symptoms to the doctor. He found that Irish and Italian patients attending an outpatient medical department in Boston presented their somatic complaints differently. The Irish tended to understate their difficulties, located their chief problem in either the eyes, ears, nose or throat, and denied having pain. Italians reported more symptoms, dramatized them, and claimed that their symptoms interfered with their interpersonal relations. Zola notes that more Italians were labeled as "psychiatric problems" by their physicians. This suggests that the manner in which the patient complains tends to influence the doctor's diagnostic reasoning. Zola points out that the doctor can block or reject the patient's communication by his reaction, or lack of it, to the patient's specific complaints. Duff and Hollingshead (25) found in their study that "Communications of patients and physicians . . . were selective so that the information sought by one and supplied by the other was usually incomplete and often misleading." Patients tend to communicate selectively that which they believe doctors expect, that is, primarily physical complaints but not psychosocial distress. Such skewed communication readily leads to diagnostic errors and mismanagement.

A patient's *actions* related to his illness may be subsumed under the heading of *coping behavior*. The latter may be adaptive or maladaptive. How the patient copes with his illness or disability depends on the various determinants of psychological reaction discussed above. Various patterns of coping behavior may be distinguished. The most desirable is active coping manifested by actions serving the purpose of recovery from or adjustment to illness and disability. Seeking expert advice, cooperation with therapeutic programs, and development of substitute sources of satisfaction are some of the adaptive strategies. They have been studied in patients suffering from poliomyelitis (26), severe burns (27), and those undergoing surgery (28).

Maladaptive coping techniques include withdrawal, passive surrender to illness (giving up), excessive dependence on others, and self-destructive behavior, including suicide. The latter may be the final flight from illness (29, 32). There is little doubt that the manner in which the patient copes, or fails to cope, influences the course and outcome of his illness. Recovery from physical disease may be protracted or absent; psychological invalidism may follow physiological recovery or complicate minor impairment of function. Duff and Hollingshead (25) found in their study of hospitalized patients that of the 155 discharged alive, 44% were "disabled from psychosocial disturbances." The practical conclusion is obvious: Assessment and management of each patient's coping behavior should be a routine in medical practice.

The Social Aspect

The social aspect pertains to the patient's interactions with others, especially his family and health professionals. This area has been studied most intensively by sociologists. Parsons (33) and his associate (34), Mechanic (35), Zola (23, 24), Bloom (36), Duff and Hollingshead (25), and others have made important contributions.

A sociological concept relevant for this discussion is that of the role of the sick person—*the sick role*—developed by Parsons (33), with Fox (34). According to them, the following expectations constitute the sick role: [1] giving up the responsibilities and obligations of the premorbid social role (for example, as wage earner); [2] surrendering to the care of competent persons; and [3] giving up the sick role as soon as possible. It is thus expected that the sick role will be a transient one. This is in accordance with the values and norms of the American society which stresses independence, action, achievement, and efficiency. The patient has several possible choices with regard to the sick role: [1] He may attempt to reject or avoid it, even if this is harmful for him; [2] he may accept it realistically and give it up upon recovery; [3] he may adopt it gladly and refuse to give it up; or [4] he may strive to avoid it, then give in to and cling to it. These patterns of playing the sick role influence the course, duration, and outcome of any illness or injury. They are determined by the interplay between the patient, his illness, and his social environment.

The readiness with which a person adopts a sick role depends on the kind, severity, and duration of disease as well as on psychological and sociocultural factors. The meaning of disease plays a part in this. For example, for some people illness means shameful weakness. Others find it difficult to be controlled by and dependent on others. A person who views dependence, helplessness, and physical vulnerability as unacceptable or threatening may have difficulties in accepting the sick role. Furthermore, once such a person has accepted the sick role, he tends to either give it up prematurely or prolong it unduly. This apparent paradox is related to the fact that overemphasis on independence and self-reliance is often a reaction formation to unconscious longing for the opposite condition.

Playing the sick role has social consequences: It generally brings disapproval if it is thought to be exaggerated or unduly prolonged. On the other hand, it may be in various ways endorsed and encouraged by one or more members of the patient's family who may derive satisfaction from being in the stronger, supporting, and controlling role. The patient himself may postpone giving up the sick role if playing it pays, psychologically or economically, or both. Psychological gains from illness and disability are diverse: satisfaction of dependent needs, avoidance of intra- and interpersonal conflicts and social responsibilities, and control of others by being vulnerable and disabled. If there is collusion between the patient's motivation, conscious or unconscious, to remain sick and a gratifying social response to his persisting complaints, prolonged disability is liable to ensue. One may then speak of psychogenic invalidism. This is manifested by continuing somatic complaints and refusal to return to some or all of the premorbid social roles.

That other psychological factors may also be responsible for psychosocial disability after physical illness must be emphasized. These factors include particularly anxiety or depression, or both, whether related to the disease proper or to other influences (37, 38). The role of iatrogenic factors must not be overlooked. Failure to explain to the patient the nature and likely prognosis of his illness may give rise to unrealistic fears and refusal to return to work (39). Treatment of psychogenic symptoms as if they were due to organic disease may have similar effect.

The quality of the doctor-patient relationship (36) is an important variable in the patient's psychological response at all phases of his illness.

REFERENCES

1. Cope, O.: *Man, Mind and Medicine,* J. B. Lippincott, Philadelphia, 1968.
2. Brown, J. H. V.: Behavioral sciences and the medical school. *Science* 163: 964, 1969.
3. Lipowski, Z. J.: Review of consultation psychiatry and psychosomatic medicine. I. General principles. *Psychosom. Med.* 29: 153, 1967.
4. Lipowski, Z. J.: Review of consultation psychiatry and psychosomatic medicine. II. Clinical aspects. *Ibid.,* p. 201.
5. Lipowski, Z. J.: Review of consultation psychiatry and psychosomatic medicine. III. Theoretical issues. *Psychosom. Med.* 30: 395, 1968.
6. MacNalty, A. S. (editor): *The British Medical Dictionary,* J. B. Lippincott, Philadelphia, 1963.
7. Bibring, G. L.: Psychiatry and medical practice in a general hospital. *New Eng. J. Med.* 254: 366, 1956.
8. Lipowski, Z. J.: Delirium, clouding of consciousness and confusion. *J. Nerv. Ment. Dis.* 145: 227, 1967.
9. Little, J. C.: The athletes' neurosis—a deprivation crisis. Paper presented at the 124th Annual Meeting of the American Psychiatric Association, Boston, May 13–17, 1968.
10. Orbach, C., E. Bard, M., Sutherland, A. M.: Fear and defensive adaptations to the loss of anal sphincter control. *Psychoanal. Rev.* 44: 121, 1957.
11. Orbach, C. E., Tallent, N.: Modification of perceived body and of body concepts. *Arch. Gen. Psychiat.* 12: 126, 1965.
12. Mann, T.: *The Magic Mountain,* A. A. Knopf, New York, 1958.
13. Solzhenitsyn, A.: *Cancer Ward,* The Bodley Head, London, 1968.
14. Pinner, M., Miller, B. F. (editors): *When Doctors are Patients,* W. W. Norton, New York, 1952.
15. Van den Berg, J. H.: *The Psychology of the Sickbed,* Duquesne University Press, Pittsburgh, 1966.
16. Barker, R. G.: *Adjustment to Physical Handicap and Illness,* Social Sciences Research Council, New York, 1953.
17. Proust, M.: *Time Regained,* Chatto and Windus, London, 1957.

18. Bard, M., Dyk, R. B.: The psychodynamic significance of beliefs regarding the cause of serious illness. *Psychoanal. Rev.* 43: 146, 1956.
19. Mabry, J. H.: Lay concepts of etiology. *J. Chron. Dis.* 17: 371, 1964.
20. Petrie, A.: *Individuality in Pain and Suffering,* University of Chicago Press, Chicago, 1967.
21. Gold, M. A.: Causes of patient's delay in disease of the breast. *Cancer* 17: 564, 1964.
22. Goldsen, R. K.: Patient delay in seeking cancer diagnosis: behavioral aspects. *J. Chron. Dis.* 16: 427, 1963.
23. Zola, I. K.: Culture and symptoms: an analysis of patients' presenting complaints. *Amer. Soc. Rev.* 31: 615, 1966.
24. Zola, I. K.: Problems of communication, diagnosis and patient care. *J. Med. Educ.* 38: 829, 1963.
25. Duff, R. S., Hollingshead, A. B.: *Sickness and Society,* Harper & Row, Publishers, New York, 1968.
26. Visotsky, H. M., Hamburg, D. A., Goss, M. E., Lebovits, B. Z.: Coping behavior under extreme stress. *Arch. Gen. Psychiat.* 5: 27, 1961.
27. Hamburg, D. A., Hamburg, B., De Goza, S.: Adaptive problems and mechanisms in severely burned patients. *Psychiatry* 16: 1, 1953.
28. Janis, I. L.: *Psychological Stress,* J. Wiley & Sons, New York, 1958.
29. Tuckman, J., Youngman, W. F., Kreizman, G.: Suicide and physical illness. *J. Gen. Psychol.* 75: 291, 1966.
30. Farberow, N. L., Shneidman, E. S., Leonard, C. V.: Suicide among general medical and surgical hospital patients with malignant neoplasms. *Vet. Adm. Med. Bull.,* No. 9, 1963.
31. Farberow, N. L., McKelligott, J. W., Cohen, S., Darbonne, A.: Suicide among patients with cardiorespiratory illness. *JAMA* 195: 422, 1966.
32. Brown, W., Pisetsky, J. E.: Suicidal behavior in a general hospital. *Amer. J. Med.* 29: 307, 1960.
33. Parsons, T.: *The Social System,* The Free Press, Glencoe, Ill., 1951.
34. Parsons, T., Fox, R.: Illness, therapy, and the modern urban American family. *J. Soc. Issues* 8: 31, 1952.
35. Mechanic, D.: The concept of illness behavior. *J. Chron. Dis.* 15: 189, 1962.
36. Bloom, S. W.: *The Doctor and His Patient,* Russell Sage Fund, New York, 1963.
37. Imboden, J. B., Canter, A., Cluff, L.: Symptomatic recovery from medical disorders. *JAMA* 178: 1182, 1961.
38. Ruesch, J.: *Chronic Disease and Psychological Invalidism,* University of California Press, Berkeley, 1951.
39. Klein, R. F., Dean, A., Wilson, M. L., Bogdonoff, M. D.: The physician and postmyocardial infarction invalidism. *JAMA* 194: 123, 1965.

3

The Nature of Suffering and the Goals of Medicine

Eric J. Cassell

THE OBLIGATION OF PHYSICIANS to relieve human suffering stretches back into antiquity. Despite this fact, little attention is explicitly given to the problem of suffering in medical education, research, or practice. I will begin by focusing on a modern paradox: Even in the best settings and with the best physicians, it is not uncommon for suffering to occur not only during the course of a disease but also as a result of its treatment. To understand this paradox and its resolution requires an understanding of what suffering is and how it relates to medical care.

Consider this case: A 35-year-old sculptor with metastatic disease of the breast was treated by competent physicians employing advanced knowledge and technology and acting out of kindness and true concern. At every stage, the treatment as well as the disease was a source of suffering to her. She was uncertain and frightened about her future, but she could get little information from her physicians, and what she was told was not always the truth. She had been unaware, for example, that the irradiated breast would be so disfigured. After an oophorectomy and a regimen of medications, she became hirsute, obese, and devoid of libido. With tumor in the supraclavicular fossa, she lost strength in the hand that she had used in sculpturing, and she became profoundly depressed. She had a pathologic fracture of the femur, and treatment was delayed while her physicians openly disagreed about pinning her hip.

Reprinted from *The New England Journal of Medicine* 306, no. 11 (1982): 639–645, with permission, Massachusetts Medical Society.

Supported in part by a Sustained Development Award for Ethics and Values in Science and Technology (NSF OSS 80-18086) from the National Science Foundation and the National Endowment for the Humanities.

Each time her disease responded to therapy and her hope was re-kindled, a new manifestation would appear. Thus, when a new course of chemotherapy was started, she was torn between a desire to live and the fear that allowing hope to emerge again would merely expose her to misery if the treatment failed. The nausea and vomiting from the che-motherapy were distressing, but no more so than the anticipation of hair loss. She feared the future. Each tomorrow was seen as heralding in-creased sickness, pain, or disability, never as the beginning of better times. She felt isolated because she was no longer like other people and could not do what other people did. She feared that her friends would stop visiting her. She was sure that she would die.

This young woman had severe pain and other physical symptoms that caused her suffering. But she also suffered from some threats that were social and from others that were personal and private. She suffered from the effects of the disease and its treatment on her appearance and abilities. She also suffered unremittingly from her perception of the future.

What can this case tell us about the ends of medicine and the relief of suffering? Three facts stand out: The first is that this woman's suffering was not confined to her physical symptoms. The second is that she suf-fered not only from her disease but also from its treatment. The third is that one could not anticipate what she would describe as a source of suffering; like other patients, she had to be asked. Some features of her condition she would call painful, upsetting, uncomfortable, and distress-ing, but not a source of suffering. In these characteristics her case was ordinary.

In discussing the matter of suffering with lay persons, I learned that they were shocked to discover that the problem of suffering was not directly addressed in medical education. My colleagues of a contemplative nature were surprised at how little they knew of the problem and how little thought they had given it, whereas medical students tended to be unsure of the relevance of the issue to their work.

The relief of suffering, it would appear, is considered one of the primary ends of medicine by patients and lay persons, but not by the medical profession. As in the care of the dying, patients and their friends and families do not make a distinction between physical and nonphysical sources of suffering in the same way that doctors do.[1]

A search of the medical and social-science literature did not help me in understanding what suffering is; the word "suffering" was most often coupled with the word "pain," as in "pain and suffering." (The data bases used were *Psychological Abstracts*, the *Citation Index*, and the *Index Medicus*.)

This phenomenon reflects a historically constrained and currently inadequate view of the ends of medicine. Medicine's traditional concern primarily for the body and for physical disease is well known, as are the widespread effects of the mind-body dichotomy on medical theory and practice. I believe that this dichotomy itself is a source of the paradoxical situation in which doctors cause suffering in their care of the sick. Today, as ideas about the separation of mind and body are called into question, physicians are concerning themselves with new aspects of the human condition. The profession of medicine is being pushed and pulled into new areas, both by its technology and by the demands of its patients. Attempting to understand what suffering is and how physicians might truly be devoted to its relief will require that medicine and its critics overcome the dichotomy between mind and body and the associated dichotomies between subjective and objective and between person and object.

In the remainder of this paper I am going to make three points. The first is that suffering is experienced by persons. In the separation between mind and body, the concept of the person, or personhood, has been associated with that of mind, spirit, and the subjective. However, as I will show, a person is not merely mind, merely spiritual, or only subjectively knowable. Personhood has many facets, and it is ignorance of them that actively contributes to patients' suffering. The understanding of the place of the person in human illness requires a rejection of the historical dualism of mind and body.

The second point derives from my interpretation of clinical observations: Suffering occurs when an impending destruction of the person is perceived; it continues until the threat of disintegration has passed or until the integrity of the person can be restored in some other manner. It follows, then, that although suffering often occurs in the presence of acute pain, shortness of breath, or other bodily symptoms, suffering extends beyond the physical. Most generally, suffering can be defined as the state of severe distress associated with events that threaten the intactness of the person.

The third point is that suffering can occur in relation to any aspect of the person, whether it is in the realm of social roles, group identification, the relation with self, body, or family, or the relation with a transpersonal, transcendent source of meaning. Below is a simplified description or "topology" of the constituents of personhood.

"PERSON" IS NOT "MIND"

The split between mind and body that has so deeply influenced our approach to medical care was proposed by Descartes to resolve certain philosophical issues. Moreover, Cartesian dualism made it possible for science to escape the control of the church by assigning the noncorporeal, spiritual realm to the church, leaving the physical world as the domain of science. In that religious age, "person," synonymous with "mind," was necessarily off limits to science.

Changes in the meaning of concepts like that of personhood occur with changes in society, while the word for the concept remains the same. This fact tends to obscure the depth of the transformations that have occurred between the 17th century and today. People simply *are* "persons" in this time, as in past times, and they have difficulty imagining that the term described something quite different in an earlier period when the concept was more constrained.

If the mind-body dichotomy results in assigning the body to medicine, and the person is not in that category, then the only remaining place for the person is in the category of mind. Where the mind is problematic (not identifiable in objective terms), its very reality diminishes for science, and so, too, does that of the person. Therefore, so long as the mind-body dichotomy is accepted, suffering is either subjective and thus not truly "real"—not within medicine's domain—or identified exclusively with bodily pain. Not only is such an identification misleading and distorting, for it depersonalizes the sick patient, but it is itself a source of suffering. It is not possible to treat sickness as something that happens solely to the body without thereby risking damage to the person. An anachronistic division of the human condition into what is medical (having to do with the body) and what is nonmedical (the remainder) has given medicine too narrow a notion of its calling. Because of this division, physicians may, in concentrating on the cure of bodily disease, do things that cause the patient as a person to suffer.

AN IMPENDING DESTRUCTION OF PERSON

Suffering is ultimately a personal matter. Patients sometimes report suffering when one does not expect it, or do not report suffering when one does expect it. Furthermore, a person can suffer enormously at the distress of another, especially a loved one.

In some theologies, suffering has been seen as bringing one closer to God. This "function" of suffering is at once its glorification and its relief. If, through great pain or deprivation, someone is brought closer to a cherished goal, that person may have no sense of having suffered but may instead feel enormous triumph. To an observer, however, only the deprivation may be apparent. This cautionary note is important because people are often said to have suffered greatly, in a religious context, when they are known only to have been injured, tortured, or in pain, not to have suffered.

Although pain and suffering are closely identified in the medical literature, they are phenomenologically distinct.[2] The difficulty of understanding pain and the problems of physicians in providing adequate relief of physical pain are well known.[3-5]

The greater the pain, the more it is believed to cause suffering. However, some pain, like that of childbirth, can be extremely severe and yet considered rewarding. The perceived meaning of pain influences the amount of medication that will be required to control it. For example, a patient reported that when she believed the pain in her leg was sciatica, she could control it with small doses of codeine, but when she discovered that it was due to the spread of malignant disease, much greater amounts of medication were required for relief. Patients can writhe in pain from kidney stones and by their own admission not be suffering, because they "know what it is"; they may also report considerable suffering from apparently minor discomfort when they do not know its source. Suffering in close relation to the intensity of pain is reported when the pain is virtually overwhelming, such as that associated with a dissecting aortic aneurysm. Suffering is also reported when the patient does not believe that the pain can be controlled. The suffering of patients with terminal cancer can often be relieved by demonstrating that their pain truly can be controlled; they will then often tolerate the same pain without any medication, preferring the pain to the side effects of their analgesics. Another type of pain that can be a source of suffering is pain that is not overwhelming but continues for a very long time.

In summary, people in pain frequently report suffering from the pain when they feel out of control, when the pain is overwhelming, when the source of the pain is unknown, when the meaning of the pain is dire, or when the pain is chronic.

In all these situations, persons perceive pain as a threat to their continued existence—not merely to their lives, but to their integrity as persons. That this is the relation of pain to suffering is strongly suggested by the fact that suffering can be relieved, in the presence of continued pain, by making the source of the pain known, changing its meaning, and demonstrating that it can be controlled and that an end is in sight.

It follows, then, that suffering has a temporal element. In order for a situation to be a source of suffering, it must influence the person's perception of future events. ("If the pain continues like this, I *will be* overwhelmed"; "If the pain comes from cancer, I *will* die"; "If the pain cannot be controlled, I *will not* be able to take it.") At the moment when the patient is saying, "If the pain continues like this, I will be overwhelmed," he or she is not overwhelmed. Fear itself always involves the future. In the case with which I opened this paper, the patient could not give up her fears of her sense of future, despite the agony they caused her. As suffering is discussed in the other dimensions of personhood, note how it would not exist if the future were not a major concern.

Two other aspects of the relation between pain and suffering should be mentioned. Suffering can occur when physicians do not validate the patient's pain. In the absence of disease, physicians may suggest that the pain is "psychological" (in the sense of not being real) or that the patient is "faking." Similarly, patients with chronic pain may believe after a time that they can no longer talk to others about their distress. In the former case the person is caused to distrust his or her perceptions of reality, and in both instances social isolation adds to the person's suffering.

Another aspect essential to an understanding of the suffering of sick persons is the relation of meaning to the way in which illness is experienced. The word "meaning" is used here in two senses. In the first, to mean is to signify, to imply. Pain in the chest may imply heart disease. We also say that we know what something means when we know how important it is. The importance of things is always personal and individual, even though meaning in this sense may be shared by others or by society as a whole. What something signifies and how important it is relative to the whole array of a person's concerns contribute to its personal meaning. "Belief" is another word for that aspect of meaning concerned with implications, and "value" concerns the degree of importance to a particular person.

The personal meaning of things does not consist exclusively of values and beliefs that are held intellectually; it includes other dimensions. For the same word, a person may simultaneously have a cognitive meaning, an affective or emotional meaning, a bodily meaning, and a transcendent or spiritual meaning. And there may be contradictions in the different levels of meaning. The nuances of personal meaning are complex, and when I speak of personal meanings I am implying this complexity in all its depth—known and unknown. Personal meaning is a fundamental dimension of personhood, and there can be no understanding of human illness or suffering without taking it into account.

A SIMPLIFIED DESCRIPTION OF THE PERSON

A simple topology of a person may be useful in understanding the relation between suffering and the goals of medicine. The features discussed below point the way to further study and to the possibility of specific action by individual physicians.

Persons have personality and character. Personality traits appear within the first few weeks of life and are remarkably durable over time. Some personalities handle some illnesses better than others. Individual persons vary in character as well. During the heyday of psychoanalysis in the 1950s, all behavior was attributed to unconscious determinants: No one was bad or good; they were merely sick or well. Fortunately, that simplistic view of human character is now out of favor. Some people do in fact have stronger characters and bear adversity better. Some are good and kind under the stress of terminal illness, whereas others become mean and offensive when even mildly ill.

A person has a past. The experiences gathered during one's life are a part of today as well as yesterday. Memory exists in the nostrils and the hands, not only in the mind. A fragrance drifts by, and a memory is evoked. My feet have not forgotten how to roller-skate, and my hands remember skills that I was hardly aware I had learned. When these past experiences involve sickness and medical care, they can influence present illness and medical care. They stimulate fear, confidence, physical symptoms, and anguish. It damages people to rob them of their past and deny their memories, or to mock their fears and worries. A person without a past is incomplete.

Life experiences—previous illness, experiences with doctors, hospitals, and medications, deformities and disabilities, pleasures and successes, miseries and failures—all form the nexus for illness. The personal meaning of the disease and its treatment arises from the past as well as the present. If cancer occurs in a patient with self-confidence from past achievements, it may give rise to optimism and a resurgence of strength. Even if it is fatal, the disease may not produce the destruction of the person but, rather, reaffirm his or her indomitability. The outcome would be different in a person for whom life had been a series of failures.

The intensity of ties to the family cannot be overemphasized; people frequently behave as though they were physical extensions of their parents. Events that might cause suffering in others may be borne without complaint by someone who believes that the disease is part of his or her family identity and hence inevitable. Even diseases for which no heritable basis is known may be borne easily by a person because others in the family have been similarly afflicted. Just as the person's past experiences give meaning to present events, so do the past experiences of his or her family. Those meanings are part of the person.

A person has a cultural background. Just as a person is part of a culture and a society, these elements are part of the person. Culture defines what is meant by masculinity or femininity, what attire is acceptable, attitudes toward the dying and sick, mating behavior, the height of chairs and steps, degrees of tolerance for odors and excreta, and how the aged and the disabled are treated. Cultural definitions have an enormous impact on the sick and can be a source of untold suffering. They influence the behavior of others toward the sick person and that of the sick toward themselves. Cultural norms and social rules regulate whether someone can be among others or will be isolated, whether the sick will be considered foul or acceptable, and whether they are to be pitied or censured.

Returning to the sculptor described earlier, we know why that young woman suffered. She was housebound and bedbound, her face was changed by steroids, she was masculinized by her treatment, one breast was scarred, and she had almost no hair. The degree of importance attached to these losses—that aspect of their personal meaning—is determined to a great degree by cultural priorities.

With this in mind, we can also realize how much someone devoid of physical pain, even devoid of "symptoms," may suffer. People suffer from what they have lost of themselves in relation to the world of objects, events, and relationships. We realize, too, that although medical care can reduce the impact of sickness, inattentive care can increase the disruption caused by illness.

A person has roles. I am a husband, a father, a physician, a teacher, a brother, an orphaned son, and an uncle. People are their roles, and each role has rules. Together, the rules that guide the performance of roles make up a complex set of entitlements and limitations of responsibility and privilege. By middle age, the roles may be so firmly set that disease can lead to the virtual destruction of a person by making the performance of his or her roles impossible. Whether the patient is a doctor who cannot doctor or a mother who cannot mother, he or she is diminished by the loss of function.

No person exists without others; there is no consciousness without a consciousness of others, no speaker without a hearer, and no act, object, or thought that does not somehow encompass others.[6] All behavior is or will be involved with others, even if only in memory or reverie. Take away others, remove sight or hearing, and the person is diminished. Everyone dreads becoming blind or deaf, but these are only the most obvious injuries to human interaction. There are many ways in which human beings can be cut off from others and then suffer the loss.

It is in relationships with others that the full range of human emotions finds expression. It is this dimension of the person that may be injured when illness disrupts the ability to express emotion. Furthermore, the extent and nature of a sick person's relationships influence the degree of suffering from a disease. There is a vast difference between going home to an empty apartment and going home to a network of friends and family after hospitalization. Illness may occur in one partner of a long and strongly bound marriage or in a union that is falling apart. Suffering from the loss of sexual function associated with some diseases will depend not only on the importance of sexual performance itself but also on its importance in the sick person's relationships.

A person is a political being. A person is in this sense equal to other persons, with rights and obligations and the ability to redress injury by others and the state. Sickness can interfere, producing the feeling of political powerlessness and lack of representation. Persons who are permanently handicapped may suffer from a feeling of exclusion from participation in the political realm.

Persons do things. They act, create, make, take apart, put together, wind, unwind, cause to be, and cause to vanish. They know themselves, and are known, by these acts. When illness restricts the range of activity of persons, they are not themselves.

Persons are often unaware of much that happens within them and why. Thus, there are things in the mind that cannot be brought to awareness by ordinary reflection. The structure of the unconscious is pictured quite differently by different scholars, but most students of human behavior accept the assertion that such an interior world exists. People can behave in ways that seem inexplicable and strange even to themselves, and the sense of powerlessness that the person may feel in the presence of such behavior can be a source of great distress.

Persons have regular behaviors. In health, we take for granted the details of our day-to-day behavior. Persons know themselves to be well as much by whether they behave as usual as by any other set of facts. Patients decide that they are ill because they cannot perform as usual, and they may suffer the loss of their routine. If they cannot do the things that they identify with the fact of their being, they are not whole.

Every person has a body. The relation with one's body may vary from identification with it to admiration, loathing, or constant fear. The body may even be perceived as a representation of a parent, so that when something happens to the person's body it is as though a parent were injured. Disease can so alter the relation that the body is no longer seen as a friend but, rather, as an untrustworthy enemy. This is intensified if the illness comes on without warning, and as illness persists, the person may feel increasingly vulnerable. Just as many people have an expanded sense of self as a result of changes in their bodies from exercise, the potential exists for a contraction of this sense through injury to the body.

Everyone has a secret life. Sometimes it takes the form of fantasies and dreams of glory; sometimes it has a real existence known to only a few. Within the secret life are fears, desires, love affairs of the past and present, hopes, and fantasies. Disease may destroy not only the public or the private person but the secret person as well. A secret beloved friend may be lost to a sick person because he or she has no legitimate place by the sickbed. When that happens, the patient may have lost the part of life that made tolerable an otherwise embittered existence. Or the loss may be only of a dream, but one that might have come true. Such loss can be a source of great distress and intensely private pain.

Everyone has a perceived future. Events that one expects to come to pass vary from expectations for one's children to a belief in one's creative ability. Intense unhappiness results from a loss of the future—the future of the individual person, of children, and of other loved ones. Hope dwells in this dimension of existence, and great suffering attends the loss of hope.

Everyone has a transcendent dimension, a life of the spirit. This is most directly expressed in religion and the mystic traditions, but the frequency with which people have intense feelings of bonding with groups, ideals, or anything larger and more enduring than the person is evidence of the universality of the transcendent dimension. The quality of being greater and more lasting than an individual life gives this aspect of the person its timeless dimension. The profession of medicine appears to ignore the human spirit. When I see patients in nursing homes who have become only bodies, I wonder whether it is not their transcendent dimension that they have lost.

THE NATURE OF SUFFERING

For purposes of explanation, I have outlined various parts that make up a person. However, persons cannot be reduced to their parts in order to be better understood. Reductionist scientific methods, so successful in human biology, do not help us to comprehend whole persons. My intent was rather to suggest the complexity of the person and the potential for injury and suffering that exists in everyone. With this in mind, any suggestion of mechanical simplicity should disappear from my definition of suffering. All the aspects of personhood—the lived past, the family's lived past, culture and society, roles, the instrumental dimension, associations and relationships, the body, the unconscious mind, the political being, the secret life, the perceived future, and the transcendent dimension— are susceptible to damage and loss.

Injuries to the integrity of the person may be expressed by sadness, anger, loneliness, depression, grief, unhappiness, melancholy, rage, withdrawal, or yearning. We acknowledge the person's right to have and express such feelings. But we often forget that the affect is merely the outward expression of the injury, not the injury itself. We know little about the nature of the injuries themselves, and what we know has been learned largely from literature, not medicine.

If the injury is sufficient, the person suffers. The only way to learn what damage is sufficient to cause suffering, or whether suffering is present, is to ask the sufferer. We all recognize certain injuries that almost invariably cause suffering: the death or distress of loved ones, powerlessness, helplessness, hopelessness, torture, the loss of a life's work, betrayal, physical agony, isolation, homelessness, memory failure, and fear. Each is both universal and individual. Each touches features common to all of us, yet each contains features that must be defined in terms of a specific person at a specific time. With the relief of suffering in mind, however, we should reflect on how remarkably little is known of these injuries.

THE AMELIORATION OF SUFFERING

One might inquire why everyone is not suffering all the time. In a busy life, almost no day passes in which one's intactness goes unchallenged. Obviously, not every challenge is a threat. Yet I suspect that there is more suffering than is known. Just as people with chronic pain learn to keep it to themselves because others lose interest, so may those with chronic suffering.

There is another reason why every injury may not cause suffering. Persons are able to enlarge themselves in response to damage, so that instead of being reduced, they may indeed grow. This response to suffering has encouraged the belief that suffering is good for people. To some degree and in some persons, this may be so. If a leg is injured so that an athlete cannot run again, the athlete may compensate for the loss by learning another sport or mode of expression. So it is with the loss of relationships, loves, roles, physical strength, dreams, and power. The human body may lack the capacity to gain a new part when one is lost, but the person has it.

The ability to recover from loss without succumbing to suffering is sometimes called resilience, as though nothing but elastic rebound were involved, but it is more as though an inner force were withdrawn from one manifestation of a person and redirected to another. If a child dies and the parent makes a successful recovery, the person is said to have "rebuilt" his or her life. The term suggests that the parts of the person are structured in a new manner, allowing expression in different dimensions. If a previously active person is confined to a wheelchair, intellectual pursuits may occupy more time.

Recovery from suffering often involves help, as though people who have lost parts of themselves can be sustained by the personhood of others until their own recovers. This is one of the latent functions of physicians: to lend strength. A group, too, may lend strength: Consider the success of groups of the similarly afflicted in easing the burden of illness (e.g., women with mastectomies, people with ostomies, and even the parents or family members of the diseased).

Meaning and transcendence offer two additional ways by which the suffering associated with destruction of a part of personhood is ameliorated. Assigning a meaning to the injurious condition often reduces or even resolves the suffering associated with it. Most often, a cause for the condition is sought within past behaviors or beliefs. Thus, the pain or threat that causes suffering is seen as not destroying a part of the person, because it is part of the person by virtue of its origin within the self. In our culture, taking the blame for harm that comes to oneself because of the unconscious mind serves the same purpose as the concept of karma in Eastern theologies; suffering is reduced when it can be located within a coherent set of meanings. Physicians are familiar with the question from the sick, "Did I do something that made this happen?" It is more tolerable for a terrible thing to happen because of something that one has done than it is to be at the mercy of chance.

Transcendence is probably the most powerful way in which one is restored to wholeness after an injury to personhood. When experienced, transcendence locates the person in a far larger landscape. The sufferer is not isolated by pain but is brought closer to a transpersonal source of meaning and to the human community that shares those meanings. Such an experience need not involve religion in any formal sense; however, in its transpersonal dimension, it is deeply spiritual. For example, patriotism can be a secular expression of transcendence.

WHEN SUFFERING CONTINUES

But what happens when suffering is not relieved? If suffering occurs when there is a threat to one's integrity or a loss of a part of a person, then suffering will continue if the person cannot be made whole again. Little is known about this aspect of suffering. Is much of what we call depression merely unrelieved suffering? Considering that depression commonly follows the loss of loved ones, business reversals, prolonged illness, profound injuries to self-esteem, and other damages to person-hood, the possibility is real. In many chronic or serious diseases, persons who "recover" or who seem to be successfully treated do not return to normal function. They may never again be employed, recover sexual function, pursue career goals, reestablish family relationships, or reenter the social world, despite a physical cure. Such patients may not have recovered from the nonphysical changes occurring with serious illness. Consider the dimensions of personhood described above, and note that each is threatened or damaged in profound illness. It should come as no surprise, then, that chronic suffering frequently follows in the wake of disease.

The paradox with which this paper began—that suffering is often caused by the treatment of the sick—no longer seems so puzzling. How could it be otherwise, when medicine has concerned itself so little with the nature and causes of suffering? This lack is not a failure of good intentions. None are more concerned about pain or loss of function than physicians. Instead, it is a failure of knowledge and understanding. We lack knowledge, because in working from a dichotomy contrived within a historical context far from our own, we have artificially circumscribed our task in caring for the sick.

Attempts to understand all the known dimensions of personhood and their relations to illness and suffering present problems of staggering complexity. The problems are no greater, however, than those initially posed by the question of how the body works—a question that we have managed to answer in extraordinary detail. If the ends of medicine are to be directed toward the relief of human suffering, the need is clear.

I am indebted to Rabbi Jack Bemporad, to Drs. Joan Cassel, Peter Dineen, Nancy McKenzie, and Richard Zaner, to Ms. Dawn McGuire, to the members of the Research Group on Death, Suffering, and Well-Being of The Hastings Center for their advice and assistance, and to the Arthur Vining Davis Foundations for support of the research group.

REFERENCES

1. Cassell E. Being and becoming dead. Soc Res. 1972; 39:528–42.
2. Bakan D. Disease, pain and sacrifice: toward a psychology of suffering. Chicago: Beacon Press, 1971.
3. Marks RM, Sachar EJ. Undertreatment of medical inpatients with narcotic analgesics. Ann Intern Med. 1973; 78:173–81.
4. Kanner RM, Foley KM. Patterns of narcotic drug use in a cancer pain clinic. Ann NY Acad Sci. 1981; 362:161–72.
5. Goodwin JS, Goodwin JM, Vogel AV. Knowledge and use of placebos by house officers and nurses. Ann Intern Med. 1979; 91:106–10.
6. Zaner R. The context of self: a phenomenological inquiry using medicine as a clue. Athens, Ohio: Ohio University Press, 1981.

4

The Patient's View of the Patient's Role

Daisy L. Tagliacozzo • *Hans O. Mauksch*

EVERY SOCIETY GRANTS to the sick person special privileges and every society also imposes on the sick person certain obligations.[1] An understanding of such general norms can provide an effective guide to the study of the behavior and attitudes of the sick in our society. However, general norms gain meaning in a specific social setting, or may be modified by intra-institutional expectations. The extent to which a sick person may feel free to seek satisfaction for his emotional needs and to assume the "rights and privileges of the sick role" may thus depend on the social context within which behavior unfolds. Even if general rules for behavior remain the same, the patient may be influenced by considerations which involve efforts to accommodate to real or imagined expectations of significant others.

The experience of being hospitalized adds another dimension to the experience of being ill. This dimension consists of the rights and obligations which are legitimated by organizational forces and which are based on the fact that admission to the hospital is tantamount to assuming an organizational position with all the implications for normative compliance and sanctions. This discussion is based on a study which sought to ascertain to what extent the attitudes and needs which are organized around these two experiences, being ill and being hospitalized, may dif-

Originally printed in *Patients, Physicians and Illness,* edited by E.G. Jaco, Macmillan Publishing Co. Inc., 1972. Reprinted by permission of the authors.

Based on a study conducted by the authors through the Department of Patient Care Research, Presbyterian St. Luke's Hospital, Chicago, Ill. This study was supported by a grant from the Commonwealth Fund.

fer or even come into conflict with each other. The attitudes and reactions of patients were viewed within the context of a system of roles and as a consequence of the patient's efforts to conform to perceived systems of expectations. The study concentrated on the implications of hospitalization, with less concern for the illness role *per se*. It explored to what extent the role of the hospitalized patient may be lacking clear definitions of rights and easily definable criteria for legitimate claims. The question was raised whether the position and the attitudes of patients deprive them of genuine means to control others in the system and thus limit their readiness to express their claims and desires without fear of sanction.

Throughout the study the patient is shown to be aware of the degree to which he is dependent on those who care for him. This dependency is based largely on the power to heal and to cure. It is also based on the power ascribed to hospital functionaries to give or to withhold those daily services which, for the hospitalized patient, can embrace some basic survival needs. The single or double rooms and the rapid patient turnover in the modern hospital do not foster an effective patient community which could serve as interpreter and modifier of hospital rules. The patient, therefore, is much more dependent on his previous learning, be it from direct or indirect experiences with the patient role. More importantly, the absence of adequate interpretations by the patient community makes the patient more dependent on hospital functionaries for clues about the appropriateness of his behavior, demands and expectations.

The fact that patients frequently remain strangers in the hospital community tends to add to the power of those who, as functionaries, are intimately familiar with the rules and expectations of the organization. The power which is vested in them can inhibit the patient to seek clarification and guidance. Also, those who are informed tend to become oblivious to the needs of their clients to be initiated into the "rules of the game."

The study was conducted in a metropolitan voluntary hospital with a capacity of 850 beds. The hospital is part of a large Midwest medical center. It is a teaching hospital for nurses and physicians. Patients occupy predominantly two-bed or private rooms.[2] This discussion rests on the analysis of 132 interviews which were administered to 86 patients. The sample was limited to patients who were admitted with cardiovascular or gastro-intestinal diagnoses. All patients in the sample were Caucasian, American-born males or females between 40 and 60 years of age. All patients had been previously hospitalized and all were married. They paid for their hospitalization in part with private or industrial insurance. During the semi-structured interview, the patient was asked to express himself freely on present and previous hospital experiences. The interviews averaged one hour and were recorded and transcribed. The average day of interviewing was the fifth day of hospitalization. When possible, second interviews were conducted.

PHYSICIANS AND NURSES: THEIR SIGNIFICANCE

Physicians and nurses are among the significant others in the network of role relationships in which the hospitalized patient becomes involved. Their significance is derived from different sources. The physician represents authority and prestige. His orders legitimize the patient's demands on others and justify otherwise deviant aspects of illness behavior. The physician is not only the "court of appeal" for exemption from normal role responsibilities,[3] he also functions as the major legitimizing agent for the patient's demands during hospitalization. Yet his orders generally do not constitute guides to behavior in specific situations and they do not consider or modify the patient's understanding of the formal and informal expectations of nurses. Although the physician's authority ranks supreme in the eyes of most patients, they are also aware that he is only intermittently present and thus not in a position to evaluate the behavior of both patients and nurses and to sanction this behavior during the everyday procedures of hospital care.

The significance of the nurse stems not only from her authority in interpreting, applying and enforcing the orders of the physician but, in addition, from the fact that she can judge and react to the patient's behavior more continuously than the physician. From the patient's point of view, he also depends upon the nurse as an intermediary in the provision of many other institutional services.

For most patients it is of greatest importance to feel that they adjust to the expectations of the nurse and of the physician. To accommodate themselves to what they feel is expected of them, patients must be able to perceive these expectations as congruent or they must cope with the strains involved in efforts to adjust to what may appear to them as conflicting demands. Conflict is thus likely to arise if the nurse executes a plan of care which, from the point of view of the patient, deviates in detail or emphasis from the patient's interpretation of the physician's orders.

Close adherence to the orders of the physician was not equally important for all patients and not all patients appear to be equally intense in their sensitivity to congruence in the plan of care and cure. Those patients who expressed concern for complete adherence to the physician's word and expected strictest observance and literal interpretation of medical orders typically expressed distrust in the reliability and efficiency of anyone except the physician. These patients frequently feared that even minor deviations may result in further physical harm. For some patients,

close adherence to medical orders appeared congruent with their conceptions of themselves; as did some patients, who resisted following certain
medical orders, they used this area of conformity to convey something
essential about themselves.

Demands for rigid adherence to medical orders were associated with
the desire for "reliable" nursing care and "efficiency." The eagerly co-
operative patient not only emphasized that he followed all orders willingly, he also expected the nurse to "co-operate" with him in his efforts
to carry out the orders of the physician as he understood them. The patient's concern typically expressed itself in close observations of hospital
personnel, in emphasis on observance of punctuality and in worry whether
"orders have been written" and "charts double-checked." Such efforts to
"co-operate with the physician" by seeing that "things get done" may
become a source of stress. The patient who is ready to act on behalf of
medical orders may have to call for services from the nurse and impose
demands on her time or ask her to alter behavior. Thus, if the patient
hears from the physician that the "specimen should be warm," he may
feel obligated to insist that a "cooling-off" delay be avoided. If the physician has told him that he may "stay in bed another day," the patient's
interpretation may lead him to actively resist a nurse's urging that he do
some things for himself: "My doctor said that I can stay in bed another
day." Patients' insistence on rigid adherence to the orders of the physician
were frequently defended in the light of one implication of the sick role—
the obligation to make efforts towards the restoration of health. Thus,
patients who were critical of deviations from medical orders justified their
criticisms by pointing out that they did not want to be "complainers" or
"troublemakers"—but that they, after all, "want to get well."

When a patient's efforts to co-operate fully and to observe the details
of medical orders expressed themselves in more frequent demands, he
also reacted to the risks involved in violating his obligation not to be
demanding of nurses. Those patients who reported that they had expressed their desire for compliance with medical orders in active demands
or complaints also tended to be very observant of the reactions of members of the nursing staff. Praise and criticism of "good" and "bad" nurses
revealed that these patients rejected the nurse who "grumbled" and that
they praised enthusiastically the nurse who responded "willingly" and
who "smiled" when she was asked to do things for the patient. Patients
also praised the nurse who "helped the patient to co-operate" and who
"did not mind" when she was reminded of an order.

Those patients for whom co-operation with a physician's order became the guiding principle during hospitalization tended to be very sensitized to the reactions of others. They appeared to be "on the alert" and
reacted quickly to facial expression, a tone of voice and the general man-

ner in which a request was received. If they felt that their demands were not well received, they frequently became angered and, when given an opportunity, expressed their antagonism in attacks on those members of the nursing staff who "do not treat you like a person," who "make you feel that you are at their mercy" and "who consider you just a case."

The conflict between the felt obligation to insist on precise implementation of medical orders and efforts not to appear demanding or inconsiderate *vis à vis* the nursing staff was often resolved in favor of striving for approval by nurses. The data indicate that many patients prefer not to risk appearing too demanding or too dependent. They accept what appears to them to be deviations from the physician's orders, and even violate what they believe is expected of them by the physician. They anxiously watch a medication being late, rather than object to the delay, and they watch the specimen get cold rather than pointing this out to a nurse. Frequently this endeavor to "please" the nurse may backfire. Patients who disobey the physician's orders and get up to do "small things" for themselves rather than call the nurse may find themselves reprimanded by her because she may view this as lack of co-operation or even protest. She also may consider such behavior an incident which could incur the anger of the physician.

Thus, patients may pay for the security of "being liked" by nurses and of having them "know that I am not demanding" with concerns over arousing the physician's criticism or harming their own recovery. But even where the obligation to be cooperative with the physician is not immediately at stake, patients may somewhat reluctantly forego the privileges which they could claim as a result of being sick. As one patient expressed it:

> If it is a hotel you won't hesitate to pick up a phone or to complain; in a hospital you think twice about it—you figure maybe they are busy or shorthanded. . . . It's a much more human thing, the hospital . . . it's more personal.

EXPECTATIONS AND CONSTRAINTS

When patients were asked what was expected of them by their physicians and by nurses, they responded with considerable consistency, indicating that several rules for "proper" conduct of patients were well defined and widely shared. The physician was seen as expecting "co-operation" and "trust and confidence." A large group of patients felt that the nurse, too, expected "co-operation." On the other hand, many patients were convinced that nurses expected them "not to be demanding," to be "respectful" and to be "considerate." Only very few patients listed these latter three categories for physicians.

Self-descriptions which patients introjected into the interviews followed a similar pattern. It was most important to patients that the interviewer saw them as having "trust and confidence" in those who took care of them. This was particularly true of those patients who also admitted to some negative reactions toward nurses or physicians. Many patients were eager to mention that they were not demanding, co-operative, not dependent and considerate. In spontaneous discussions of the obligations of the hospitalized patient, the pattern did not change significantly.

One of the factors underlying the patient's hesitation to impose demands on hospital personnel is his awareness of the presence of other, often sicker patients. Observation of other patients introduces restraints. Comparisons of "my illness" with the illness of the roommate appeared to intensify the moral obligation to "leave them free to take care of the seriously ill" and comparisons of one's own claims or criticisms with the behavior of a very ill person seemed to intensify restrained. behavior: "After I observed him I felt kind of bad. I felt that I should be grateful and not ask for anything." It is well nigh impossible and a latent source of difficulty for the patient to judge his comparative status relative to patients in other rooms. The nurse summoned to give him a glass of water may have been called away from "a critical case." The isolation of the patient and the ensuing inability to establish relative claims serve as restraining forces on the expression of needs,[4] even though this concern is counterbalanced with an occasionally voiced concern about "getting one's share."

The patient's perceived entitlement for service is also linked to his definition of the severity of his illness. Patients apparently feel more secure in ascertaining their rights if their understanding of their condition permits them to rank themselves in the upper strata of a "hierarchy of illness." However, a secure assessment of "my case" may be difficult. Communications from the physician are general and understanding of the relative severity of the illness does not appear to be facilitated by his explanations. In many cases, a statement such as "I want you to stay in bed" does not legitimize the demand for a glass of water—the patient gets up to avoid being considered "too demanding."

Patients therefore seem to link the extent of their claims on service to readily perceived and objectively visible indices. Thus, being in traction, having tubes attached or being restrained by dressings are highly ranked legitimators for patients' demands. Fever also serves as a criterion for claims; the patient who asks the nurse what his temperature might be not only may inquire about the severity of his illness but indirectly may also ask: "To what services am I entitled today?" Hospital rules which prevent the nurse from giving such information may deny the patient guidelines for the rules applicable to his behavior.

Two-thirds of all patients in the sample indicated that they had refrained from expressing their needs and criticisms at least once. The observation that nurses are too busy, rushed and overworked was given as the most frequent reason for this reluctance. Beliefs about the conditions under which hospital personnel work serve thus as another limiting factor in the patient's expression of demands. One has to keep in mind the admiration for nurses and for "all those who do such difficult work" to understand why some patients may spend a night helping another patient when being told "that there is a shortage on the nightshift." Some patients did not engage in these activities without some conflict. They admitted that they were concerned with the physician's reactions "if he finds out," and that they were fearful of the consequences of such activity for their health. Even though they never admitted it directly, many responses revealed indirectly their desire to take more advantage of the privileges of the sick.

Constraint in voicing demands was also reinforced by the patient's assessment of the power of hospital personnel and physicians relative to his own. Over one-fourth of those patients who admitted to restraint of their demands also expressed their often resentful assessment of their own helplessness. Efforts to be "considerate" of the conditions which limit services may thus be convenient rationalizations of the patient's fears of offending others and of endangering his good relationship with them. "Being on good terms" was seen by these patients not only as a convenient but as an essential factor for their welfare. They directly expressed their awareness of their inability to control those who are in charge of their care. Patients felt that they were subject to rewards and punishment and that essential services can be withheld unless they make themselves acceptable. Some of these patients were dependent upon intimate forms of physical assistance, and their points of view reflected their awareness of this dependence upon others.

Feelings of helplessness were directly expressed in observations that "one is at their mercy," that "trying to change things is futile" and "won't get you anywhere" and that patients feel "helpless." The recognition of the power of others to withhold services also found expression in fears that one does not want to be considered a "complainer," or "troublemaker" or a "demanding patient," and in such apprehensions as "they can refuse to answer your bell, you know," or "they can refuse to make your bed." The same fears were expressed in efforts "to save that button so they come when I really need them" or in enthusiastic reactions to nurses who "come in to inquire why you never call for them" or who "do not mind if you ring once too often."

Patients very rarely expressed openly a concern that their physician may impose sanctions on inappropriate behavior. They tried to be intensely considerate toward him, since he, too, is considered "very busy" and "on his way" to other sick patients. Attempts to accommodate demands to these pressures on the physician serve as a considerable restraint on the patient's willingness to ask questions.

The admiration for the physician was in most cases tied to a very personal and emotionally charged attachment to the man who is "so kind and understanding." Gratitude intensified efforts to "make things easy" for him. Although hostility or annoyances toward nurses was often directly expressed, patients actively resisted direct verbalization of any negative feelings toward "the physician." Typically, complaints were expressed reluctantly and in terms of "I wish he could" coupled with quick modifications such as "I know he can't—he is too busy."

Patients may also be concretely limited by the observation that the physician is "on the go." Thus, a patient may want to ask questions and feel that "taking his time" is legitimate, but may feel that the time is simply not made available:

> He'll say well, we'll talk about it next time. And next time he'll talk fast, he out-talks you—and rushes out of the room and then when he's out of the room you think, well, I was supposed to ask him what he's going to do about my medicine . . . you run in the hall and he has disappeared that fast.

A patient who was impressed with the fact that his physician was "over-burdened and rushed" tried to describe how the resulting pressure of his own tensions and anxiety prevented him from fully comprehending what he was told:

> All I know is that your mind sort of runs ahead. You sort of anticipate what they are going to say, and you finish what they are going to say in your mind. I guess it's because perhaps sometimes you have trouble following them or maybe you would want them to say certain things, and you are listening—well, I don't know . . . you try to think what they are going to say, because otherwise, you have difficulty understanding them, but then, when they are out of the room, you don't remember a thing about what they have said.

In view of the above, it is not surprising that patients who were asked directly what they "considered their rights" had some difficulties responding. One-fourth of the respondents admitted that they did not know what their rights were; some patients stated outright that they had no rights. The majority of respondents limited themselves to general answers such as "good care," followed by the modification that specific claims depended upon the "seriousness of the illness." The belief that claims for service had to be justified in terms of immediate physical needs overshadowed any inclination to voice the rights of paying consumers. Few patients justified their demands in relation to their monetary payment and many of those who introduced the criteria of a paying consumer quickly added to their demands other legitimizing factors, such as the nature of their illness or the fact that they had been considerate in other respects. Conceptions of rights and obligations provide guidelines for alternative actions. They are used and "fitted" in accordance with the exigencies of situations and the developing meanings which individuals and groups bring to bear upon them. The general patterns which have been discussed should not conceal that differences in the characteristics of patients may contribute to significant variations in the more general theme. The following observations will illustrate the importance of further research in this area.

Patients who do not experience active and well-defined symptoms and whose activities are not visibly impaired may hesitate to present themselves to others as seriously ill and may find "co-operation" at times more difficult. Patients with cardio-vascular illness tended to focus more frequently on behavior involving co-operation with physicians and nurses; particularly in relation to the physician, this obligation appeared to preoccupy these patients. They were also more intent on presenting themselves as co-operative to the interviewer. Some of these patients were severely ill from the medical point of view, requiring complete bed rest and its concomitant extensive services. However, they seemed to have a difficult time accepting this state without concern that they may be considered "too dependent" or overly "demanding." At times, these difficulties appeared enhanced by social and economic pressures to leave the hospital, and by psychological needs for denial which also seemed to find expression in the insistence that they "really did not need any special attention" and that they were "not worried about their illness."

Some of the subtle difficulties of these patients are not easily verbalized. Only rarely can a patient formulate as forcefully the aftermath of a heart attack as did the patient quoted below. His statement sums up the illusions and hints dropped by other patients with a cardiac problem:

> Well, you know, a heart patient is a peculiar animal. That heart attack has done something to him, not only physically but mentally. I can tell you this because I have been through it. It brings up something which you don't want to let go of. If he tells you you must stay in bed, well, how come this sudden change? I don't want to stay in bed, and if he tells you that you cannot walk upstairs, he is telling you that you are weak, that you are no longer strong. He has taken something away from you—ah, your pride. You suddenly want to do what you are not supposed to do, what you have been doing all your life and that you have every right to do. Besides, a heart patient has an excitability built up in him.

Patients with cardio-vascular conditions verbalized criticisms less frequently than other patients. On the other hand, they stressed the importance of "dedication and interest" when discussing their ideal expectations of nurses and physicians.

One explanation for these tendencies may be found in some common fears which occur among patients who suffer from a type of illness in which the onset of a crisis can be sudden and unpredictable. For a patient with a cardio-vascular illness, as probably for all patients who fear a sudden turn for the worse, it is of utmost importance to know that someone will be there when the patient really needs help. The need for this type of security is revealed in the following responses of cardio-vascular patients:

> I think that there should be somebody out in front there all the time. I think the hospital would back me up on that. . . . If the patient was really ill, rang the buzzer and nobody was there to get it—no telling what would happen.
> Well, as I said, some patients may need more care because they have a more serious illness and when you have a heart disease then you need to be watched much more, also you are more frightened and it is important that somebody is around to watch your pulse.

Patients with non-specific gastro-intestinal conditions were more likely to be preoccupied with cancer. At times this was accompanied by the suspicion that the physician "really knows but will not tell me." Such apprehensions seemed to make it more difficult for the patient to sustain trust and confidence in personnel, particularly the physician.

Openly anxious and critical patients were found more frequently within the gastro-intestinal category. While patients with cardio-vascular conditions appeared to focus attention on concrete services which assured their safety, gastro-intestinal patients seemed more inclined to focus on the qualitative nature of their interactions with nurses and physicians. They were more easily threatened by the attitudes of others, more responsive to "personalized care" and more openly critical when these areas of expectations were not satisfied.

In each culture there is the recognition that it is legitimate to deviate from normal behavior under certain extreme conditions. For these conditions most societies develop differential standards for men and women. In our society men and women are generally not expected to respond in an identical fashion to pain nor are they expected to react identically to illness. We expect that expressive behavior (complaining or moaning) should be more controlled by men, and we frown less when women appear to exploit the illness role through passive and dependent behavior. All patients generally agreed that it was more difficult for men to be patients.

The data indicate that the sex of a patient may substantially affect orientations, needs and reactions to physicians and nurses. Evidence for such differences can be found in many areas. Women were considerably more critical of nursing care than were men, and more frequently expressed fear of negative sanctions from nurses. Women, more than men, emphasized personalized relationships when they discussed the needs of patients. Women were less concerned with problems of co-operation. On the other hand, they tended to focus on nurses' expectations for consideration and respect. When describing their expectations of nurses or when evaluating them, women focused more on personality attributes than men and also gave more emphasis to efficient and prompt care. Women were more critical when a quick response was not forthcoming and they were generally more concerned with efficiency. It is compatible with the male role to receive care and to have someone else maintain the physical surroundings. Women, however, are typically the managers of the home and the performers of major housekeeping tasks. They "know" from experience the standards of personal care and housekeeping, and thus tend to apply them to their judgment of the nursing team. The female patient's concern that the nurse may be critical of her may be indirectly an expression of her awareness that she tends to be demanding.

The more intense emphasis of women on "personality" and "personalized care" may also stem from a relationship which tends to be less personal and less informal than the relationship between nurses and male patients. Unlike his female counterpart, the male patient is probably not too critical of the technical aspect of those functions of the nurse which are reminiscent of the homemaker and mother. He may also derive satisfaction from his relationship to a member of the opposite sex. All this may not only contribute to tolerance of nursing care in general but may give the appearance of more "personalized" relationships. These conjectures may also help to explain the well-known preference nurses have for male patients.

FEARS AND APPREHENSIONS

Apprehensions and fears are the frequent companions of illness. The nature of the patient's concern springs, on the one hand, from his intense preoccupations with himself, with *his* body and with *his* state of mind. His dependence on others, on the other hand, prompts simultaneous concern with the meaning and consequences of their activities. Once the patient enters the hospital his attention may shift back and forth from himself to others. He is sensitive to any physical changes and watchful of any new and unexplained symptoms. He wonders about the outcome of an examination and about the effectiveness of his treatment. He ponders the reliability of those who are responsible for the many procedures and activities which to the patient remain unknown or unknowable, albeit essential.

Patients are preoccupied with safety in the hospital. This is revealed in the preoccupation with protection from mistakes and neglect which prevails when patients talk about their own needs or the needs of other patients. It is expressed in the nature of their recall of past experiences. Not only do patients concentrate on negative experiences, but they select those occurrences which signify the dangers of neglect and lack of attention. Although patients generally deny that they, themselves, are fearful, they have a tendency to ascribe such feelings to other patients.

These apprehensions cannot be entirely alleviated by admiration for the professional groups who are responsible for his treatment, or by a very favorable relationship to the personal physician. Realistic awareness of the complexity of large organizations or simply the fact that among many competent and interested doctors and nurses there may always be a "few who are not competent" may at least put the patient on the alert. In the words of a male patient with gastro-intestinal illness this fear is expressed as follows:

> When you are really sick, you are at the mercy of the hospital staff. In my opinion, you've got to have luck on your side. You've got to be lucky enough to get key people in the hospital who are really alert and who wish to do a job; and have someone on the shift at the time you need them who want to give the service or you are just out of luck. I think you could die in one of these hospitals of a heart attack before anybody came in to help you.

Perceptions of the patient role make it unlikely that such fears will be openly expresed by many patients. It is one of the obligations of a patient to have "trust and confidence" in those who care for him. The expression of these concerns could thus be interpreted as a failure to conform to these obligations. Also a free expression of concerns is inhibited by the belief that the courageous, sick persons rather than "sissies" are valued and rewarded.

Apprehensions of certain "dangers" may be directly derived from previous experiences which were, to the patient, indicative of lack of competence, neglect, or lack of interest. They also may be derived indirectly from certain widely held conceptions about the nature of "some" doctors and nurses and the conditions under which they work. Thus, the belief that some nurses do not like "demanding patients" leads to the concern of many patients that asking for too much may result in a slow response to a call or in reduced attention to their needs. The belief that some nurses and some physicians may be prone to oversights because they are inevitably overworked and rushed may further contribute to insecurity. Some patients observed with concern that physicians occasionally are "too busy" to spend enough time to listen to their patients or that a nurse "under the pressure of work" may overlook a physician's order or fail to carry it out in time.

There is evidence in the data that both physicians and nurses, in effect, continuously have to prove themselves. Beliefs such as "some doctors are only interested in money," "some doctors are not interested in their patients," "some doctors are hard-hearted," appear as conceptions about "possibilities" which the patient is ready to have dispelled or confirmed upon first contact with a nurse or a physician in the hospital. Negative conceptions about physicians and nurses, therefore, are typically limited to specific individuals. Without this "specificity" in orientation, patients would find it difficult to sustain the trust and confidence which they consider so important.

The patient's search for safety and security in the hospital may also be indirectly expressed in expectations of good physicians and good nurses. Their behavior or attitudes are seen by the patient as being instrumental in recovery and recuperation. The attitudes of others in the hospital function as clues which are symbolic of good care. From the patient's point of view, the "dedicated nurse" or the nurse who gives "spontaneous and willing services" is a reliable nurse; the "kind" physician who visits the patient regularly is "trustworthy" and "thorough." Mistakes and neglect are more obviously avoided if the nurse responds promptly, if the physician "knows what is going on" and if the nurse is informed about the doctor's intent. A "prompt response" from a nurse appears as one of the most significant indices for establishing trust and confidence in nursing care.

Patients' perspectives are also shaped by the nature of the social process into which they have entered and by the nature of the interactions to which they are exposed. Those patients who were very responsive to the more impersonal phases of patient-care also tended to be among the more apprehensive. Such patients often felt that they were functioning in a situation in which they could not establish effective and meaningful relationships with others. Feelings of "unrelatedness" were expressed directly in the observation that other patients are often "lonely" and "fearful" or that one sometimes feels like "just a case":

> You're no more . . . no more a patient but just a number . . . you dare not ask a question; you know, they're too busy. And they come around, fine, that's it, "we'll see you next time" and that's it. . . .

The very isolation he fears may be aggravated by the patient himself. In his efforts to be "considerate" and "not demanding" he may intensify the consequences of the anonymity and segmentalization he observes in the modern hospital. Efforts to be a "good patient" may, therefore, trigger disappointments and criticisms of those who do not provide services "spontaneously." The demand for "spontaneous services" appears also to stem from the desire to obtain all necessary services and attentions without having to initiate action. Spontaneous services curtail those interactions in which the patient may be viewed as "too demanding" or "difficult."

The interviews suggest that conformity to the patient role may lead to discrepancies between the behavior and the emotional condition of a patient. The calm appearance of the "good patient" may often hide anxieties and tensions which may not come to the attention of physicians or nurses unless relationships develop which do not trigger fear of criticism or sanction. When patients fail to exercise the restraints on behavior which they think appropriate, guilt or fear may be the consequence. Deviation from the good patient model can be threatening to a patient, unless he is convinced that his behavior was, in the eyes of others, legitimate and/or justified by the condition of his illness:

> I know myself that I talked very rudely to my doctor on one occasion. Afterwards I was ashamed of myself. I was sick or I would never act that way. He is kind and understanding. When I apologized, he acted as if nothing happened. He didn't walk out of the room or tell me off or any of the things that I might do after someone talked to me that way. But I know they have to have a lot of patience with us.

Patients practice an economy of demands, based on their own "principles of exchange." They will indeed curtail their less urgent demands to assure for themselves a prompt response during times when they "really need it." Some patients appear to consider themselves entitled to a certain finite quantity of services which they use sparingly to draw upon during periods of crisis, and many patients seem to feel that their entitlement to service is more severely cut by a demand which does not meet the approval of doctors and nurses:

> I says, "I'm saving that button," I says, "When I push that thing you'll know I need help." She smiled . . . they kind of appreciate that. And from that day, all the times I've been in the hospital I have never pushed the button unless it was something that I actually needed . . . not like some people that drive these nurses crazy; pushing it to raise the bed up; five minutes later push it again. "Oh that's a little too high." To me it paid dividends, because every time I pushed that button I got service, every dog-gone time.

DISCUSSION

The hospitalized patient is a "captive" who cannot leave the hospital without serious consequence to himself. These consequences do not only apply to the patient's physical condition. Our society expects efforts of the sick to do everything in their power to get well as soon as possible. Open rebellion against the care by competent professional personnel is, therefore, subject to severe criticism. The obligation to be a "co-operative patient" is learned early in life and, as has been indicated, apparently taken very seriously by most patients. More aggressive interpretations of the patient role are not easily verbalized and, apparently, not often realistic alternatives for the patient. Prevalent images of the hospital as a crisis institution, the conception that rights and demands should be governed by the seriousness of the illness and consideration for other, possibly sicker patients, makes it extremely difficult to play the "consumer role" openly and without fear of criticism. Thus, self-assertion as a "client" is controlled by moral commitments to the hospital community as well as by considerations of practical and necessary self-interest.

The norms of our society permit the sick person conditionally passive withdrawal and dependence but, at the same time, emphasize the sick person's responsibility to co-operate in efforts to regain his health.[5] The prevailing image of the hospital increases the pressure to get well fast by enhancing the patient's awareness of the relative degree of the seriousness of his case. Many patients do not have to look far to find and hear about patients who seem more seriously ill. This pressure to get well also is intensified by the observation of "over-worked" and "rushed" nurses and physicians. The pattern of hospital relationships which, for the most part, prevents the development of those relationships which would reduce fears of being rejected or criticized, further discourages patients from exploiting the leniency to which illness *per se* may entitle them. A moral commitment to physicians and nurses is also strengthened by the gratitude and admiration of the sick for those who are "trying to help."

Patterns of interaction are also affected by the controls which the participants can exert over each other and the understanding which they can have of the function of others. For a variety of reasons, the patient sees few areas in which he has control.

A prerequisite for controlling the actions of others is the capacity to feel competent to judge their achievements. Most patients feel quite helpless in evaluating the knowledge, skill and competence of nurses and physicians. This may be one reason for their intense emphasis on "personality." "Personality" is felt to be associated with, and an indicator of, those more technical qualities which patients do not feel qualified to judge.

Control does not only depend on the capacity to judge the competence or efficiency of others. It also involves the freedom to convey and impose judgments. Even if patients feel quite certain about their judgments, they may feel reluctant to express them if such action may portend a reduction in good patient care.

The institutional context affects the way the patients balance their perceived claims and obligations. They manage to communicate the conditional nature of their claims, the undesirability of their state and, therefore, the importance of their obligations. Their persistent verbal assertions that they should co-operate, that they must not be demanding, underscore their motivation to get well. The problem of patients does not stem from a rejection of major social values but rather from the dissonance created between the desire to broaden the boundaries of what seems a legitimate sphere of control and the tendency to adhere compulsively to behavior which reflects conformity to obligations.[6] The data confirm Parsons' contention that dependence is, in our society, a primary threat to the valued achievement capacity and that the sick, to this extent, are called upon to work for their own recovery.[7]

Efforts to adhere to obligations are accompanied by the complementary hope that others will meet their obligations in turn and thus will satisfy the patient's expectations. Recognition of the limitations under which hospital functionaries work does not prevent patients from forming "ideal" expectations which call for a model of care which the on-going work processes of the hospital do not readily approximate.[8] The restraint which is exercised by the hospitalized patient is partly an expression of his fears that he may be deprived of important service if he should deviate from acceptable behavior. However, while patients have some notions of the sanctions which can be applied should they violate standards for appropriate behavior, they appear much less certain what they could do if nurses or physicians do not meet their obligations. The feeling of helplessness of patients is partly derived from an incapacity to judge adequately the competence of those who take care of them—in part, from the fact that their experiences do not provide easily defendable criteria for asserting their rights; and partly from their reluctance to use the controls which are available to them.

The interviews showed that patients always knew what they should not be like or what qualities or behavior would make them acceptable to others. Even much more difficult for them was to define what specific tasks they had a right to expect and what expectations could be transformed into active demands without deviating from general norms of behavior. A lack of familiarity with what constitutes proper care and cure procedures as well as the fact that a slight change in their condition could alter the legitimacy of demands appears to contribute to this difficulty. Rigid adherence to general rules of conduct appeared to be one way out of this dilemma.

Patients were also limited in the expression of their feelings by the fact that personalized and supportive care was not considered to lie within the sphere of the essential. They clearly felt that they had to subordinate such demands to their own or other patients' needs for physical care. The point of view of patients parallels the common distinction between the legitimacy of somatic and mental illness—a distinction which is accompanied by the notion that somatic illness legitimately entitles the ill to accept dependence as a result of manifestly impaired *physical* capacity for task performance. This dependence is narrowly defined in terms of permitting hospital functionaries to do things for the patient only as long as it is really *physically* necessary. Emotional dependence or other deviations from adult role performance are considered legitimate by most patients only in cases of extreme illness.[9]

The opportunities to obtain personalized care are limited and they are further restricted by patients who as "good patients" withdraw from those on whom they depend and with whom they wish to communicate but whom they do not wish "to bother." The control of the desire to obtain and demand more personal care tends to intensify alienation.[10] The expression of such emotional needs is checked not only by the various pressures to conform to the patient role, but also by the fact that those patient-care activities which direct themselves to the emotional needs of the patient are not institutionalized as role obligations of personnel in the general hospital. Personal concern, support or other emotionally therapeutic efforts tend to be from the patient's point of view pleasant (often unexpected) attributes of otherwise task-oriented personnel. Such activities are quickly praised and even "ideally" seen as the major attributes of the "good" nurse and of the "good" physician. But, since these do not really belong to the manifestly legitimate obligations, they are only reluctantly criticized when missing and rarely directly demanded.

Efforts to adhere to rules of conduct involve also the desire to project a specific image of self.[11] Being accepted is of more than passing importance to the hospitalized patient.[12] Self-consciousness about the norms to which one tries to conform may also suggest that the role is in certain respects alien to the performers and that they are not secure in essential social relationships. Efforts to reiterate conformity to general rules of conduct may thus, at least in part, stem from the patient's limited knowledge of the reality of the institutional setting and from fears that he may not be able to measure up to institutionalized expectations. Thus, uncertain about how far he can go before violating prescribed rules for behavior, patients may find their security in efforts to live up to the "letter of the law."[13]

The frequently expressed obligation to co-operate and the persistent attempt to seek approval is, within this frame of reference, not only a diplomatic effort to manipulate relationships to one's own advantage, but also an expression of the patient's perception of the degree of dependency associated with his status. The associated attitudes are thus not merely psychological consequences of the sick role but also reflect the patient's common sense assessments of the abrogation of independence and decisionmaking associated with his status in the hospital.[14] These deprivations are communicated to the patient beginning with the possessive gesture of the identification bracelet affixed during admission to the hospital, and they are continuously reinforced in daily experiences. The hospital preempts control and jurisdiction, ranging from the assumption of accountability of body functions to the withholding of information about medical procedures.[15]

The interviews reflect a degree of uncertainty whether physicians and nurses operate as effective teams in close communication or whether the patient ought to function as interpreter and intermediary between these two all important functionaries. Sometimes patients wonder whether they are sources of conflict and competition between medicine and nursing. The physician is seen as supreme authority and patients repeatedly stress that "if something is really seriously wrong," they would turn to the physician. The physician, however, is for the most part not present to observe, respond or intervene. The nurse is continually present, or at least within reach of the call system. She is the physician's representative and interpreter, but she also is the one who has to bear the brunt of work resulting from the physician's orders. She represents hospital rules, and yet she is not infrequently seen by the patient as a potential spokesman for his needs and interests. These perceptions reflect remarkably well the organization of the hospital and the ambiguous position of the nurse at the crossroads of the care and cure structures.[16]

This study suggests that the patient role, like other comparable behavior syndromes organized around a status, are not adequately described by isolating attitudinal and normative responses to the role theme itself, i.e., illness. The full repertory of role behavior must be placed into the context of organizational processes if it is to encompass realistic orientations and behavior display.

The patient role described in this paper is specific to the hospital. The data support and amplify the implication of Merton's use of the role-set as an analytic concept.[17] The patient gropes for appropriate criteria and distinctions in defining his role with reference to a variety of significant relationships. The concept points to the importance of the difference in the power of the members of the role-set *vis-à-vis* the status occupant who has to manipulate between correspondents and to the significance of the support which the status occupant receives from others in like circumstances. However, the relatively isolated patient in the modern single or double hospital room is frequently left to his own devices in coping with differences in real or perceived expectations. This adds to the conditions favoring manifestations of withdrawal or dependence on the approval of others as realistic responses to institutionalized impotence.

The data also suggests a further elaboration of certain aspects of the theoretical model of role behavior. The concept of the role-set refines the differential system of expectations attached to a status from the point of view of the range of counter roles. The data reported in this paper suggest that an additional dimension of role expectation would be a useful addition to theory. Expectations which define a role are normally attributed to the social system surrounding a status.[18] It is suggested that a distinguishable difference exists between the pattern of expectations arising from the structural aspects of the status and those expectations which are attached to the function ascribed to the role. Thus, the role concomitants of being ill can be defined as the functional role segment of the patient role while the consequences of hospitalization, be they perceived or real, could be termed positional role segments.

Concern with the functional segment of the patient role has been evidenced in most previous treatments of the sick role in the literature.[19] The positional role segment in this study is specific to the hospital. Yet in other settings for patient behavior—be it the home, the clinic or the physician's office—these structural components of the patient role would also bear fruitful sociological investigation. This conceptual scheme aids in structuring the observations of potential strain and conflict between different aspects of the patient role.

This study suggests that a prevailing theme of successful role behavior is the ability of the status occupant to integrate into his own behavior and responses different components from the system of expectations surrounding him. In the case of the patient his efforts to be "a good patient," to meet the obligations as he perceives them and to strive to cooperate in recovery are handicapped by the inadequacy of the communications system within which he functions.[20] Were it more effective, it may permit the patient to cope with his role with greater certainty about rights and obligations, the controls at his disposal and the risks inherent in behavioral experimentation.

FOOTNOTES

1. Parsons, T., "Definitions of Health and Illness in the Light of American Values and Social Structure," in E. G. Jaco (ed.), *Patients, Physicians and Illness*, New York: Free Press, 1958, pp. 165–187.
2. Thirty-two per cent of the patients in this sample occupied a private room; 61 per cent occupied a two-bed room and 7 per cent shared a room with two other patients.
3. Parsons, T., *The Social System*, New York: Free Press, 1951, pp. 433–477.
4. This phenomenon suggests a parallel to the concept of "relative deprivation" described by R. K. Merton and P. Lazarsfeld (eds.), *Continuities in Social Research*, New York: Free Press, 1950. Just as deprivation is experienced in relation to relative norms, legitimacy of claims rests on a relative basis. If this basis is not ascertainable, uncertainty functions as restraining force.
5. Parsons, T., and R. Fox, "Illness, Therapy and the Modern Urban American

Family," in E. G. Jaco (ed.), *Patients, Physicians and Illness*, New York: Free Press, 1st ed., 1958, p. 236.

6. At times the patient and his significant others among hospital functionaries may be less in disagreement over proper role relationships than significant others involved in their social network. Thus, in some cases patients were found to define their obligations in terms of all the previously discussed considerations. Their relatives, however, emphasized the rights of the paying consumer and expressed their opinion that the patient was "not asking for enough." For a discussion of the role of the third part see W. J. Goode, "A Theory of Role Strain," *American Sociological Review*, 25:483–496, August, 1960.

7. Parsons, "Definitions of Health and Illness . . .," *op. cit.* p. 185.

8. Reactions to experiences in the hospital assume, therefore, meaning not only in relation to "realistic" anticipations but also in relation to more subtly held "ideal" expectations. The relative discrepancy between "realistic" and "ideal" experiences is a significant variable in the patients' responses to actual experiences.

9. Patients were not interviewed during the critical phases of their illness when, indeed, their claims may have been different. However, only a few patients in the sample considered themselves recovered. The majority of patients in the cardio-vascular category were recuperating from severe illness and were under orders for bedrest. The majority of the patients in the gastro-intestinal category were under treatment for ulcers or hospitalized for other chronic or acute gastro-intestinal conditions. In all of these cases the conditional nature of rights was bound to create some difficulties— either because of the absence of visible symptoms of illness or because the illness was not considered very serious. Case studies of the more seriously ill patients indicate that anxiety may cause them to "break through" the limits set by their role but that such a breakthrough often demands added efforts since claims, demands or irritations have to be justified. To reestablish an acceptable view of themselves seems to often constitute a major effort for these patients.

10. Parsons, "Definitions of Health and Illness . . .," *op. cit.*, p. 186. The author points out that the supportive treatment of the sick person "undercuts the alienative component of the motivational structure of his illness."

11. Goffman, E., "The Nature of Deference and Demeanor," *Amer. Anthropologist,* 58:473–502, June, 1956; E. Goffman, *Encounters: Two Studies in the Sociology of Interaction,* Indianapolis, Ind.: Bobbs-Merrill, 1961, pp. 99–105.

12. Efforts to give verbal evidence of conformity may aim at protection from criticism. Deviations tend to be viewed as forgiveable as long as a person gives evidence of "good will." Goode emphasized that failure in role behavior tends to arouse less criticism than failure in emotional commitment to general norms. This principle may be particularly applicable to situations where it is also an obligation of alters to tolerate failures in role behavior. See W. J. Goode, "Norm Commitment and Conformity to Role Status Obligations," *Amer. J. Soc.,* 66:246–258, November, 1960.

13. See Merton's discussion of ritualism. Anxiety over the ability to live up to institutional expectations may contribute to compulsive adherence to institutional norms. R. K. Merton, *Social Theory and Social Structure,* New York: Free Press, Rev. Ed., 1957, pp. 184–187.

14. Parsons and Fox stressed the need for a "well-timed, well-chosen, well-balanced exercise of supportive and the disciplinary components of the

therapeutic process." Institutional factors as well as widely held social values may tend to shift the emphasis too much to the disciplinary components particularly in the setting of the general hospital which incorporate structurally as well as in terms of explicitly or implicitly held attitudes the distinction between the emotionally sick and the physically sick (Parsons and Fox, *op. cit.*, p. 244).

15. Mauksch, H. O., "Patients View Their Roles," *Hospital Progress*, 43:136–138, October, 1962.
16. Mauksch, H. O., "The Organizational Context of Nursing Practice," in F. Davis (ed.), *The Nursing Profession*, New York: Wiley, 1966, pp. 109–137.
17. Merton, R. K., "The Role Set," *British J. Sociology*, 8:106–120, June, 1957.
18. *Ibid.*, p. 113f.
19. Parons, *The Social System, loc. cit.* Other writers, notably R. Coser, *Life in the Ward*, Lansing, Mich.: Michigan State Univ. Press, 1962, include positional considerations to a greater extent.
20. Skipper, Jr., J. K., D. L. Tagliacozzo and H. O. Mauksch, "Some Possible Consequences of Limited Communication Between Patients and Hospital Functionaries," *J. Health and Human Behavior*, 5:34–39, Spring, 1964; J. K. Skipper, Jr., "Communication and the Hospitalized Patient", in J. K. Skipper and R. C. Leonard (eds.), *Social Interaction and Patient Care*, Philadelphia: Lippincott, 1965, pp. 61–82.

PART

III

Practicing Humane Care—
The Caregiver

Introduction to Part III

CAREGIVERS' PHILOSOPHICAL COMMITMENT, good intentions, and conceptual understanding have little meaning unless acted upon and integral to their day-to-day activities. In this section, we focus on how caregivers can interact with patients more compassionately. To this end, we present three articles that discuss specific techniques the caregiver can use to communicate effectively. They illustrate that there *are* methods the caregiver can apply to build the caring relationship.

In "Reassurance Reconsidered," David Buchsbaum examines the role of reassurance as an effective therapeutic intervention. After describing the meaning of reassurance, he presents several illustrations to help the reader understand when and how to reassure. Reassurance can relieve patients' anxiety and restore their sense of autonomy. Buchsbaum encourages the caregiver to clarify the meaning that the illness has for the patient, identify the patient's needs for information, and address these needs in an empathetic and unambiguous way.

Reframing—redirecting patients' perspectives on their illness—is also useful in making rapid and effective professional interventions. In "Reframing Techniques in the General Hospital," Stuart Eisendrath explains how the caregiver can help patients comprehend the constructive aspects of their circumstances and thus lessen their fear and anxiety. The resulting shift in attitude can markedly improve the patient's outlook and interest in doing what needs to be done to get well. Similarly, when staff who are having difficulty with a patient reframe their own perceptions, they can improve both their own morale and patient care.

Humanistic care cannot take place without direct human contact, and many significant aspects of this interaction are nonverbal in nature. The article by Howard Friedman, "Nonverbal Communication Between Patients and Medical Practitioners," suggests that effective nonverbal communication—voice, tone, facial expressions—is therefore essential to the patient-caregiver relationship. Major aspects of nonverbal communication that are directly relevant to health care have been studied scientifically but have not, as yet, been systematically used. Friedman reviews several promising ways in which caregivers can draw on nonverbal skills in the provision of humane care.

5

Reassurance Reconsidered

David G. Buchsbaum

THE ABILITY TO REASSURE THE PATIENT in need is one of the most commonly appreciated, clinically important and least understood functions that the physician performs in his daily practice of medicine. Often reassurance is the intentional goal of the physician while at other times it is the by product of information learned during the session [1].

When is reassurance indicated? Although physicians commonly associate the need for reassurance in patients with symptomatic but benign disease [2], there is a role for reassurance in patients with chronic and progressive disease as well.

Webster's International Dictionary defines reassurance as the restoration of confidence [3]. Confidence, or the individual's faith in his ability to live and perform to his expectations, is a common casualty of illness and is therefore, the focus of the physician's intervention. This requires that the physician clarify the meaning that the illness carries for the patient, characterize the patient's information needs and convey a message that addresses these needs in an empathic and unambiguous way. This paper reviews the process of reassuring patients in the clinical setting. Vignettes, drawn from a library of videotaped physician-patient visits are provided to clarify the communications important to this process.

UNCOVERING PERSONAL MEANING

When a person is ill or believes he may be ill because he experiences unfamiliar symptoms or learns of asymptomatic physical or chemical ab-

Reprinted from *Social Science and Medicine* 23, no. 4 (1986): 423–427, with permission, Pergamon Journals Ltd.

normalities, he is likely to fantasize about his condition and the uncertain consequence of this condition upon his life. Anxiety, fear and feelings of vulnerability are common emotional sequela of these ruminations. The following vignette involves a young female physician and a young female college student referred to the university clinic by another health agency. The patient has a strong family history of diabetes mellitus.

Doctor: I'm Dr. Yallow, how are you doing?
Patient: (quietly) okay.
Doctor: Well, how did you end up coming to the clinic?
Patient: When I went for my yearly checkup . . . They said I had some sugar in my blood.
Doctor: (looking at referral sheet). I see . . . anybody in your family have diabetes?
Patient: (looking over doctor's shoulder). My father.
Doctor: Sometimes when you have high sugar you have symptoms like being thirsty or passing your water frequently.
Patient: (sits upright). I drink all the time, and last night I passed my water five times . . . I've never done that before.
Doctor: I see. Any cramps or numbness down your arms or legs?
Patient: (appears anxious, rubbing her legs). I have cramps sometimes, even last night while in bed.
Doctor: I see. Well, we'll need to repeat the blood tests, but in the meantime I'm going to examine you.

Exit interview

Doctor: (rest hand on top of the patient's record and looks at patient). Well, you probably have diabetes and we'll need to check your blood. You know that diabetes is very serious and can affect your legs, circulation, heart, brain and kidneys. Your pancreas puts out insulin and it may be overworked. Now, you're 21 and will have diabetes for a long time so we need to control it. I recommend that we start insulin. I'll have you come back Monday after the results return and we'll take it from there. Now . . .
Patient: (sits back in chair startled). Who will have to go on insulin?
Doctor: (quizzically). You will, as I've just explained.
Patient: (emphatically). I don't need insulin!

In this encounter the patient's startled response and resistance to insulin management suggests that she harbors powerful beliefs and fears that are not easily assuaged by rational explanations of physiology.

The houseofficer's responsibility to the patient does not end with providing a diagnosis or a rationale for her management. She must consider, appraise and address the meaning that the illness carries for her patient. All patients invest their illness with personal meaning that is derived from the perceived impact the illness will have upon his or her life. This in turn is influenced by a number of coalescing forces including the patient's age, social circumstances, emotional state, personality and previous experience with the diagnosed disorder [4–6].

In this session the physician can uncover the meaning that diabetes has for her patient by asking her what she understands about diabetes. Furthermore, by eliciting the patient's concerns, or by clarifying questions she may pose, the physician can dispel misconceptions the patient may have regarding the potential consequences of this disorder upon her life.

The physician must keep in mind that illness may threaten the individual's sense of autonomy, while at the same time awaken dependency needs and fears of abandonment [7, 8]. The physician can address these needs by conveying genuine interest and by offering her patient respectful and unconditional support. These are communications that are common to all successful helping relationships [9, 10].

Patients may vary in their need for the physician's support [11], but in times of the emotional turbulence that often accompanies illness, the patient's trust that the physician will provide consistent and compassionate care is quite reassuring.

CONVEYING EMPATHY

A number of investigations cite empathy as a principal feature of all helping relationships [9, 10]. By empathizing with his patient, the physician bridges the emotional distance separating the patient from the world of the healthy. It is reassuring to the patient to believe that the physician understands his predicament and cares. Yet, the ability to feel empathy is not automatic and a number of factors may constrain its expression. The following vignette describes a session in which physician empathy fails to materialize. The patient is middle aged and overweight.

Doctor: Hello, I'm Dr. Xavier (extends hand, looks at chart).
Patient: I'm Mrs. Perry (shakes hand).
Doctor: (looking at desk). So, what brings you here today?
Patient: I need to get a work-up for blood pressure. I've been off medication for many years and need to get back on to stay on Social Security (extends hand with bottles enclosed). I take this medication for my nerves.

Doctor: (looks at bottle then down at chart). You take thorazine for your nerves . . . I see, so you've come to get your blood pressure checked.

Patient: (rocking to and fro). And get back on my medication.

Doctor: (cross, looks up). You know that once you're on blood pressure medicines you're supposed to stay on them (patient looks down). Well, how have you been feeling?

Patient: (looks up). Well, I've been getting those headaches and when I get up fast my heart beats like I'm going to have a heart attack (makes fluttering movement with hand over chest).

Doctor: Has this been going on for a long time?

Patient: Well, it's gotten bad since I've got more weight on me.

Doctor: (curt). Well, you know this weight is very dangerous to your heart.

Patient: Well, the medicine makes me gain weight (points to Thorazine).

Doctor: (emphatically shaking head). This medicine doesn't do that much to your appetite. Have you ever tried to lose weight?

Patient: I've tried but it doesn't work (looks down and resumes rocking).

Doctor: Look, we're not talking about getting down to normal, but maybe if you lost a significant part it would help you tremendously. I'll tell you what, we have a special clinic here today.

Patient: I've tried that. I've got to stop on my own, first.

Doctor: Well, it's not going to work on your own.

Patient: (quietly). I don't want to go.

Doctor: (scolding). Well what do you think's going to happen. Do you think you're going to be able to fit on the scales the next time you come here?

If a goal of reassurance is to reinforce or restore the patient's self esteem, this session can be considered counter-reassuring. The physician has responded to the patient in an emotional way that conveys rejection.

The intense emotions that constrain the physician's feeling of empathy for his patient in the vignette may have been triggered by specific features of the patient or her condition [12–15]. For example, obesity is a condition that is largely a result of patient behaviors. The physician may regard these behaviors and their inevitable outcome as undesirable. The stronger the physician's attitude, and the more rigid his personality, the more hostile his response is likely to be. Additionally, the physician's response may be magnified by his automatic weighing of the consequences he believes will result from his treatment efforts. If he anticipates that treating hypertension in this patient will be an aggravating and ultimately futile experience, he will approach this challenge with ambivalence and reluctance at best.

Alternatively, a patient may provoke intense emotions in the physician because she demonstrates behaviors or personality features that are similar to those of a significant person in the physician's life, or to himself [16]. Young houseofficers often have difficulty caring for seriously ill patients of similar age [17]. In this situation the physician's empathic feelings yield to painful identification.

Discomfort may also arise when the physician is confronted with unresolved psychodynamic issues. Two areas of particular difficulty for young physicians are sexuality and death [17, 18]. One common physician response to severe patient illness is a flight into science that protects the physician but isolates the patient [19].

A number of external factors may prime the physician to respond in a particularly emotional manner. These include the physician's physical and emotional health at the time of the patient's visit, the pressures of time and competing responsibilities, the relative stability of physicians' family and home life, and adequacy of sleep [22, 23].

Empathy conveys caring, the *sine qua non* of the doctor-patient relationship. Importantly, Kasteler [22] and Hayes-Bautista [23] both found that the most common reason for patients terminating the physician-patient relationship was the patient's perception that the physician was uncaring.

ADDRESSING THE PATIENT'S INFORMATION NEEDS

During the period of uncertainty that accompanies the threat of illness, the information that the physician shares with the patient can be a powerful and stabilizing force. Timely and meaningful information can dispel inordinate fears and enable the patient to chart a coherent and organized course of action.

The following vignette demonstrates one possible outcome when a physician withholds information from a patient who expresses a need for information. The patient is a carefully groomed and college educated middle aged woman visiting the physician for the first time.

Doctor: Hello, I'm Dr. Harding. What can I do for you?
Patient: I would like to get a mammogram.
Doctor: (shifts backward, looks at patient). I see. Well, we can determine the need for that after I examine you—now, you're a new patient to the clinic?

Patient: Yes I am.

Doctor: How have you been doing?

Patient: (looking at physician). I've been doing fine but I think it would be a good idea if I got a mammogram. I was examining myself last month and I felt a lump.

Doctor: Uh huh, have you ever felt one before?

Patient: No but . . .

Doctor: (looking at patient). Have you noticed any lumps anywhere else or lost any weight?

Patient: No, I've been feeling quite well physically.

Further review of systems followed by physical examination.

Exit interview

Doctor: Well, Mrs. Myers, after examining you I agree we should get a mammogram.

Patient: Yes, you never know what a lump might be.

Doctor: (begins filling out requisition, shielding his writing from patient's view with right arm). That's true, that's why I think this test is necessary.

Patient: (straining neck to see over physician's arm). I hope the mammogram can tell what it is.

Doctor: (moves body in position to further block patient's view of writing). uh huh.

Patient: (climbing over physician's arm to see record).

Doctor: (startled, looks up at patient).

It is clear in this vignette that the patient needs information. Initially she is quite assertive about her needs. As the session continues she becomes verbally less demanding, but as her behavior suggests she is no less anxious. Although the patient is apparently concerned about the possibility of cancer, the physician, perhaps in an effort to 'protect' the patient, withholds the information that she desperately needs.

Illness, or the threat of illness casts the patient into a landscape of uncertain dimensions. Information is a map that can help the individual gain a sense of boundaries and control over her predicament, an important step to reestablishing a sense of control and self confidence.

All patients, to varying degrees, have preconceived notions, expectations and hidden questions about their symptoms and the need for investigation of these symptoms. Often the likelihood of reassurance is conditioned upon the physician meeting the patient's information needs [1]. If the physician tries to reassure the patient without considering her needs, his intervention is unlikely to meet with success. Moreover, the physician's recognition and successful address of his patients' information needs can influence the duration and severity of experienced symptoms and functional impairment, the patient's sense of participation and the patient's satisfaction with the clinical session [1, 24–26].

How much information should the physician impart? Not all patients are capable of assimilating the same type and amount of information. The physician's message must be individualized, taking into consideration the patient's cognitive function, formal education, cultural background and prominent personality features as well as the circumstantial impact of the message [11].

Returning to this vignette, the patient provides ample personal and behavioral evidence that she requires factual information. Reassurance will not occur by ignoring her request for information but by addressing these needs. The physician should discuss the obvious diagnostic possibilities and an organized plan of investigation and management. The patients' questions will guide the physician in the extent of his elaboration.

By encouraging the patient to express her fears or by verbalizing her fears, the physician reassures the patient that her fears are an expected and normal response; a reassurance that is likely to relieve the patient's sense of isolation and strengthen the doctor-patient relationship. By 'protecting' the patient through withholding information, the physician infantilizes the patient, a process that at once discounts the patient's identity as an autonomous and capable adult and fosters dependency upon the physician. In terms of reassurance this is a counter productive strategy.

PROVIDING A CLEAR MESSAGE

The way the physician presents information to his patient can be as important to patient reassurance as the content of the information. Most medical decisions are based on the evaluation of incomplete data. At times an investigation will uncover information that was not intentionally sought and of uncertain significance. A number of articles have been written that address this clinical quandary [27, 28]. The manner in which the physician manages uncertainty can be reassuring to his patient or provoke anxiety in his patient. The following exchange captures the distressing effect that a physician's ambiguous message has upon a patient's perception of his health status. The patient is a 30 year old male with a family history of hypertension. He has returned 2 weeks after an initial health maintenance exam.

Doctor: (leafing through the medical record). Well Mr. Tyler, how have you been today?

Patient: (rubbing hands on knees). Great Doctor. I feel fine.

Doctor: (still reviewing chart). uh huh (looks up). Well, we have the results of the labs we sent a couple of weeks ago.

Patient: (sits upright). Yea, I was wondering. How is it?

Doctor: (looks up and smiles). Fine, everything checks out . . . more or less (looks down).

Patient: Good. I was kind of worried, you know with my father having kidney problems.

Doctor: Well, its fine, the only thing . . . your cholesterol and creatinine are a little high, but nothing to really worry about (looks down at chart).

Patient: (concerned look). How high?

Doctor: (biting lip). Well I don't want to make a big deal of it really, but mildly elevated.

Patient: Anything to worry about?

Doctor: No, not really. Look, you're a healthy young man. I'm sure there's no problem. I usually wouldn't do anything (rubs his chin, scratches his head then writes out requisition slip) but . . . I'm going to draw some blood to separate your cholesterol. You know there's good and bad cholesterol. I'd also like to get a 24 hr urine specimen from you to check your kidney function, and we may need to schedule special X-rays.

Patient: (hand running through hair). But I'm okay?

Doctor: Oh yea, you're fine.

In this vignette the physician tries to reassure the patient by minimizing the importance of the uncovered laboratory abnormalities. He initially states that the tests are fine but qualifies his statement by adding that there are a couple of abnormalities that require further investigation. The message he conveys is ambiguous and contradictory. If everything is fine, then why the need for more tests?

The message that the patient gleans from what the physician says is gathered from the verbal information that the physician presents and the affective or non-verbal behavior that accompanies the information [29, 30]. As in all interpersonal situations, the patient is simultaneously reading these complementary forms of communication for consistency. If the physician is inconsistent in his communication, the patient will question the validity of his verbal message.

In this exchange the physician's presentation of his information is more threatening to the patient than the uncertain nature of the information itself. The physician must realize that most patients can accommodate short term uncertainty without any serious adverse effects [31].

With this in mind the physician may acknowledge his uncertainty but at the same time convey the message that he can competently manage this uncertainty through implementing and pursuing a strategy for its resolution. Although patients want to participate in their care, they also need the physician to assist and at times, guide them in their decisions [32].

CONCLUSION

Reassurance is a therapeutic intervention that requires careful consideration prior to implementation. The purpose of reassurance is to relieve anxiety and restore the patient's confidence in his or her ability to live as an autonomous and functioning individual. Accordingly, reassurance is a timely intervention in any clinical situation where the patient feels that this ability to function is threatened. In this regard, the patient's perceptions and fantasies of illness, whether aroused by the experience of transient and self terminating disease or a disorder that is chronic and progressive, are the focus of attention.

In this expanded consideration of reassurance the physician's power resides not only in his words, but in his behavior and commitment to the doctor-patient relationship, and to the empathic, respectful and competent care he extends to his patient.

Acknowledgement—Grant support in part by Bureau of Health Professions, HRSA, grant for residency training in general internal medicine.

REFERENCES

1. Sox H. C., Margolles T. and Sox C. H. Psychologically mediated effects of diagnostic tests. *Ann. intern. Med.* 95, 680–685, 1981.
2. Sapira J. D. Reassurance therapy. What to say to symptomatic patients with benign disease. *Ann. intern. Med.* 97, 603–604, 1972.
3. *Webster's Third New International Dictionary* (Edited by Gove P. B.). Mirriam, Springfield, Mass., 1976.
4. Barlund D. C. The mystification of meaning: The doctor-patient encounter. *J. med. Educ.* 57, 716–725, 1976.
5. Lipowski F. J. Psychosocial aspects of disease. *Ann. intern. Med.* 7, 1197–1206, 1969.
6. Mechanic D. Social psychologic factors effecting the presentation of bodily complaints. *New Engl. J. Med.* 286, 1132–1139, 1972.
7. Bowlby J. *Attachment and Loss*, Vol. 1. Basic Book, New York, 1969.
8. Rabin D., Rabin P. L. and Rabin R. Compounding the ordeal of ALS: Isolation, from my fellow physicians. *New Engl. J. Med.* 307, 506–509, 1982.
9. Truax C. B. and Wargio D. G. Psychotherapeutic encounters that change behaviors for better or for worse. *Am. J. Psycho-Ther.* 20, 499–520, 1966.
10. Rogers C. R. The characteristics of a helping relationship. In *On Becoming a Person* (Edited by Rogers C. R.), pp. 39–58. Houghton Mifflin, Boston.

11. Leigh H. and Reiser M. R. The patient's personality. In *The Patient* (Edited by Leigh H. and Reiser M. R.), pp. 253–269. Plenum Medical Book Co., New York 1980.
12. Drucker E. Hidden values and health care. *Med. Care* 12, 266–273, 1974.
13. Carey K. and Logan W. S. Exploration of factors influencing physician decisions to refer patients for mental health services. *Med. Care* 9, 55–56, 1971.
14. Dardick L. and Grady K. Openness between gay persons and health professionals. *Ann. intern. Med.* 93, 115–119, 1980.
15. Ajzen I. and Fishbein M. *Understanding Attitudes and Predicting Social Behaviors*. Prentice Hall, Englewood Cliffs, N. J., 1980.
16. Langs R. *Psychoanalytic Psychotherapy*, Vol. 1. Jason Aronson, New York, 1976.
17. Artis K. L. and Levine A. S. Doctor-patient relation in serious illness. *New Engl. J. Med.* 288, 1210–1214, 1973.
18. Mudd J. W. and Geigel R. J. Sexuality. The experience and anxieties of medical students. *New Engl. J. Med.* 281, 1397–1403, 1969.
19. Pond D. A. Doctors' mental health. *N.Z. med. J.* 69, 131–135, 1969.
20. McCue J. D. The effects of stress on physicians and their medical practice. *New Engl. J. Med.* 287, 373–375, 1982.
21. Friedman R. C., Bigger J. and Kornfield D. S. The intern and sleep loss. *New Engl. J. Med.* 285, 201–203, 1971.
22. Hayes-Bautista D. Termination of the doctor-patient relationship: Divorce style. *J. Hlth soc. Behav.* 17, 12, 1976.
23. Kasteler J., Kane R. L., Olsen D. M. and Thefford C. Issues underlying prevalence of "doctor-shopping" behavior. *J. Hlth soc. Behav.* 17, 328–339, 1976.
24. Starfield B., Steinwachs E., Morris I., Bause G., Siebert S. and Westin C. Patient-doctor agreement about problems: Influence on outcome of care. *J. Am. med. Ass.* 242, 344–346, 1979.
25. Vertinsky I. B., Thompson W. A. and Uyeno D. Measuring consumer desire for participation in clinical decision making. *Hlth Res.* 9, 121–134, 1974.
26. Woolley F. R., Kane R. L., Hughes C. C. and Wright D. D. The effects of doctor-patient communication on satisfaction and outcome of care. *Soc. Sci. Med.* 12, 123–128, 1978.
27. Link K., Centor R., Buchsbaum D. and Witherspoon J. Why physicians don't pursue abnormal laboratory tests: An investigation of hypercalcemia and the follow-up of abnormal tests results. *Hum. Path.* 15, 75–78, 1984.
28. Werner M. and Althschuler C. H. Cost-effectiveness of multiphasic screening: Old controversies and a new rationale. *Hum. Path.* 12, 111, 1981.
29. Dimatteo M. R., Friedman H. S. and Taranta A. Sensitivity to bodily communication as a factor in practitioner-patient rapport. *J. Nonverbal Behav.* 1, 18–26, 1979.
30. Ekman P. and Friessen W. V. Nonverbal leakage and clues to deception. *Psychiatry* 32, 88–106, 1969.
31. Hornsby L. H., Sappington J. T., Monjan P., Guellen W. H., Bono S. F. and Altekruse F. Risk for bladder cancer. *J. Am. med. Ass.* 253, 1899–1902, 1985.
32. Strull W. M., Lo B. and Charles G. Do patients want to participate in medical decision making. *J. Am. med. Ass.* 252, 2990–2994, 1984.

6

Reframing Techniques in the General Hospital

Stuart J. Eisendrath

PATIENTS IN THE GENERAL HOSPITAL usually face major life stresses in the form of medical illness. The potential losses of self-esteem, autonomous functioning, valued body parts, and usual coping mechanisms can be significant. Fear of losing important objects, through death or the loss of relationships, can add to the stress of illness. The physician who treats these patients is confronted with helping them cope in the face of these potential major losses and disruptions. Psychosocial interventions in the general hospital differ considerably from those made in the outpatient office. Usually there is little luxury of time. The stressed patients cling desperately to their characteristic psychological defenses. The primary physician or psychiatric consultant has the task of entering the patient's system and making effective interventions rapidly. Reframing is a particularly useful method for doing so. This article will examine the technique of reframing for physicians and consultants.

Most physicians and consultants are already familiar with some aspects of reframing. For example, a physician who explains that a non-compliant patient is suffering from an organic brain syndrome rather than a personality disorder, may help reframe the patient in the staff's view. The staff may feel less angry and better able to cope with the patient. As this illustrates, reframing can be useful with either staff or patients. Indeed, reframing techniques may be very helpful in enabling staff to deal with difficult situations.

Communication theorists have highlighted the therapeutic potential

---

Reprinted from *Family Systems Medicine* 4, no. 1 (1986): 91–95, with permission, Brunner/Mazel, Inc.

of reframing. Watzlawick (6) has described reframing as a technique that is aimed at altering the opinions a person holds. It is a "means to change the conceptual and/or emotional setting or viewpoint in relation to which a situation is experienced and to place it in another frame which fits the 'facts' of the same concrete situation equally well or even better, and thereby change its entire meaning" (6). Reframing allows patient and staff to view a set of circumstances from a different light.

Therapeutic reframing does not require the situation itself to change, and thus is exceptionally valuable when a patient has a medical condition that is unlikely to change. It does not require the patient to alter his/her characteristic psychological defenses—in some instances it may enhance them. In fact, it often increases the patient's sense of control and mastery over a difficult situation. The patient does not feel threatened by being required to give up a coping mechanism that has been successful in the past, even though it may not be completely adequate for the stress of medical illness in the hospital.

The technique of reframing builds upon other psychotherapeutic techniques such as clarification and suggestion. The physician often uses clarification (3, 4) to demonstrate to a patient another way in which such a situation can be viewed. When the consultant reframes the situation by presenting a different view of the same situation, suggestion may be utilized. For example, many patients experience a significant regression in the face of medical illnesss (5). The positive transference that is often generated in that situation allows the consultant to make readily accepted suggestions about the way a patient might be able to view his or her situation.

Because reframing may involve an element of persuasion, it can be considered a form of manipulation (1, 2). Although manipulation has been considered pejoratively as a psychotherapeutic technique by some, this view is short-sighted. Manipulation, in the sense it is utilized for reframing, implies a goal of achieving what is in the patient's or staff's best interest. For example, reframing a frightening medical situation so that a patient can tolerate it more easily is clearly in the patient's best interest. The examples that follow will demonstrate that reframing's manipulative quality benefits the patient primarily, although other components of the system (such as the family) may benefit as well.

PATIENT EXAMPLES

Case 1: A Russian Matriarch
A 65-year-old Russian female immigrated to the U.S. with her daughter, son-in-law, and grandchildren. In her native Russian culture she played an active role in assisting her children; she helped provide

some financial assistance, childcare, and sage advice. One year after immigrating, she developed angina. She eventually had a successful coronary artery bypass procedure but became seriously depressed postoperatively. She stopped participating in her convalescence, preferring to spend the day in her hospital bed. The psychiatric consultant developed a supportive relationship with her. He learned that she felt she no longer could help her family and, in fact, would be a burden henceforth. He asserted that she was feeling depressed because she felt the illness would rob her of her usual role. He suggested that she not only could continue her matriarchal advising, but could show her offspring how to deal courageously with a serious medical problem by actively participating in her own recuperation. Her recovery then began to be viewed by her as a way of reestablishing her matriarchal role. She became progressively more active and her successful convalescence from cardiac surgery actually helped her to feel that she still had much to give to her family. Reframing her illness as an opportunity to aid her children's education on how to cope with adversity successfully countered her depressive view.

Case 2: Macho in the CCU

A 44-year-old black male laborer was admitted to the Coronary Care Unit (CCU) for typical symptoms of a myocardial infarction. His electrocardiogram, laboratory findings, and clinical picture suggested a massive infarction. When this information was conveyed to him, he became less compliant with the medical staff who were urging him to rest, lest he extend his infarct. When staff tried to impress him with the gravity of his situation, he began to voice comments suggesting he didn't believe his doctors had the right diagnosis; he even proposed signing himself out of the hospital. His attending physician spoke with the patient and his family. He learned the patient perceived the infarction and attempts at enforced bedrest by the instillation of fear as threats to his masculinity. The physician then reframed the situation for the patient by saying, "It takes a real man to put up with all that we are asking." Coping with the bedrest and the attendant passivity were pictured as requiring a great deal of macho, rather than implying a loss of manhood. With this view of his situation, the patient tolerated his stay in the CCU without further difficulty.

STAFF EXAMPLES

As noted earlier reframes can be useful with staff as well. Consider the following examples:

Case 3: The Dying Patient

A seriously ill 60-year-old man was transferred to an Intensive Care Unit for treatment. When accepted into the unit, he was seen as someone whose survival would require a miracle. His devoted wife and children clung to their fragile hopes. Within a few days the staff realized that the patient would not survive, and because of their attachment to this attractive patient, began to feel depressed and demoralized. These feelings were expressed in a staff meeting which a liaison psychiatrist regularly attended. When the feelings were explored in the meeting, it became clear that the staff felt they had let the patient and his family down. The psychiatrist dealt with this by making clear that the staff had done all that was medically possible. Then the psychiatrist reframed the situation: Instead of being helplessly frustrated by a patient dying, the staff had an opportunity both to help the patient die with dignity and also to help his family begin the bereavement process. After discussing how these interventions could be implemented, the staff had a change in attitude. Satisfaction in helping the family through the dying process replaced the earlier sense of impotence.

Case 4: Nurse Frustration

The staff nurses in a medical-surgical ICU were accustomed to patients who improved or worsened over a short time span. Only rarely did they have to care for a patient over a long time period. Mr. B was a Guillain-Barré syndrome patient who was admitted with almost complete paralysis and needed mechanical ventilation during a long and gradual recovery. He required extensive nursing support because he was unable to provide any care for himself. He was unable to turn or even to signal a nurse if he became disconnected from the ventilator. In a staff meeting attended by the ICU's Medical Director, the nurses voiced their frustrations. They complained that little was happening with the patient's medical situation and that they felt rather useless—merely caretakers. The ICU Medical Director reframed the nurses' situation utilizing the following points: Patients with severe Guillain-Barré syndrome required intensive *nursing* support for their survival. Autonomic instability, respiratory failure, and the severe emotional trauma of the disease required maximal support. In contrast to surgical cases, with Guillain-Barré patients, the nurses were the main agent of treatment. It was also pointed out that although the progress was slow, their patient had an excellent prognosis. In many ways their patient typified the ideal ICU patient: highly salvageable and requiring intensive nursing care. Following this discussion the nurses developed an organized care plan which they carried through with enthusiasm during the patient's stay.

DISCUSSION

As can be seen in the above examples, reframing exerts its beneficial action in various ways. A successful reframing conveys a sense of understanding, which is markedly therapeutic in itself. In addition, reframing often helps patients or staff feel more in control, less impotent, and more hopeful. This often leads to improved self-concepts and esteem. In Case 1, reframing allowed the Russian matriarch to feel less helpless, more hopeful about her future, and restored the role that produced much of her self-esteem. In Case 2, the threat to the man's masculinity was reframed to allow him to feel more in control of his immediate situation. In Case 3, the staff's sense of impotence was markedly diminished, resulting in improved esteem. In Case 4, the staff's role was clarified and reformulated in keeping with their own high ideals, leading to lessened frustration and improved esteem.

As the examples illustrate, reframing requires the consultant to obtain a clear understanding of how the situation is perceived. Once the consultant has obtained this understanding, he or she must creatively search for another view that is valid, believable, and congruous with the situation. If this is not done, the reframing may appear as inappropriate or insensitive. It must also be remembered that there are some limits to the use of reframing. Some situations cannot yield an alternative view that ameliorates the distress. For example, the loss of a loved one can hardly be reframed, but rather must be grieved. As with other forms of intervention, clinical judgment should prevail in deciding when to appropriately utilize reframing.

Reframing is only one tool for the physician and consultant on a medical-surgical floor. Generally it is best utilized after the consultant has begun to develop a sense of rapport with the patient or staff. In practice, it is usually combined with other interventions such as ventilation, clarification, suggestion, interpretation, and reassurance. For some individuals, reframing will not be sufficient to improve the situation; interventions requiring more extended efforts will be needed. Nonetheless, as a specific, short-term technique, reframing can be extremely useful in the general hospital setting. When used judiciously, it can enhance the physician's sense of efficacy, creativity, and satisfaction.

REFERENCES

1. Bibring, E. Psychoanalysis and the dynamic psychotherapies. *Journal of the American Psychoanalytic Association*, 1954, 2, 745–770.
2. Briggins, C. & Zinberg, N. Manipulation and its clinical application. *American Journal of Psychotherapy*, 1969, 23, 198–206.
3. Langs, R. *The technique of psychoanalytic psychotherapy.* New York: Jason Aronson, 1973.

4. Rogers, C. *Client-centered therapy*. Boston: Houghton-Mifflin, 1951.
5. Viederman, M. & Perry, S. Use of a psychodynamic life narrative in the treatment of depression in the physically ill. *General Hospital Psychiatry*, 1980, 3, 177–185.
6. Watzlawick, P. The gentle art of reframing. In P. Watzlawick, J. Weakland, & R. Fisch (Eds.), *Change—Principles of problem formation and problem resolution*. New York: Norton, 1974.

7

Nonverbal Communication Between Patients and Medical Practitioners

Howard S. Friedman

SINCE ANCIENT TIMES, physicians and other healers have relied upon careful observation to diagnose illness, and have developed appropriate bedside manners to promote recovery. Medical education emphasizes the need for careful attention to the patient's subtle clues of pain, anxiety, emotion, and disease (O'Brien, 1974). Medical lore offers numerous suggestions for proper comforting of patients, for correct demeanor, and for appropriate reactions to patient behavior (DiMatteo, 1979). In practice, many experienced practitioners rely heavily on the subtleties of face-to-face interaction. However, although scientific procedures have replaced art in much of medical practice, the dynamics of interpersonal interaction remain mostly unattended by systematic research (Bennett, 1976). Even in the face of the past decade's advances in behavioral science and communication (e.g., Korsch, Gozzi, & Francis, 1968), intuition, faith, morale, empathy, sensitivity, caring, comfort, will to live, and similar pregnant but imprecise terms are still the by-words of nursing and direct patient care. Actually, there is a quantity of available scientific information on the use and meaning of *nonverbal communication* which can be applied to medical interactions.

Nonverbal communication involves those subtle cues which complement and illustrate aspects of the verbal interaction and often provide messages and express feelings that are not subject to direct conscious

Reprinted from the *Journal of Social Issues* 35, no. 1 (1979): 82–99, with permission, The Society for the Psychological Study of Social Issues.

analysis by the interactants. A patient's grimace, smile, or expression of fear, as well as a nurse's comforting touch or facial expression of disgust, are communicative acts which may be even more important than the matter under verbal discussion.

For a number of reasons, nonverbal communication is especially crucial in medical settings. Medical care is increasingly complex. Doctors, nurses, patients, family members, and allied health personnel all affect each other, and systems approaches have become useful. Such approaches shift attention away from considering only what doctors prescribe for patients, and instead focus attention on the nature of the ongoing interaction, the responses of each interactant, and the *process* of health care— all areas where nonverbal communication becomes important (Daubenmire, 1976).

HEALTH CARE TRANSACTIONS

Analysis of what actually occurs in health transactions can be usefully divided into those cues which the patient receives and those which the patient expresses or sends.

Patient Sensitivity

A number of factors combine to make it likely that most patients will be especially observant of and sensitive to the nonverbal communication of health practitioners. First of all, illness generally provokes fear, anxiety, and emotional uncertainty not only because of the possibility of disability or death, but also because of encounters with unfamiliar scientific terminology and medical jargon, reactions to drugs, the presence of imposing new machinery and novel environments, and separation from loved ones and familiar surroundings. Under these conditions, many patients will have a strong need for social comparison, and will look to those around them—health care personnel—for subtle clues as to how and what they are or ought to be feeling (cf. Schachter, 1959; Ellsworth, Friedman, Perlick, & Hoyt, 1978). Second, most patients are likely to be searching for factual information about the nature of their disease, its severity, its course, and their prognosis. Of course, some of this information is provided in the form of a verbal diagnosis, lab reports, and statements of current condition. However, this information may not be fully understood by patients. More importantly, it may not be fully believed. Furthermore, practitioners may withhold or distort the whole truth for a variety of legitimate and not-so-legitimate reasons and patients know that this may be true in their cases. Since people commonly believe that clues about possible deception are expressed and "leaked" through nonverbal channels (Knapp, Hart, and Dennis, 1974), such cues are likely to be afforded special consideration by patients. Furthermore, patients playing the role of the "good" patient (Taylor, 1979) may be hesitant to question a busy, high-status professional in detail and prefer to rely on messages left "unsaid" for clues about their medical condition. Third, patients are especially likely to attend to nonverbal cues because of their position of weakness. There is evidence that subordinates will closely monitor the nonverbal cues of their bosses, perhaps to assess the mood and ascertain which actions are having a positive and which a negative effect (Exline, 1972; Henley, 1977). Patients are often completely at the mercy of the practitioner and are probably especially motivated by such concerns. Finally, certain medical matters that interfere with normal verbal communication, such as speech or throat impairments, orders to hold still, attachment to a respirator, need for the practitioner to concentrate, and even a thermometer in the mouth, all limit the patient's ability to question the practitioner and increase the importance of nonverbal cues.

Patient Expressiveness

Some of these same factors and some additional ones make it likely that patients will be especially nonverbally expressive and that some important information will be emitted solely through nonverbal channels. First of all, patients are likely to experience a number of emotions, which are often more clearly revealed nonverbally than verbally, especially through facial expressions (Argyle, 1975; Ekman, Friesen, & Ellsworth, 1972). Furthermore, some of these emotional states, such as pain, fear, depression and various bodily disturbances, may be states that the patient rarely experiences otherwise and thus are not readily described in words. Second, patients are unlikely to have had much experience hiding or controlling these emotions, especially in medical settings. Thus, anger at an interpersonal slight in a supermarket may be controlled, but fear, surprise, or pain at a doctor's probing may be directly revealed. Third, patients may be hesitant to communicate their feelings about certain difficult matters—concerning death, embarrassing disabilities, desires for additional services, and so on—and thus communicate them only through channels that are not deliberate, that is, through nonverbal communication. Fourth, many illnesses affect a patient's movements, odors, facial expressions and other nonverbal signals in ways not fully recognized by the patient. Such cues cannot be described or controlled by the patient, but could be important clues to practitioners. Finally, various medical conditions resulting from disease, drugs, or other treatment may disrupt verbal communication and leave the patient communicating only by nonverbal means. For example, weakness of the seriously ill may make verbal conversation too difficult but leave nonverbal message, such as a glance or gesture, still available (Blondis & Jackson, 1977).

Thus it is probable that patients will: 1) be especially observant of and sensitive to the nonverbal cues emitted by health practitioners; and 2) communicate a significant amount of important information through their own nonverbal cues. Since so much valuable information is revealed by the patient through nonverbal communication, the importance of practitioner sensitivity to these matters in diagnosis and monitoring of treatment is obvious. The relations of specific nonverbal cues to diagnosis and maintenance are presented throughout the remainder of this paper. The importance of practitioner nonverbal expressiveness—the other side of the coin of patient nonverbal sensitivity—is perhaps not so obvious: ignorance of this factor may be one of the most serious deficiencies of the practice of modern medicine.

Practitioner Communication and the Placebo Effect

In most medical research involving patients, the methodological safeguard known as the "double-blind" procedure is essential. In this procedure, neither the patient nor the physician (or clinician) knows whether the patient has received the experimental treatment or is in the control group. For example, in a pharmacological study of pain reduction, neither the patient nor the physician is told whether the patient is receiving a traditional analgesic such as aspirin or a new experimental narcotic. This procedure is necessary to protect the validity of the experimental design from the well-known but poorly understood placebo effect—the psychological or psychophysiological effect of a therapy that does not have specific activity for the condition being treated (Shapiro, 1971). Often, improvement results from the expectation of improvement. However, this research "problem" points up two processes essential to many aspects of healing: the patient's expectations and the practitioner's role in creating these expectations.

The placebo effect remains overlooked and underresearched, although it is central to the healing process. Much of the history of medicine before modern times was the history of the placebo effect, and it is understandable that medical practitioners would want to disavow any association between modern medicine and such therapies as bleeding, leeching, purging, shocking, and such drugs as crocodile dung, eunuch fat, and swine's teeth. Yet throughout history, physicians have retained relatively high status because such treatments often worked (Shapiro, 1960, 1971). They worked, in part, because of the importance of psychological and emotional factors to "physical" health. Yet such factors have been so belittled and have met such resistance in recent times that a 1975 article in the *Journal of the American Medical Association* urged physicians to reconsider this "neglected and berated aspect of patient care" (Benson & Epstein, 1975). Rather than a threat to the science of medicine, placebo effects are intimately related to the well-being of many patients. Placebos may produce definite, severe physiological effects (Shapiro, 1971) and placebo effects may disrupt the usual action of a treatment.

It is likely that one prime element of a placebo effect is expectation (Shapiro, 1971; Rosenthal, 1976; Jones, 1977; Frank, 1978). If the practitioner can transmit positive expectations to the patient, real benefits may ensue; negative expectations may produce negative effects. It is important to understand and keep in mind that placebo effects involve a therapy with nonspecific activity for the condition being treated; drugs or pills may function as placebos but so may various other therapies, including psychotherapy (Shapiro, 1971). In fact, it seems likely that placebo effects more often result from procedures—exercise regimens, extensive testing, diets, and other medical rituals—than from pills. Certainly in such areas as pain reduction, which have relatively strong psychological components (Johnson, J. E., 1973), expectation can significantly influence outcome (cf. Jones, 1977). Yet, positive expectations do not arise miraculously. Patients' expectations arise from interactions with health practitioners. Expectations are social-psychological in nature. And, for the various reasons described above, patients are especially likely to obtain information on which these expectations are based through nonverbal cues. Patients will observe the nonverbal actions of the health providers and decide whether they are liked, respected, and expected to improve, or are repugnant, worthless, or untreatable.

ELEMENTS OF NONVERBAL COMMUNICATION

A number of recent writers in medical psychology recognize the importance of the face-to-face practitioner-patient interaction itself, discussing such matters as tone, warmth, rapport, empathy, and support. They sometimes specifically refer to nonverbal communication (e.g. Adler, 1979; Blondis & Jackson, 1977; DiMatteo, 1979; Korsch et al., 1968; Stone, 1979; Wortman & Dunkel-Schetter, 1979). Unfortunately, relatively little use has been made of the advances of the last decade in the field of nonverbal communication. This field has identified specific nonverbal cues and has begun to examine how they combine with other cues and with the social situation to produce unique meanings. A number of ideas, hypotheses, and findings concerning facial expression, touch, smells, gestures, and related cues, are directly relevant to medical settings.

Touch

For hundreds of years during the Middle Ages, Europeans sought relief from the disease of scrofula (a tubercular lymphatic disease) through the "King's touch" or the "royal touch" (Bloch, 1973). The persistence of the belief in the curative powers of the royal touch, despite a very low "cure" rate, attests to the tremendous symbolic value of touch in healing as well as to the important role of expectation in health care. The healing power of the royal touch tended to wane with the disappearing divinity of kings, but it may in fact have been transferred to physicians. Patients may feel much better after a routine physical exam in which the doctor uses his or her special expertise to examine rather than merely question them. Certainly the desire to be touched by high-status political leaders, entertainers, sports figures, and the like, has not disappeared in this modern age; touch has retained its symbolic value as a kind of blessing involving the transfer of special powers.

Faith healers have long used the technique of the "laying on of hands" and this "therapy" is still popular in American society. Since its efficacy is supposedly derived from the transfer of a healing spirit, just as the King transferred the divine spirit, this technique is generally viewed as quackery by modern medicine. Some sophisticated proponents have explained it as involving the operation of electromagnetic fields, but it may be more fruitfully seen as a special sort of placebo effect (cf. Riscalla, 1975). The practitioner's touch may indeed promote healing if it is imbued with a special symbolic value. In the last two decades, the concept of touching as basic to the process of healing has been enthusiastically adopted by the so-called "human potential movement." In fact, even "the most timid and conservative T-groups are assailing cultural taboos against touching. It is rare to find a group whose members do not at some point take turns being lifted up in the air from below by the hands of others" (Howard, 1970, p. 146). At the very least, touching may have a significant psychological effect on many patients.

Not all benefits of touching are due to expectation. Since Harlow's classic studies of monkeys raised with wire and cloth surrogate mothers (Harlow & Zimmerman, 1959), the importance of touch to healthy social development has been widely accepted. The comfort of contact is physiologically based; indeed, lack of touch has been implicated in skin disease (Montague, 1978). Certainly backscratching, patting, gentle massaging, and other touches can be tension-reducing. The successful use of waterbeds in hospitals, supposedly to reduce the incidence of bedsores ("Making Waves," 1975), may in fact partly result from an increased need for tactual stimulation in a tense atmosphere removed from usual family touching. In fact, nursing instructors will now acknowledge that "in nursing, touch may be the most important of all nonverbal behaviors" (Blondis & Jackson, 1977, p. 6). An ill, anxious patient, surrounded by cold equipment, may be especially reassured by a warm touch. A similar conclusion was reached by Ashley Montague (1978) who wrote that "in every branch of the practice of medicine touching should be considered an indispensable part of the doctor's art. . . . Touch always enhances the doctor's therapeutic abilities" (p. 223).

Although therapeutic touching has been left as a relatively unresearched "art," medical practitioners are well-trained to palpate, poke, feel, and otherwise touch their patients for purposes of diagnosis. Furthermore, diagnostic procedures such as temperature-taking, blood-testing, ear, nose and throat examinations, stethoscopic examination, blood pressure taking, and reflex testing all necessitate invading the patient's bodily integrity with a scientific instrument. Often, as in routine examination of the breasts, vagina, anus, prostate, and groin, the touch is in intimate areas not usually invaded by relative strangers. This touching will produce reactions on two levels: emotional and interpersonal.

There is little doubt that being touched is sometimes comforting and sometimes emotionally (or sexually) arousing. However, whether a certain type of touch at a certain part of the body can be shown to have a general, predictable effect is doubtful. First of all, there are tremendous individual differences in responses to different types of touches, ranging from the type of pat that is reassuring to the type of touch that is sexually arousing. Furthermore, many differences arise from interpersonal matters: the meaning of the touch for the specific matter at hand.

Two likely interpersonal meanings of touch involve intimacy and power. In usual interaction, the part of the body touched is generally clearly related to the intimacy of the relationship (Jourard, 1966); for example, the genitals are generally only touched by an opposite-sex close friend. Violation of such norms in the medical setting may produce confusion. Nurses often report incidents in which patients begin disclosing very personal information or become flirtatious during or after a backrub, a bath, or other usually "intimate" forms of touching, even though such behavior violates role constraints (Johnson, B. S., 1965). Touching also communicates power (Henley, 1977). Practitioners may touch patients routinely, but there is usually very little occasion for the patient to touch the practitioner. The practitioner is of higher status. Of course, most of this one-sided touching is for instrumental purposes in the technical side of medical care. But the implication of a power difference remains.

In sum, touch has various significant functions and meanings in medical settings. Touch may have symbolic value in healing, may create positive expectations, may have important physiological effects, and, even when used for strictly diagnostic purposes, may affect the interpersonal nature of the practitioner-patient interaction. Certainly this topic is deserving of much additional research which reflects the multidimensional meaning of touching.

Gaze

One of the most influential nonverbal cues is gaze. People generally know and respond when they are stared at (Ellsworth, 1975). Eye behavior is like touching in that its meaning depends upon other factors in the situation: a stare may be comforting if it intensifies a pleasant situation or opens communication in an uncertain situation, but a stare may be arousing or threatening if the context is negative (Ellsworth, 1975; Ellsworth et al., 1978). Glances from a sympathetic nurse or an unhurried doctor may encourage a patient who is having a difficult time or help a patient bring up a sensitive subject. Failure to look a patient in the eye, on the other hand, may be part of the process of dehumanization, common in medical settings, in which the patient is seen as (and comes to feel like) a body not a person.

Excessive staring at a patient, with no apparent cause, will likely have a negative effect, perhaps making the patient feel like a freak or like a bad person. Presumably, health providers will generally not stare at a patient's physical deformity, but constant eye contact to avoid so doing is also likely to be noticed and reacted to by a patient. Although studies have not found systematic effects of stigmata on eye contact behavior, interaction with a handicapped person (including eye contact) does tend to be less variable, that is, more rigid and unchanging (Kleck, 1968). Refusal to look at or constant staring at the chest of a mastectomy patient, or avoidance of or excessive eye contact with a dying patient, may have similar effects: a signal to the patient that something is awry in the interaction and an intensification of the emotions being communicated through other channels.

The Face and Facial Expression

The most specific and detailed information about states and emotions is communicated through facial expression (Izard, 1977). First of all, the face is a key area for diagnosis because it has many muscles, detailed ennervation, several sense organs, and high visibility. Long ago, Hippocrates urged the physician to study the patient's face first. A face with "the nose sharp, the eyes sunken, the temples fallen in, the ears cold and drawn in and their lobes distorted, the skin of the face hard, stretched and dry, and the colour of the face pale or dusky," usually portends death (Hippocrates, 1950 ed., p. 113). In modern times, facial features have proved very useful in diagnosing genetic disorders (Goodman & Gorlin, 1970).

Facial expression is an important element in the communication of pain. While pain is not one of the basic facial expressions of emotion in current categorizations, it is closely related to them (Izard, 1977; Ekman & Friesen, 1975). There is little doubt that valuable information about the intensity and stage of pain and related negtive feelings (fear, distress, sadness) is communicated to the health practitioner through the face, even when the patient is not fully conscious. For example, facial expression has been used to assess amount of distress of women in labor (Leventhal & Sharp, 1965). In fact, the concept of pain itself has a communicative component in that its expression generally brings help from others (Szasz, 1957); pain is, in part, a request for comfort. Facial expression of pain may thus be expected to vary in part as a function of the nature of interpersonal relationships. If the expression of pain brings rewards other than pain relief, the patient may show more and more pain. On the other hand, if the expression of pain is ignored or punished, it may decrease, though at the cost of the possibility of relief through treatment.

This communicative function of pain expression is especially important because recent theory and research suggest a role for facial expression in the perception and management of pain. At the very least, facial expression plays an important mediational role in the subjective experience of emotion (Izard, 1977). Controlling the facial expression of pain (hiding pain) may help to reduce the pain (Lanzetta, Cartwright-Smith, & Kleck, 1976). Thus it may be advantageous for health providers to reinforce patients' suppression of facial expressions of pain. However, since such suppression will, in turn, affect other responses of the health care providers, the issue is a complex one, and research efforts should continue in this field.

The practitioner's expectations are often clearly and forcefully communicated through facial expression. The human face is fantastically expressive and is most often the object of our attention (Vine, 1970). People can easily and quickly recognize distinct emotional states from facial expression (Ekman et al., 1972; Ekman & Friesen, 1975) and thus such expression can effectively communicate a nurse's digust at a wound or deformity, a physician's anger at a patient's failure to follow treatment regimens, or a technician's fear of a patient's deterioration. On the other hand, facial expressions can be effectively controlled by most people (Ekman & Friesen, 1975). With proper training and motivation, practitioners' expressions might just as effectively communicate a nurse's sympathy and understanding or a physician's positive outlook and expectations. This psychological power of facial expression was not lost on tribal medicine men who wore elaborate masks during healing. In fact, in Ceylon, different masks were worn for each disease (Liggett, 1974). Patients, paying special attention to nonverbal cues and especially influenced by the affective nature of the interaction (Ben-Sira, 1976), will usually be heavily influenced by the provider's facial expression.

Voice

As with facial expressions, the specific emotional and motivational states of patients and practitioners may be revealed through their tone of voice (cf. Davitz, 1964). The tone of voice refers to those sounds, primarily pitch variations, which accompany the spoken word but are independent of the verbal content. Feelings like fear, anger, sadness, joy, and pain are readily transmitted through vocal cues. Furthermore, voice tone may be especially important where possible deception is involved (cf. DePaulo, Rosenthal, Eisenstat, Rogers, & Finklestein, 1978). However, the practitioner must be willing to spend some time talking to and listening to the patient in order to perceive and transmit many of these cues.

Although tone of voice is probably an important element of the overall "tone" the practitioner sets for an interaction, surprisingly little research has been conducted in this area. Voice has, however, been implicated in the transmission of experimenter expectancies (Duncan & Rosenthal, 1968) and thus is likely important in placebo effects. One study found a negative correlation between the amount of "anger" judged to be present in a doctor's voice and his success in dealing with alcoholic patients (Milmoe, Rosenthal, Blane, Chafetz, & Wolf, 1967). Another showed a relationship between a physician's ability to express emotions through voice tone or face and voice and the way the physician was evaluated by his or her patients (Friedman, DiMatteo & Taranta, [1980]). Thus, additional research should continue to address such questions as the effects of the voice tones of health care providers on the expectations and emotional reactions of various types of patients. Aspects of vocal communication that are unique to the health care setting should also be identified.

Olfaction

Although communication through odors is very important throughout much of the animal world, it appears relatively insignificant among humans, especially in American society (e.g., Knapp, 1978). However, the medical field may be an important exception. Some illnesses and treatments may act directly to produce unpleasant odors in the patient, while others affect patient odor through actions on the gastro-intestinal tract. There is even some promise of a breathalyzer device for diagnosis ("Breath and body odors," 1978). On the other hand, practitioners too may be associated with particular odors. The use of disinfectants, chemical treatments, anesthesia, alcohol, and so on, as well as the lingering odors of other patients, may all transmit olfactory messages to the patient. And there is no doubt that many of these patient and practitioner odors arouse strong negative feelings.

In the area of person perception, negative personal attributes are often associated with malodor. A bad person may be labelled a "stinker" or "stinkpot." In fact, perceiving the outgroup as smelly is a prime characteristic of prejudice (Largey & Watson, 1972; Allport, 1954). Thus, the diseased person suffering from malodor may be reacted to with negative feelings. Some health care personnel may come to see foul-smelling patients as less good or moral, especially if the patient has at least some control over the odor. Such reactions of distaste are then likely to be transmitted to patients through facial expressions and the distances used in face-to-face interaction (cf. Hall, 1966).

The particular, uncommon smells of medical settings may also affect the health care process in another way. For unknown reasons, odors often have tremendous power to evoke memories of forgotten times and places (Meerloo, 1964; Allport, 1954). Hence, a doctor's office or a hospital or sickroom may evoke vivid memories of the previous negative experiences of an ill relative or a childhood trauma and thus may create significant negative expectations. The many implications of olfactory communication in medical settings remain to be systematically investigated. The first step probably should be the collection of impressions and observations regarding odor in medical settings to serve as a basis for more systematic research.

Other Nonverbal Cues

There are many other nonverbal cues which are important to face-to-face interaction and take on a special meaning in medical settings. Although relatively little is known about these cues (with a few exceptions), the terminology and approach of the field of nonverbal communication can do much to inform the untrained observer of medical interactions.

A major category of nonverbal communication involves body positions and gestures. Posture, hand movements, gait, lean, foot-tapping and so on are combined in this category because they generally receive little attention from the interactants and little is known about the meaning of individual actions. However, such behaviors do have important effects on the "immediacy" or mutual stimulation of an interaction (Mehrabian, 1972). One especially active area of research involves the nonverbal detection of deception. There is theoretical and empirical reason to suspect that cues of deception are often emitted through body behavior rather than through facial expression, presumably because the body is under less conscious control (Ekman & Friesen, 1969). Nurses learn to recognize a patient's squirming, gesturing, pacing, and similar body signs of general restlessness (Blondis & Jackson, 1977), but should also learn to watch these cues when questioning a patient. The issue of whether patients with their heightened vigilance can detect practitioner lying and thus develop negative expectations is unresearched but certainly deserving of immediate attention. Practitioners often speculate that certain patients who have been denied the whole truth really "know" it anyway, and if so, it is possible that deception actually hurts rather than helps treatment.

There are also a number of sounds which may affect the nature of face-to-face interaction and are more likely to appear among patients than in the general population. For example, stomach rumbles, belches, flatulence, sneezes, coughs, and so on may be especially common. Although these signs may be valuable for diagnostic purposes, they also may violate some subcultural norms of polite society. The effects of such disturbances on practitioner-patient interactions has not been investigated, but could be addressed using the paradigms established for studying other nonverbal cues.

Finally, many other factors in the health care environment, ranging from the clothing worn by practitioners and patients to the color and design of hospital rooms, will likely have a significant effect on the health care process. However, the present paper focuses mainly on the dynamic aspects of face-to-face practitioner-patient interaction, since these elements are likely to be psychologically most salient. Nevertheless, environmental factors are also deserving of increased research efforts.

VERBAL AND NONVERBAL COMMUNICATION

One of the most critical aspects of effective treatment involves neither just what is said nor just how it is said. Rather, what is often more important is the degree of consistency between verbal and nonverbal cues. Stigmatized people in general are quite vigilant in watching for clues as to how they will "really" be treated (cf. Goffman, 1963). As noted above, such vigilance is probably even greater in the ill who are also seeking factual information about the nature and severity of their illness and social comparison information as to what they should be feeling in a time of emotional uncertainty. So even the slightest inconsistency is unlikely to go unnoticed.

A positive verbal communication such as "You're looking better today" accompanied by a negative nonverbal cue is likely to be perceived as insincere (Argyle, 1975; Friedman, [1979]). If there is some anger in the communicator's face, sarcasm and nastiness may be perceived. However, if the practitioner saying positive words shows a sad face, the overall message may be seen as one of indifference (cf. Friedman, [1979]). On the other hand, a relatively submissive, negative verbal message such as "I hope you won't mind if I tell you that you need some additional tests" will probably be perceived as sincere and sympathetic, despite the negative content, if accompanied by a sad face, but might be seen as patronizing if accompanied by a happy face. The degree and type of consistency between verbal and nonverbal cues create the "innuendo" that can be very distressing or comforting to an ill person. Additional research is needed before we can fully understand such subtleties of cue combinations but the illustrations given here show that we need not remain tied to vague notions of "empathy" and "sincerity" but can define specific behaviors and researchable questions.

It seems likely that nonverbal communication increases in efficiency and utility as a relationship between two people develops (Altman, 1974). Spouses are probably better than strangers at quickly communicating and detecting distress, encouragement, understanding. However, illness brings practitioners and patients into an intimate relationship (especially from the patient's perspective) involving verbal self-disclosure in which nonverbal communication channels have *not* been fully developed. The relationship is intimate but its development has been forced or abrupt. Confusions and omissions may result, as patients emit special cues that practitioners miss or misunderstand. Unfortunately, an absence of research on such matters precludes any solution at present other than helping the parties involved recognize that mistakes in nonverbal communication are likely to occur.

Finally, it is important to note that in the name of increased efficiency, various modern forces tend to decrease the amount of face-to-face interaction between practitioners and patients. Such technological advances include the use of computer diagnosis (cf. Slack, 1971) and the use of telephone and even television in diagnosis and especially in treatment. Since patient-practitioner nonverbal communication may be disrupted or even eliminated by such techniques, the quality of health care may suffer.

CONCLUSION

For a number of reasons, nonverbal communication takes on a special importance in the medical setting. Although this importance is increasingly recognized, the topic is generally not approached with the scientific rigor applied to most other medical matters. Fortunately, it is no longer necessary for medical practitioners to rely solely on vague concepts like intuition, sincerity and empathy in dealing with the subtle interpersonal aspects of health care. Further, it is an oversimplification for behavioral scientists studying medical care to discuss the "tone," the "atmosphere," or the "rapport" of practitioner-patient interactions. There is a growing scientific literature on the meaning and impact of touch, facial expressions, voice tone, and related elements of nonverbal communication. This literature provides the concepts, tools, and strategies necessary to learn more about the crucial face-to-face aspects of health care. Attention to nonverbal cues deserves a key place in diagnosis and monitoring, alongside the newest computerized, mechanized techniques. And appropriate expectancies and encouragement, communicated both verbally and nonverbally, must be an important part of medical regimens.

REFERENCES

Adler, N. E. Abortion: a social-psychological perspective. *Journal of Social Issues,* 1979, *35,*(1).

Allport, G. W. *The Nature of Prejudice.* Garden City: Addison-Wesley Publishing Company, Inc., 1954.

Altman, I. The communication of interpersonal attitudes: an ecological approach. In T. L. Huston (Ed.), *Foundations of Interpersonal Attraction.* New York: Academic Press, 1974.

Argyle, M. *Bodily Communication.* New York: International Universities Press, Inc., 1975.

Bennett, A. E. *Communication Between Doctors and Patients.* Oxford: Oxford University Press, 1976.

Ben-Sira, Z. The function of the professional's affective behavior in client satisfaction: a revised approach to social interaction theory. *Journal of Health and Social Behavior,* 1976, *17,* 3–11.

Benson, H., & Epstein, M. The placebo effect: A neglected asset in the care of patients. *Journal of the American Medical Association,* 1975, *232* (12), 1225–1226.

Bloch, M. *The Royal Touch* (F. E. Anderson trans.). Montreal: McGill-Queen's University Press, 1973. (Originally published, 1961.)

Blondis, M. N., & Jackson, B. E. *Nonverbal Communication with Patients.* New York: John Wiley & Sons, Inc., 1977.

Breath and body odors may be diagnostic tools. *UPI* (Chicago), December 3, 1978.

Daubenmire, M. J. Nurse-patient-physician communicative interaction process. In H. Werley, A. Zuzich, M. Zajkowski, & A. Zngornik (Eds.), *Health Research: The Systems Approach.* Springer Publishing Co., Inc., 1976.

Davitz, J. R. *The Communication of Emotional Meaning.* New York: McGraw-Hill, Inc., 1964.

DePaulo, B. M., Rosenthal, R., Eisenstat, R. A., Rogers, P. L., & Finkelstein, S. Decoding discrepant nonverbal cues. *Journal of Personality and Social Psychology,* 1978, *36,* 313–323.

DiMatteo, M. R., A social-psychological analysis of physician-patient rapport: Toward a science of the art of medicine. *Journal of Social Issues,* 1979, *35*(1).

Duncan, D. S., Jr., & Rosenthal, R. Vocal emphasis in experimenters' introduction reading as unintended determinant of subjects' responses. *Language and Speech*, 1968, *11*, 20–26.

Ekman, P., & Friesen, W. Nonverbal leakage and clues to deception. *Psychiatry*, 1969, *32*, 88–105.

Ekman, P., & Friesen, W. *Unmasking the Face*. Englewood Cliffs, N.J.: Prentice-Hall, Inc., 1975.

Ekman, P., Friesen, W. & Ellsworth, P. *Emotion in the Human Face*. New York: Pergamon Press, Inc., 1972.

Ellsworth, P. Direct gaze as a social stimulus: the example of aggression. In P. Pliner, L. Krames, and T. Alloway (Eds.). *Nonverbal Communication of Aggression*. New York: Plenum Publishing, 1975.

Ellsworth, P., Friedman, H., Perlick, D., & Hoyt, M. Some effects of gaze on subjects motivated to seek or to avoid social comparison. *Journal of Experimental Social Psychology*, 1978, *14*, 69–87.

Exline, R. V. Visual Interaction: The glance of power and preference. In J. Cole (Ed.), *Nebraska Symposium on Motivation 1971*. Lincoln: University of Nebraska Press, 1972.

Frank, J. D. The medical power of faith. *Human Nature*, 1978, 1, 40–47.

Friedman, H. S. The interactive effects of facial expressions of emotion and verbal messages on perceptions of affective meaning. *Journal of Experimental Social Psychology* [1979, *15(5)*, 453–469].

Friedman, H. S., DiMatteo, M. R., & Taranta, A. A study on the relationship between individual differences in nonverbal expressiveness and factors of personality and social interaction. *Journal of Research in Personality* [1980, *14(3)*, 351–364].

Goffman, E. *Stigma*. Englewood Cliffs: Prentice-Hall, Inc., 1963.

Goodman, R., & Gorlin, R. *The Face in Genetic Disorders*. St. Louis: C. V. Mosby Co., 1970.

Hall, E. T. *The Hidden Dimension*. Garden City: Doubleday & Company, Inc., 1966.

Harlow, H. F., & Zimmermann, R. R. Affectional responses in the infant monkey. *Science*, 1959, *130*, 421–432.

Henley, N. M. *Body Politics*. Englewood Cliffs: Prentice-Hall Inc., 1977.

Hippocrates. *The Medical Works of Hippocrates* (J. Chadwick and W. N. Mann, trans.). Oxford: Blackwell Scientific Publications, 1950.

Howard, J. *Please Touch*. New York: Dell Publishing Co. Inc., 1970.

Izard, C. E. *Human Emotions*. New York: Plenum Press, 1977.

Johnson, B. S. The meaning of touch in nursing. *Nursing Outlook*, 1965, *13*, 59–60.

Johnson, J. E. Effects of accurate expectations about sensations on the sensory and distress components of pain. *Journal of Personality and Social Psychology*, 1973, *27*, 261–275.

Jones, R. A. *Self-fulfilling Prophecies*. New York: Lawrence Erlbaum Associates, Inc., 1977.

Jourard, S. M. An exploratory study of body-accessibility. *British Journal of Social and Clinical Psychology*, 1966, *5*, 221–231.

Kleck, R. Physical stigma and nonverbal cues emitted in face-to-face interaction. *Human Relations*, 1968, *21*, 119–128.

Knapp, M. L. *Nonverbal Communication in Human Interaction*. New York: Holt, Rinehart and Winston, 1978.

Knapp, M. L., Hart, R. P., & Dennis, H. S. An exploration of deception as a communication construct. *Human Communication Research*, 1974, *1*, 15–29.

Korsch, B. M., Gozzi, E. K., & Francis, V. Gaps in doctor-patient communication. I: Doctor-patient interaction and patient satisfaction. *Pediatrics*, 1968, *42*, 855–871.

Lanzetta, J. T., Cartwright-Smith, J., & Kleck, R. Effects of nonverbal dissimulation on emotional experience and autonomic arousal. *Journal of Personality and Social Psychology*, 1976, *33*, 354–370.

Largey, G. P., & Watson, D. R. The sociology of odors. *American Journal of Sociology*, 1972, *77*, 1021–1033.

Leventhal, H., & Sharp, E. Facial expressions as indicators of distress. In S. S. Tomkins & C. E. Izard (Eds.), *Affect, Cognition and Personality: Empirical Studies*. New York: Springer, 1965.

Liggett, J. *The Human Face*. New York: Stein and Day, 1974.

Making waves. *Newsweek*, March 24, 1975, page 91.

Meerloo, J. A. M. *Unobtrusive Communication*. Assen, The Netherlands: Koninklijke Van Gorcum & Comp. N. V., 1964.

Mehrabian, A. *Nonverbal Communication*. Chicago: Aldine-Atherton, 1972.

Milmoe, S., Rosenthal, R., Blane, H. T., Chafetz, M. E., & Wolf, I. The doctor's voice: postdictor of successful referral of alcoholic patients. *Journal of Abnormal Psychology*, 1967, *72*, 78–84.

Montague, A. *Touching*. New York: Harper & Row, 1978.

O'Brien, M. J. *Communications and Relationships in Nursing*. St. Louis: The C. V. Mosby Company, 1974.

Riscalla, L. Healing by laying on of hands: myth or fact. *Ethics in Science and Medicine*, 1975, *2*, 167–171.

Rosenthal, R. *Experimenter Effects in Behavioral Research*. New York: Irvington Publishers, Inc., 1976.

Schachter, S. *The Psychology of Affiliation*. Stanford: Stanford University Press, 1959.

Shapiro, A. K. A contribution to a history of the placebo effect. *Behavioral Science*, 1960, *V*, 109–135.

Shapiro, A. K. Placebo effects in medicine, psychotherapy, and psychoanalysis. In A. Bergin & S. Garfield (Eds.), *Handbook of Psychotherapy and Behavior Change*. New York: John Wiley & Sons, Inc., 1971.

Slack, W. Computer-based interviewing system dealing with nonverbal behavior as well as keyboard responses. *Science*, 1971, *171*, 84–87.

Stone, G. C. Patient compliance and the role of the expert. *Journal of Social Issues*, 1979, *35*(1).

Szasz, T. S. *Pain and Pleasure: A Study of Bodily Feelings*. New York: Basic Books, 1957.

Taylor, S. E. Hospital patient behavior: reactance, helplessness, or control? *Journal of Social Issues*, 1979, *35*(1).

Vine, I. Communication by facial-visual signals. In J. H. Crook (Eds.), *Social Behavior in Birds and Mammals*. London & New York: Academic Press, 1970.

Wortman, C. B. & Dunkel-Schetter, C. Interpersonal relationships and cancer: a theoretical analysis. *Journal of Social Issues*, 1979, *35*(1).

PART

IV

Practicing Humane Care—
The Institution

Introduction to Part IV

THE PREVIOUS SECTION examined how caregivers can interact with their patients more effectively. For the most part, these interactions are taking place in institutional contexts such as hospitals, nursing homes, outpatient clinics, group practices, and other health care organizations. Most health care is, in fact, delivered in an institutional setting which, by its very complexity, tends to be impersonal and potentially dehumanizing. It is therefore incumbent upon institutional leadership to make every effort to humanize the services that the institution provides.

This means a great deal more than providing the setting in which health care can be practiced competently, safely, efficiently, and legally. Essentially, it entails the development and maintenance of policies, programs, and organizational environments that motivate, encourage, and support the caregiver to render personalized care.

The article by Edward Speedling and Gary Rosenberg, "Patient Well-Being: A Responsibility for Hospital Managers," presents an insightful analysis of the substantive influence that health care managers have in creating a supportive environment conducive to humane service. The authors cite specific areas in an organization where administrative intervention can indeed make a difference. Their focus on management of human resources, for example, is particularly instructive as it emphasizes the importance of nurturing the most vital element of any organization—its staff. Perhaps the greatest contribution of the article is its attempt to give managers an appreciation of the opportunities they have to effect humane patient care. This challenge should not go unheeded.

8

Patient Well-Being: A Responsibility for Hospital Managers

Edward J. Speedling • *Gary Rosenberg*

AS HOSPITAL MANAGERS SEEK WAYS of adapting their institutions to a rapidly changing health care scene, they are paying closer attention to patients' opinions of hospital care. This attention has crystallized around the concept of patient satisfaction. The sheer volume of editorials and articles on this subject is testimony to its importance on management's agenda. It is becoming increasingly clear that a satisfied clientele and a favorable public image regarding the quality of services rendered are as important to the viability and vitality of a health care organization as they are to other enterprises striving to achieve in a competitive environment.

In attempting to increase patients' satisfaction with hospital care, managers face a formidable and complex challenge. First, they are serving a clientele that is becoming more informed about health and health care and less reticent about questioning traditional medical authority.[1] Moreover, patients' evaluation of the quality of their health care includes a concern for both the technical dimensions of their care *and* how well their social and emotional needs are met while being treated for their illnesses.[2,3] Patients place a high value on care that is delivered with warmth, compassion, and attention to the needs of the whole person.[4] In their study of the determinants of patient commitment to the therapeutic relationship, DiMatteo and colleagues[5] found that hospitalized patients were more strongly influenced by the way their psychosocial needs were met

Reprinted from *Health Care Management Review*, Vol. 11, No. 3, pp. 9–19, with permission of Aspen Publishers, Inc., © Summer 1986.

than by their perceptions of the competence of their physicians. Patient satisfaction can be enhanced by an environment that provides for the preservation of personal dignity, comforts and responds to stress and suffering inherent in hospitalization, and supports patients' legitimate concerns regarding information and participation in matters of their care.

By helping shape such an environment, managers contribute to the well-being of patients since the issues we have touched on, and which will be elaborated on throughout this article, have significance not only for satisfaction but also for patients' ability to reach their potential for healing. Also of significance is the fact that by promoting patient satisfaction, managers advance the interests of their institutions since it is clear that satisfaction influences consumers' health care utilization behavior.[6,7]

This article provides a framework, based largely on empirical research from a behavioral science perspective, for understanding the significance of the manager's role for patients' well-being, i.e., maximizing health and alleviating suffering. It also presents examples of how the framework can be applied by hospital managers, those at the top and those in the middle of the administrative hierarchy. Moreover, this is an attempt to close the gap, both in theory and practice, that exists between the roles of patient and manager. The gap is evident in the way the problem of patient satisfaction is presented in the health care literature. Managers are perceived as having influence over those matters that expose patients to health care, such as access to the system and availability of services; that provide technical and organizational support necessary for clinical practice; or that add comfort to the patient's experience, such as the quality of the physical environment, the convenience of services, and the courtesy of hospital employees.

Matters that are significant in terms of patients' response to their medical care, such as the quality of their participation in the therapeutic process, the ability to cope with uncertainty and maintain a positive attitude, the avoidance of excessive stress, and loss of ego defenses are not presented as issues relevant to the management function.[8] On the job, the typical hospital manager spends so little time in direct interaction with patients that it is hardly possible to gain much understanding or appreciation of the far-reaching significance of hospital services to patients.[9] There is also some question as to whether managers' professional education prepares them to enact a patient-centered role.[10,11]

In order to more closely link the manager's role to the quality of patient well-being, the patient's experience in the hospital is examined with reference to those aspects of the therapeutic process that managers are in a position to influence.

PATIENT PARTICIPATION IN THE THERAPEUTIC PROCESS

During hospitalization much is done to and for patients. Their physical limitations and need for care require patients to accept a certain amount of dependency during the process of diagnosing their conditions and developing treatment strategies for them. This does not imply, however, that the hospitalized patient's role is a passive one. On the contrary, the most effective therapeutic strategy is one that encourages patients to become active participants with their caregivers in their care.

Cognitive and Behavioral Aspects

Without the patient's active cooperation not even the most sophisticated technology can give the clinician a clear and complete understanding of what is wrong and what will help. The introduction to a well-known medical text cautions physicians to stay attuned to "the important personal and clinical information that is not perceived with 'scientific' equipment or expressed in 'scientific' dimensions."[12] The quality of information provided by the patient during the course of his or her hospitalization has a critical influence on the quality of care provided by clinical staff. The accuracy of the physician's diagnosis depends at least as much on the patient's own account of the onset and development of symptoms as it does on data from the laboratory. By the same token, assessments of the patient's response to treatment are contingent upon what the patient reveals. Clinicians need access to information about the emotional and physical dimensions of the patient's experience. Patients who are reticent about expressing their emotional reactions to diagnostic and therapeutic interventions present clinicians with a real problem in interpreting the clinical data. A calm exterior can mask emotional tension that may be effecting the results of tests or influencing measures of various bodily functions.

For many health problems there is no single course of action available to physicians. Illness often presents alternative treatment choices, each with its own set of benefits and risks. Using the discipline of decision analysis the physician can, by calculating the probability of occurrence of various outcomes including risks and survival rates, arrive at a theoretically "best" choice of treatment option.[13] But whether this theoretically best option is the best appropriate choice of treatment for the individual patient cannot be determined without knowledge of both the patient's willingness to take the risks involved and the value (utility) of the proposed outcome to the patient. Patients must weigh the possible treatment options according to considerations that bear on the quality of their lives. The physician can help the patient by presenting the viable options and by supporting the patient's struggle to clarify his or her feelings and preferences regarding the trade-offs inherent in the treatment choices. But ultimately, except under extraordinary circumstances, the best decision is one that is made, not for the patient, but with the patient's active participation.

Participating in decisions regarding medical care is an example of the importance of patient input during hospitalization. It is also an indication of the effort that is required in order to be a full participant in one's medical care. A substantial part of that effort involves active listening and learning. Many patients leave the hospital with complex regimens involving medications, diet, and behavior modifications. During hospitalization, patients must learn the skills for implementing the instructions given by their caregivers. Hospitalization can be considered a socialization experience for adapting to life with a chronic illness. Developing knowledge and skills is only part of what is involved. The rationale for the prescribed regimen must be understood and accepted. Patient compliance depends on a belief in the efficacy of the regimen and confidence in being able to carry it out. Unfortunately, many patients adapt to the hospital experience in ways that are dysfunctional for developing the cognitive and emotional competence they require. Most people when they are hospitalized behave like "good" patients in that they do what they are told and voice few objections about their treatment.[14] Closer scrutiny, however, reveals that patients often comply ritualistically, without full understanding or acceptance of the instructions they are given. Rigid adherence to medical and nursing instructions often indicates a desire on the part of the patient for nurturance and acceptance rather than a reasoned commitment to the instructions.[15] The extent to which physicians misperceive the amount of knowledge patients have about their conditions plus the serious problem of noncompliance after hospital discharge suggest that an effective dialogue is not occurring. This article does not address one important aspect of this problem, namely, the failure of physicians and nurses to encourage patients to express their uncertainties, voice their concerns, and test their abilities while in the hospital, particularly patients' ability to follow medical regimens after hospital discharge, e.g., dietary and life style changes, complex medication schedules, and self-monitoring of various physiological states such a blood sugar. Patients are often told what they must do once they return home but are not given the opportunity to demonstrate their understanding or practice the skills they will need to perform complex therapeutic tasks.

This article emphasizes how the conditions of hospitalization over which managers have influence contribute to patient passivity and non-involvement in the therapeutic process.

The patient role is a demanding one. Burdened both physically and emotionally, patients are asked to provide precise information, to reveal their fears, and to expose their uncertainties. They are required to make hard decisions about matters that will affect the quality of their lives, and they are expected to master the intricacies of complex treatment regimens. Meeting these demands depends not only on will, but on emotional and psychological factors particularly having to do with maintaining a sense of personal control over the situation, avoiding debilitating stress, and maintaining optimism and a strong sense of self.

Psychosocial Aspects

Sense of Control. The consequences for health of a person's sense of personal control over life events have recently been shown in a study by Seeman and Seeman. Employing a longitudinal design for assessing the health beliefs, health habits, and illness experiences of a probability sample of the population of Los Angeles County, the results were that "a low sense of control is . . . significantly associated with (1) less self-initiated preventive care; (2) less optimism concerning the efficacy of early treatment; (3) poorer self-rated health; and (4) more illness episodes, more bed confinement and greater dependence upon the physician."[16]

There is ample reason to assert that sense of control is an important matter for the hospitalized patient. Seligman[17] reports numerous studies in which subjects whose ability to control events in their environment was temporarily suspended learned significantly less effectively than those who were permitted to maintain personal control over events. Seeman and Evans in a seminal work entitled "Alienation and Learning in a Hospital Setting"[18] demonstrated that being in a state of low control or experiencing powerlessness interferes with the ability to learn about matters related to one's illness while in the hospital.

Environments that confine people to an unaccustomed state of powerlessness generate adverse reactions. Taylor[19] points out that in the case of hospitalized patients the initial reaction to loss of personal control is likely to be anger, which can be transformed to helplessness if repeated efforts to establish personal control are thwarted. Neither feelings of helplessness nor chronic anger advance the cause of recovery for patients. People who feel helpless have great difficulty mobilizing themselves or changing their circumstances. Taylor argues that a specific consequence is the patient's "tending to refrain from disclosing information that would help staff members manage him or her more effectively."[20] One of the most adverse and insidious effects of helplessness occurs when, as Seligman[21] demonstrates in his work, it leads to depression, which can be a serious medical problem in its own right. Even mild depression reduces patients' involvement in their care,[22] and if conditions that foster the problem are not abated the result can be a condition known as "learned helplessness."[23] In other words, patients can become conditioned to helplessness in the hospital that persists even when external conditions change to permit control, for example, at home.

The other response to conditions that diminish a sense of personal control, anger, can have consequences equally as serious. An angry patient may "get back" at staff by refusing to follow instructions, behaving inappropriately and in ways designed to provoke a hostile response. There is some evidence[24] that staff members react to "bad patient" behavior in ways that do little to correct the source of the problem. Such patients may be avoided and their complaints attributed to hostility rather than to their illnesses or their feelings of powerlessness. They may be controlled by medication or turfed, i.e., transferred, to another hospital location. Anger can also cause adverse physiological reactions in sick patients. Reviewing the data, Taylor[25] reports the following as possible consequences of anger: heightened catecholamine secretion and hydrocortisone production, possible aggravation of blood pressure, hypertension, tachycardia, angina, and adrenaline depletion.

If a diminished sense of personal control can be an obstacle in the patient's path, then enhancement of control ought to benefit the patient. Research shows this to be the case. Egbert et al.[26] demonstrated that when patients are provided with information about what to expect after their surgery and are encouraged to take measures on their own behalf to cope with their pain, narcotic usage can be reduced by half and patients are able to be discharged sooner than those who receive no such support. Much can be accomplished simply by allowing patients to anticipate what is ahead for them. Without predictability there can be little control; with it one can at least prepare psychologically for what will occur and perhaps take steps to influence the outcome.[27,28]

Unfortunately, there seems to be much about hospitalization that encourages a sense of helplessness. Raps et al. found that "the longer medical patients were in the hospital, the worse they did on cognitive tasks that index learned helplessness . . . increased hospitalization produced increased depressive symptoms that covaried with poor performance. . . ."[29] Hospitalized patients are keenly aware of their dependency on others. These others certainly include physicians and nurses. But, as Tagliacozzo and Mauksch report, feelings of dependency are also based on "the power ascribed to hospital functionaries to give or withhold those daily services which, for the hospitalized patient, can embrace some basic survival needs."[30] The control that patients perceive they can exercise in the hospital setting depends, therefore, on experience with all staff, not just physicians and nurses. Strauss sums up the problem in the following terms: "There is a growing body of literature which describes hospitalization in terms of the patient's deprivation of his normal roles and identity, the stripping away of all that's familiar, and the imposition of a new 'sick role' involving enforced passivity and dependency."[31]

Stress. Stress, like loss of personal control, is something most hospitalized patients have to cope with. Stress is, according to Strain and Grossman, a normal and predictable response to illness and hospitalization which is typically experienced by patients as "unpleasant affect or a series of unpleasant affects."[32] While some amount of stress is unavoidable and may even be a necessary response to illness, when it is not contained serious psychological as well as physiological consequences can occur. Volicer, for example, found that "patients scoring high in hospital stress reported lower physical status, less improvement after discharge, and lower degree of return to usual activities than patients scoring low in hospital stress."[33]

Moderately stressful experiences have value, according to Janis,[34] because they generally stimulate effective coping mechanisms that increase a person's tolerance for stress. Stress, when received in proportions that can be handled with normal defenses, can, according to this view, function as "emotional inoculation" (Janis's analogy) building emotional resistance to threatening situations. Shielding patients from a realistic awareness of the threat associated with their illnesses or the inherent uncertainty of treatment can prevent emotional inoculation from taking place, leaving the patient vulnerable to greater psychological damage later.

The reverse is more likely to occur in hospitals, that is, not protecting patients enough from stressful experiences, resulting in adverse reactions such as panic or defensive indifference and denial.[35] The typical hospital environment has such a potential for demanding more from patients emotionally than they can cope with that Kornfeld has stated, "To consider the impact of the hospital environment on patients is not mere compassion, but a medical necessity."[36]

Since illness makes manifest one's vulnerability it is not surprising that patients in hospitals are keenly attuned to whatever may threaten their safety and security.[37] Even the food they are served and the cleanliness of their surroundings are perceived as matters of significance to their health, whereas in another context they would be assessed in terms of taste, comfort, and convenience. The physical environment has meaning for patients primarily around issues of safety and security, and secondarily around comfort and convenience. The physical environment may be a source of stress when it buffets the patient with images that accentuate the threat of illness rather than buffering against sights and sounds that can create negative emotions by virtue of the exaggerated fears and apprehension they evoke. To paraphrase Sommer: A hospital's physical plant should mirror its patient care philosophy.[38]

"The central question to be asked about hospitals," Cousins remarked, ". . . is whether they inspire the patient with confidence that he or she is in the right place; whether they enable him to have trust in those who seek to heal him; in short, whether he has the expectation that good things will happen."[39] This is one of the unrecognized consequences of stress—it robs patients of the expectation that good things will happen. A positive outlook makes a significant contribution to healing. It creates "a psychological environment that is congenial to the physician's ministrations."[40] It may be difficult to have confidence in one's ability to get well in a hospital where the climate is foreboding or when conditions suggest a lack of meticulous regard for accuracy, efficiency, and hygiene. This has not been researched, but it is plausible that a healthful atmosphere has a kind of placebo effect. Environments that engender in patients a belief that healing will occur sow the seeds of healing by stimulating emotions that can trigger beneficial biological mechanisms. Studies of the placebo effect usually involve drug regimens. A similar psychobiological process may be triggered by cues in the patient's environment. Although this possibility exists, it has not been demonstrated empirically.

Avoiding feelings of isolation is one key to managing stress.[41] Patients can be enabled to cope with a stressful environment through supportive interaction with fellow patients.[42,43] A potential resource is lost when patient interaction is not encouraged either because of staff's lack of appreciation for its value or because physical facilities are not allocated to this purpose. Ironically, patients in multiple-bed accommodations can be at risk for developing feelings of isolation. This is due to the fact that unless environmental conditions exist that permit patients the option to participate in or withdraw from what is going on around them, they will erect psychological barriers to insulate themselves against unwanted exposure to the suffering taking place around them.[44] Withdrawal into oneself is an attempt to preserve personal integrity against repeated violations of one's personal space. The cost, however, is that one feels isolated in a strange, uncontrollable environment.

Relief of Suffering. One of the foremost tasks of any health care institution is to relieve suffering. Unlike pain, however, suffering is not well understood in biomedical terms and therefore is not relieved by medications or standard medical treatments. Cassell describes suffering as "the state of severe distress associated with events that threaten the intactness of the person."[45] Understood in these terms, suffering is relieved through making a person whole, not in a physical sense but in a social-psychological sense.

Illness is a threat to the intactness of the person because it can undermine the basis of social functioning and personal identity. For some hospitalized patients illness necessitates profound departure from past patterns. New ways will have to be found to accomplish many tasks of everyday living. The skills that brought success on the job may no longer be achievable; the ease with which one managed interpersonal relationships may be made more difficult by disability. Under these circumstances patients are likely to be highly sensitive to the manner in which others relate to them. Do people treat them in a condescending manner that exacerbates their fears of permanent invalidism? Are they made to feel isolated or unwanted because of their condition? Do others give the impression that their care is a burden? Interaction with others that confirms the inherent value of the person will relieve patients' suffering, giving them reason for being optimistic in the future.

Patients suffer when circumstances during hospitalization compromise their dignity. Embarrassment due to having to be helped manage bodily functions and the visibility of their ailment to others is a frequent occurrence. The problem was well articulated by one observer as follows: "It's a kind of humiliation that seems to grow out of vulnerability, nakedness, of being handled, left exposed to be clinically peered at and examined like a grapefruit in a grocery."[46]

Most of us have experienced occasions when simple companionship gave relief from real or imagined fears, anxieties, and worries. The fact is that in times of distress we seek out others to comfort and reassure us. Research conducted by Lynch[47] has demonstrated just how important human contact, in its most basic form, can be to patients, even those in an acute state. The reassurance of a simple touch such as occurs when a nurse holds a patient's hand to take his pulse was shown to evoke such positive emotions that arrhythmias that had been occurring were, in many cases, completely suppressed.[48] The more forbidding the environment the more significant will be the value of supportive human contact. In reviewing his findings, Lynch stated, "The fact that the effects of something as routine as human touch or quiet comforting could still be observed, despite all the factors that could potentially mask its influence, serves to underscore the vital importance it has for our hearts."[49]

These data tell us that every contact a patient has with another person, regardless of that person's rank or function in the hospital, will have some effect. Rarely will human contact be neutral. A relatively untapped resource for relieving hospital patients' suffering is the hospital employee who in the course of cleaning, repairing, delivering meals, or performing a myriad of other tasks has the occasion to interact with patients. Little systematic study has been done to demonstrate the effect on patient morale of contact with nonclinical service employees. Nevertheless, there can be little doubt that the sheer amount of face-to-face interaction between service employees and patients has some effect, either positive or negative.

THE MANAGER'S CONTRIBUTION TO PATIENT WELL-BEING

Medical and nursing interventions are important elements contributing to the quality of care for hospitalized patients. But the capacity of the patient to direct his or her efforts toward active cooperation in activities designed to bring about recovery from illness also depends on a supportive environment. Here is where the role of the manager comes into play.

Below are examples of opportunities for managers to shape a health-promoting environment. They were selected from the authors' own experiences in attempting to bridge the gap between manager and patient roles, and are presented here to provide stimulus for a more meaningful discussion among managers in their own institutions about initiatives most needed and most opportune, given local circumstances. Each of the suggested activities addresses one or more of the issues presented above.

Maximizing the Predictability of the Environment

Given the uncertainty inherent in the diagnosis and treatment of illness, a predictable hospital environment is a boon to the patient's ability to cope. Studies indicate that "if a normal person is given accurate prior warning of impending pain and discomfort, together with sufficient reassurances so that fear does not mount to a very high level, he will be less likely to develop acute emotional disturbances than a person who is not warned."[50] Managers can help here through establishment of norms and procedures that support patients' need to understand and negotiate their environment. A specific example involves the matter of scheduling.

Diagnostic testing is trying for patients under the best of circumstances.[51] In addition to being physically unpleasant, a test or procedure is an emotionally charged event because of what it may reveal about the nature of the medical problem. When schedules are not adhered to, or if patients are given vague information about what will happen when, opportunities for preparing psychologically for the event are compromised by the frustration, anxiety, and anger that result from this kind of depersonalization. Not only is control diminished but suffering is increased as well. If an unpleasant event may occur at any time, concern about it begins immediately, earlier than would be the case if the patient knew when he or she was scheduled to experience the event.

The research of Schulz[52] points out that well-intentioned efforts to add enjoyment and diversion to a patient's day fail to fulfill desired results when the activity is not able to be anticipated by the patient. Activities that bring relief and boost the emotions, such as meal service, visits from volunteers, and amusements, take on additional value when their scheduling and presentation allow patients to exercise choice and control. Hospital administrators are familiar with complaints expressed by patients when they are not informed about changes in their therapeutic diets, or when they are moved to a different room without adequate notice. Even seemingly minor deviations from the expected, such as menu substitutions or changes in room cleaning schedules, can upset patients. What needs to be emphasized about patients' reactions to system breakdowns like these is the erosion of autonomy and corresponding sense of powerlessness that results from being in an environment where the activities of daily living cannot be predicted with any degree of certainty.

Making First Impressions Positive

Information, it was pointed out, can increase patients' coping abilities by allowing them to anticipate and prepare for upcoming experiences. Information received in advance of hospital admission can serve this purpose by explaining standard routines and special features associated with the specific service the patient is being admitted to. The hospital can also make explicit the ways in which it is accountable to the patient, emphasizing what the patient has a right to expect and whom to contact for what problems. In this regard, the specifics of what is presented are less important than the general message that caregivers can serve patients best when they tell caregivers what they need.

Hospitals communicate a great deal about their capacity for caring by the way they respond to patients upon admission. It takes a great deal of sensitivity to complete the instrumental tasks associated with the patient's admission in a manner that allays anxiety and establishes a caring relationship. Too often caregivers focus on the speed and efficiency of the admitting process as if the quality of the experience is measured in terms of time alone. The significance to patients is how they are responded to while in this setting. Admission offices ought to be thought of as the place where patients begin to receive care, perhaps not through medical intervention, but through support, nurturance, and attentiveness.

Preserving Privacy

The need for privacy is an obvious one, but it is something patients often express concern over. The first step in addressing the concern is recognizing its implications for patient care. As mentioned, lack of privacy can cause patients to erect strong emotional defenses against intrusions into their personal space. This, however, poses a danger to the extent that it isolates a patient socially. Respect for privacy helps maintain a patient's dignity at a time when an intact ego and a strong sense of self are vitally important. "The invasion of personal space," Sommer warns, "is an intrusion into a person's self boundaries."[53]

As any experienced hospital observer can tell, more intrusions occur than are necessary. Hospital administrators can protect the integrity of patients' personal space by providing the physical means for maximizing their privacy and by establishing norms to guide employee behavior. The physical environment must allow the patient the means to secure his or her privacy whether in a private room or ward or in transit. Employees can be taught to knock before entering a patient's room and once invited inside to exhibit the same kind of deference as would be expected when entering someone's home. Schedules for housecleaning can be made flexible enough to accommodate patients who wish to be alone at the time their room is scheduled for cleaning. Patients can be made to feel they have the right to control their space subject only to limitations arising out of medical or other necessity.

Decreasing Social Isolation

Once it is recognized that social isolation is a stressor that may heighten patients' sensitivity to pain and interfere with the healing process, managers may become more creative in providing opportunities for patients' social interaction. Decisions about whether to spend money designing comfortable lounges where patients can talk among themselves or with their families ought to be made from a perspective of patient well-being, not merely comfort. Recreational programs that encourage patients to socialize is another way of preventing the feeling of isolation. Ambulatory feeding programs that allow patients to choose to eat with others outside their rooms, perhaps even with staff members present, can be a help in this regard as well. The possibilities are limited only by the degree of willingness of managers to engage in creative thinking about their role in the therapeutic mission of their hospitals.

Buffering Patients from Threatening Elements of the Environment

Anyone who has spent time in a hospital is aware of being emotionally affected by the experience. Seeing other human beings sick and suffering can cause even the well—employees and visitors—to reflect on their own vulnerability. Patients are particularly prone to draw inferences about their conditions based on cues received from the environment. Anxiety about the diagnosis and uncertainty regarding prognosis and treatment coupled with patients' unfamiliarity with the setting make them highly susceptible to what is suggested by the sights and sounds around them. When what is suggested reinforces their worst fears and feelings of vulnerability, the environment becomes a contributor to patient stress. This is why patient complaints about cold, sterile, and cheerless rooms, or about having roommates who are in the throes of acute suffering, are matters that have consequences for well-being, not merely comfort or convenience. As such, these kinds of conditions should be treated with the utmost seriousness. An environment that is devoid of symbols of health can have a deleterious effect on patients' morale and can contribute to an overly negative perception of their condition. Hospitals that provide bright, cheerful, life-affirming surroundings for patients are not providing luxuries; these are essential ingredients of positive patient attitudes toward their recovery and their health.

Comforting the Patient

A source of suffering for hospitalized patients is actual or anticipated, real or imagined deterioration of human relationships as a consequence of illness or the sick role. Loneliness in a hospital, for example, is not a function of opportunity for interaction, but a reaction to what the patient perceives as the probable quality of the interaction. Interaction that suggests that others are relating to the patient primarily on the basis of his or her condition can have a dehumanizing effect. It feeds a not uncommon fantasy that changes associated with surgery or medical treatment make one less lovable, less valued.[54] Unfortunately, in our society people are stigmatized by virtue of their disease or disability,[55] so that the fear of being socially devalued is not without a rational basis.

Hospital employees, at all levels, ought to be considered a vital resource on behalf of the hospital's mission to alleviate suffering. Members of the support staff, those who clean and maintain patients' rooms, deliver meals, escort patients to various locations, deliver packages, and provide other supportive services are witness to the vulnerability that is an inherent part of being a patient. As such, their presence takes on a significance that reflects patients' need for supportive, understanding, and sensitive human responses to their situation. The challenge to hospital managers is to develop in their employees both an awareness of the impact of their behavior on patients, and the interpersonal skills necessary to act with sensitivity and discretion in performing their assigned duties. This means going a step beyond expecting courteousness and includes investing in training that recognizes both the frequency and significance of employee-patient interaction.

There is a reason managers can approach with cautious optimism the task of inculcating in their employees attitudinal and behavioral qualities supportive of the needs of patients, as outlined above. Many hospital service workers take a good deal of pride and satisfaction from the human service aspects of their jobs. Wessen discovered in comparing the ideological commitments of different groups of hospital personnel that as far as lower-status employees were concerned, "such intangible advantages as security and the *satisfaction of 'helping people'* mean more to them than the increased salaries they could earn on the 'outside' "[56] (emphasis added). This should not be a surprising finding since the capacity for helping others, which is a basis of social order, is something humankind is uniquely prepared to do. The social psychology underlying this capacity can be found in Mead's essay "The Nature of Sympathy."[57]

The capacity for employees to perform their duties in a manner that communicates a sense of concern for the well-being of patients is something that needs to be nurtured. In developing programs for this purpose managers may want to consider the following recommendations:

1. Start by assuming that employees want to play a role in the hospital's patient-care mission. Emphasize their value to patient well-being. New employees who will work in proximity to patients may be receptive to such a message conveyed by experienced workers who affirm the sense of self-worth that comes from comforting the sick.

2. Provide guidelines for employees to follow in various circumstances in which they encounter patients. Nursing staff can assist in this. Again, using experienced employees as a resource can help identify situations that employees find difficult to deal with such as how to withdraw from interaction with patients, or how to respond to difficult patients. Role playing and discussion of simulated experiences can enhance employees' interpersonal competence.

3. Establish reward and evaluation systems that reflect the significance of employees' caring attitudes and sensitive behavior.

4. Recognize the emotional demands placed on employees who work near and have contact with sick people. Some mechanisms will be needed to screen out those who are unable to cope with close contact with illness and place them in low-patient-contact areas. Employees working in areas that are highly charged emotionally, such as some pediatric services, intensive care areas, or areas where patients are in a terminal phase, will need special attention to ensure that they are able to cope with the demands of the environment.

5. Enlist the support of nursing staff in recognizing employees' contributions to patient well-being.

Interventions managers choose to make in their own hospital environments will require activity at three levels. Delivery systems will need to be modified and tailored to patients' psychosocial and physical needs. Linkages between groups and departments will need to be structured to support an interdisciplinary approach that is essential to patient-centered service delivery. Individuals at all levels of the organization will need to be made aware of and involved in the hospital's patient care mission.

The forces that are causing hospital managers to recognize and respond to consumers' views of the quality of their care experiences may be leading to a new level of understanding of hospital-based patient care. Areas of concern that have emerged from patient satisfaction studies suggest that patients perceive a need to be more informed about their care and need to be enabled to participate in their care with minimal loss of dignity and control. These are variables that influence the healing process in its broadest and most meaningful sense. If the response of the hospital management community is to be consistent with the health care implications of these data, managers will have to incorporate into their role definition an explicit patient care perspective. Anything less will fail to meet the challenges that are now before us.

Although emphasis here has been on what managers can do to advance patients' well-being, it is not implied that managers need to or should act apart from their colleagues in medicine, nursing, or other clinical fields. Discussion of these relationships requires more than the scope of this article allows. It needs to be said, however, that patients are served best when care is delivered in an interdisciplinary manner since their needs are not confined within the boundaries of any single discipline or department. Health care cannot be delivered piecemeal as if patients' needs were of a different order than those of autonomous human beings. Managers can take the lead in fostering a team approach to hospital care by first affirming their role in helping patients reach their potential for wellness and by opening a dialogue with their clinical colleagues on a subject of mutual interest and responsibility: patient well-being.

REFERENCES

1. Haug, M.R., and Lavin, B. "Public Challenge to Physician Authority." *Medical Care* 17 (1979): 844–58.
2. Ware, J.E., and Snyder, M.K. "Dimensions of Patient Attitudes Regarding Doctors and Medical Care Services." *Medical Care* 13 (1975): 669–82.

3. Ben-Sira, Z. "The Function of the Professional's Affective Behavior in Client Satisfaction: A Revised Approach to Social Interaction Theory." *Journal of Health and Social Behavior* 17 (March 1976): 3–11.
4. DiMatteo, M.R., and Hays, R. "The Significance of Patient's Perceptions of Physician Conduct: A Study of Patient Satisfaction in a Family Practice Center." *Journal of Community Health* 6, no. 1 (1980): 18–34.
5. DiMatteo, M.R., Prince, L.M., and Taranta, A. "Patients' Perception of Physicians' Behavior: Determinants of Patient Commitment to the Therapeutic Relationship." *Journal of Community Health* 4 (1979): 280–90.
6. Kasteler, J., et al. "Issues Underlying Prevalence of Doctor-Shopping Behavior." *Journal of Health and Social Behavior* 17 (1976): 328–39.
7. Ware, J.E., and Ross-Davies, A. "Effects of the Doctor-Patient Relationship on Subsequent Patient Behavior." Paper presented at the 111th Annual Meeting of the American Public Health Association, Dallas, Texas, November 1983.
8. Mitry, N.W., and Smith, H.L. "Consumer Satisfaction: A Model for Health Services Administrators." *Health Care Management Review* 4 (Summer 1979): 7–14.
9. Weaver, J.L. *Conflicts and Control in Health Care Administration*. Beverly Hills, Calif.: Sage, 1975.
10. McCool, B.P. "Dimensions of Professional Development: The Case for Health Administration." *Health Care Management Review* 4 (Fall 1979): 7–21.
11. Bergman, A.B. "Needed: Humanism in Health Program Managers." *Journal of Health Politics, Policy and Law* 3 (1978): 298–302.
12. Feinstein, A.R. "Science, Clinical Medicine and the Spectrum of Disease." In *Textbook of Medicine*. Vol. 1, edited by P.B. Beeson and W. McDermott. Philadelphia: W.B. Saunders, 1975, p. 6.
13. Kassier, J.P. "The Principles of Clinical Decision Making: An Introduction to Decision Analysis." *Yale Journal of Biology and Medicine* 49 (1976): 149–64.
14. Lorber, J. "Good Patients and Problem Patients: Conformity and Deviance in a General Hospital." *Journal of Health and Social Behavior* 16 (1975): 213–25.
15. Tagliacozzo, D.L., and Mauksch, H.O. "The Patient's View of the Patient's Role." In *Patients, Physicians and Illness: A Sourcebook in Behavioral Science and Health*. 2nd ed., edited by E.G. Jaco. New York: Free Press, 1972, pp. 172–85.
16. Seeman, M., and Seeman, T.E. "Health Behavior and Personal Autonomy: A Longitudinal Study of the Sense of Control in Illness." *Journal of Health and Social Behavior* 24 (1983): 144.
17. Seligman, M.E. *Helplessness*. San Francisco: Freeman, 1975.
18. Seeman, M., and Evans, J.W. "Alienation and Learning in a Hospital Setting." *American Sociological Review* 27 (1962): 772–83.
19. Taylor, S.E. "Hospital Patient Behavior: Reactance, Helplessness or Control?" *Journal of Social Issues* 35 (1979): 156–85.
20. Ibid., 168.
21. Seligman, *Helplessness*.
22. Raps, C.S., et al. "Patient Behavior in Hospitals: Helplessness, Reactance, or Both?" *Journal of Personality and Social Psychology* 2 (1982): 1036–41.
23. Seligman, *Helplessness*.
24. Lorber, "Good Patients and Problem Patients."
25. Taylor, "Hospital Patient Behavior," 175.
26. Egbert, L.D., et al. "Reduction of Postoperative Pain by Encouragement and

Instruction of Patients." *New England Journal of Medicine* 270 (1964): 825–27.

27. Schulz, R. "Effects of Control and Predictability on the Physical and Psychological Well-Being of the Institutionalized Aged." *Journal of Personality and Social Psychology* 33 (1976): 563–73.

28. Hartfield, M.T., Cason, C.I., and Cason, G.J. "Effects of Information about a Threatening Procedure on Patients' Expectations and Emotional Distress." *Nursing Research* 31 (1982): 202–6.

29. Raps, et al., "Patient Behavior in Hospitals," 1040.

30. Tagliacozzo and Mauksch, "The Patient's View of the Patient's Role," 172.

31. Strauss, R. "Hospital Organization from the Viewpoint of Patient-centered Goals." In *Organization Research on Health Institutions*, edited by B.S. Georgopoulos. Ann Arbor: University of Michigan Press, 1972, p. 211.

32. Strain, J.J., and Grossman, S., eds. "Psychological Reactions to Medical Illness and Hospitalization." In *Psychological Care of the Medically Ill*. New York: Appleton-Century-Crofts, 1975, p. 29.

33. Volicer, B.J. "Hospital Stress and Patient Reports of Pain and Physical Status." *Journal of Human Stress* 4, no. 2 (1978): 35.

34. Janis, I.L. "Vigilance and Decision Making in Personal Crises." In *Coping and Adaptation*, edited by G.V. Coelho, D.A. Hamburg, and J.E. Adams. New York: Basic Books, 1974.

35. Ibid.

36. Kornfeld, D.S. "The Hospital Environment: Its Impact on the Patient." *Advances in Psychosomatic Medicine* 8 (1972): 253.

37. Taglizcozzo and Mauksch, "The Patient's View of the Patient's Role."

38. Sommer, R. *Personal Space: The Behavioral Basis of Design*. Englewood Cliffs, N.J.: Prentice-Hall, 1969, p. 98.

39. Cousins, N. *Anatomy of an Illness as Perceived by the Patient: Reflections on Healing and Regeneration*. New York: Bantam Books, 1979, p. 154.

40. Ibid., 197.

41. Volicer, "Hospital Stress."

42. Ahmadi, K.S. "The Experience of Being Hospitalized: Stress, Social Support and Satisfaction." *International Journal of Nursing Research* 22, no. 2 (1985): 137.

43. Duff, R.S., and Hollingshead, A.B. *Sickness and Society*. New York: Harper & Row, 1968.

44. Sommer, *Personal Space*, 36–37.

45. Cassell, E.J. "The Nature of Suffering and the Goals of Medicine." *New England Journal of Medicine* 306 (1982): 640.

46. Altman, L.K. "Hospital Patients Can Suffer Twice when Staff Adds Insult to Injury." *New York Times* (February 22, 1983): C1.

47. Lynch, J.J. *The Broken Heart: Medical Consequences of Loneliness*. New York: Basic Books, 1979.

48. Ibid., 140.

49. Ibid., 150.

50. Janis, "Vigilance and Decision Making in Personal Crises," 140.

51. Kornfeld, "The Hospital Environment."

52. Schulz, "Effects of Control and Predictability."

53. Sommer, *Personal Space*, 27.

54. Strain and Grossman, "Psychological Reactions."

55. Freidson, E. "Disability as Social Deviance." In *Sociology and Rehabilitation*, edited by M. Sussman. Washington, D.C.: American Sociological Association, 1965.

56. Wessen, A.F. "Hospital Ideology and Communication between Ward Personnel." In *Patients, Physicians and Illness*, edited by Jaco, 341.
57. Mead, G.H. "The Nature of Sympathy." In *Mind, Self and Society*. Edited by C. Morris. Chicago: University of Chicago Press, 1934.

PART
V

Humane Care of the Elderly

Introduction to Part V

THE FACTS ARE CLEAR. The incidence of illness increases with age, and more and more of our patients are older. On average, the population aged 65 years and over, and even more strikingly, those 75 and over, use more health services, particularly hospital services, than the rest of the population. Given the rate of demographic change and its profound effects on the health system, we examine in this section the meaning of humane care in relation to the aged individual. The articles identify and focus attention on the special needs of the elderly.

The article by Margaret Bagshaw and Mary Adams, "Nursing Home Nurses' Attitudes, Empathy, and Ideologic Orientation," presents a fascinating study of how nurses feel about elderly patients and the way in which they care for elderly patients. The sample comprised 363 volunteers representing all levels of nursing personnel in seven nursing homes. The data analysis indicated a significant correlation between a highly controlled, custodial orientation toward treatment and a low level of empathy and negative attitudes toward the elderly. Conversely, the authors found a direct link between nurses' positive attitudes and therapeutic interactions with patients—interactions that maximized patients' opportunities for decision making, control, and meaningful social contacts.

In their article "The Doctor/Patient Relationship in Geriatric Care," Dennis Jahnigen and Robert Schrier draw upon their own experience as clinicians to explain the distinct issues and dilemmas associated with caring for the elderly. They emphasize the key role of the primary care physician in geriatric care and make a cogent argument for the establishment of primary care relationships for elderly persons. They suggest a five-step process by which primary care physicians can individualize the care they give their older patients.

Adding to Bagshaw and Adams's attitudinal perspective and Jahnigen and Schrier's insight on the caregiver-patient relationship, Susan Blumenfield's article takes a look at the dynamics of hospitalization for elderly patients and the role social workers play in their care. "The Hospital Center and Aging: A Challenge for the Social Worker," uses both theory and case studies to give the reader an appreciation for the characteristics and needs of hospitalized elderly patients, and for the four major components of gerontological social work. She provides a thoughtful analysis of the assessment and intervention skills necessary in the effective care of the patient.

Audrey Olsen Faulkner's article, "Interdisciplinary Health Care Teams: An Educational Approach to Improvement of Health Care for the Aged," stresses the need to develop a strong collaborative approach to the care of the elderly. To be effective, Faulkner suggests that health care professionals should be educated for interdisciplinary team practice. She discusses barriers to interdisciplinary teamwork and proposes the goal, structure, and orientation for such teams. She cites faculty role modeling as an essential part of an interdisciplinary educational effort. She concludes, appropriately, that the nucleus of the health care team should always be the patient.

9

Nursing Home Nurses' Attitudes, Empathy, and Ideologic Orientation

Margaret Bagshaw • *Mary Adams*

ALTHOUGH THE NURSING HOME is one of the most policy-ridden agencies in the United States, the variables of care that ultimately influence the quality of life of the institutionalized elderly cannot be mandated by the most stringent policies. According to Vladeck, "the quality of nursing service is probably the single most important aspect of care in a nursing home," [1, p. 55] because "nurses are the primary providers of care in nursing homes" [1, p. 21]. Therefore, it can be logically concluded that it is mainly the nursing personnel who make the difference as to whether or not institutionalized elderly persons enjoy a high quality of life. It is in the way that these personnel relate in the giving of care that ultimately determines whether the institutionalized elderly survive and thrive.

This study focuses on nursing personnel within seven nursing homes. The study was designed to explore the nature of the relationships among those psychosocial variables that are thought to affect the staff's therapeutic work with elderly persons. Specifically, the psychosocial variables studied were: levels of empathy, attitudes toward the elderly persons, and ideologic orientation toward treatment (custodial or therapeutic).

Previous studies have indicated the individual importance of each of these variables for therapeutic interaction and intervention. For example, Palmore states that it is the negative attitudes of health personnel toward elderly persons that leads to behavior that encourages and main-

Reprinted from *International Journal of Aging and Human Development* 22, no. 3 (1985–86): 235–246, with permission. © 1986, Baywood Publishing Co., Inc.

tains psychosocial atrophy [2]. Moreover, these negative attitudes lead to a custodial rather than a therapeutic orientation toward care, with the main danger being that such prejudice will encourage or excuse discriminatory behaviors which are the direct causes of, or at least contributory factors in, the problems of the elderly. A similar prejudice is that many elderly persons are "senile" and that mental illness among most of them is inevitable and untreatable. The belief can become a "self-fulfilling prophecy" in that the belief leads to lack of prevention and treatment, which in turn serves to confirm the original belief. The result of these negative attitudes is that the institutionalized elderly receive minimal care, inadequate care, or custodial care rather than therapeutic care in a humane environment [3].

In geriatric settings, where nursing personnel are often the only social and emotional companions left to the elderly person, it is imperative to locate and foster those environmental variables that will enhance the maximal health of the elderly person. A major focus of this research is upon the critical variable of empathy in fostering positive, psychosocial change. According to Carkhuff, an essential part of effective, therapeutic interaction is independent of the helper's orientation and techniques, but rather is dependent upon the level of facilitative and action-oriented conditions offered by the helper [4]. He states that the key ingredient of helping is the interpersonal skill of empathy without which there is no basis for helping. Joyce and Krawczyk conclude that, in order to change from an ideology of custodial care to a therapeutic philosophy which attempts to reestablish meaningful relationships for the elderly person, nursing interventions must be empathetic [5]. The importance of these variables are further discussed in Layton, Rogers, Truax and Carkhuff, and Wilmer [6–10]. The interrelationships among empathy, attitudes, and ideologic orientation toward treatment require examination because they influence the incidence of either psychosocial development or atrophy. However, no research was found on the relationships among the three. Furthermore, no earlier clinical investigations have demonstrated conclusively that specific levels of nursing personnel or individual nursing homes differ significantly from one another in regard to these variables.

The conceptual framework upon which this study is based is the Nurse-Patient Interaction Model [11]. Acccording to this conceptual framework, people are subjected to two simultaneous but contradictory processes: development and atrophy. Promoted by a therapeutic environment, psychosocial development refers to an increase in the ability to develop optimally in areas not immediately connected to the biochemical maintenance of biological life. Specifically, one such ability is that of developing healthy interpersonal relationships in the interests of both self and enjoyment. Psychosocial atrophy, which is fostered by a custodial environment, refers to a decrease in the ability to develop and function in cognitive and emotional areas, hindering the optimal interpersonal use of self [9]. A major part of the psychosocial atrophy commonly seen in the institutionalized elderly is produced and maintained by the conscious or unconscious, verbal and nonverbal behavior of the institutional nursing personnel [12]. Thus, psychosocial atrophy is not an antecedent event followed by social and physical disengagement, but a consequent event preceded by social and physical isolation and deprivation [13]. As such, psychosocial atrophy can be minimized, if not prevented, through the medium of staff-patient interpersonal interactions.

One premise of the present study is that the nature of the nurse-patient interaction in the nursing home depends upon the active, facilitative, psychosocial assets of the nursing staff, who directly mold the institutional psychosocial environment. By facilitating either custodial or therapeutic treatment, these personnel are critical determinants of the well-being of institutionalized elderly persons. A custodial environment is a weakness of institutionalization because it provides a highly controlled, rigid setting concerned mainly with the physical maintenance and safety of the patients but exerts little or no effort to rehabilitate the person to his or her optimal level of functioning. Communication within and across status lines is minimal and is task oriented rather than person oriented. Conversely, a therapeutic environment furnishes a flexible, supportive setting where patient opportunities for decision making, control, and meaningful social contacts are maximized. It fosters optimal physical, psychological, and social functioning, primarily through humanistic, therapeutic, interpersonal relationships [14]. The institutional staff's ideologic orientation toward treatment directly influences whether patients experience atrophy or development.

Another premise of the present study is that a high level of empathy and a low level of negative attitudes are critical psychosocial components directly related to the staff's therapeutic orientation toward treatment of the various problems encountered by elderly persons in nursing homes. These problems include withdrawal and isolation [15], learned helplessness [16], and much physical debility [2]. Tarbox states that a certain degree of childlike regressive behaviors in institutionalized elderly persons is a result of "infantilization" by staff. He adds that "characteristic of 'infantilization' would be manifestations of confusion, disorientation, helplessness, dependency, and poor vision and hearing" [17, p. 42]. The final result of this malady is deterioration into a severely depressed state that mimics psychosis or organic brain disease [17]. Furthermore, Tarbox argues that the current poor mental health treatment of elderly nursing home populations will only serve to increase the prevalence of psychological disturbance and emotional problems [17]. Aside from the commonly occurring physically debilitating problems, mental distress in nursing homes is estimated to range as high as 80 percent [18], much of which can be attributed to psychosocial atrophy [11]. These observations necessitate immediate attention into the etiology of psychosocial atrophy and its arrestment if enhancement of the quality of institutional life is to be realized.

Examination of the gerontological literature reveals two research categories focusing on the condition of institutionalized elderly persons who are susceptible to the processes of psychosocial atrophy. One group of studies emphasizes the vulnerability of elderly persons to the deleterious effects of institutionalization. They cite such characteristics of the nursing home population as frailty, multiple losses, and lack of support from others which make these elderly a high-risk population [19–21]. This first group of writers focuses on the nature of the psychosocial environment, rather than institutionalization *per se,* as being at least partially responsible for the unhealthy, maladaptive behaviors observed in elderly residents of nursing homes [22].

The aspects of the psychosocial environment thought to be responsible for fostering psychosocial atrophy were primarily the caregiver's negative attitudes toward the elderly [2, 15, 23]. The negative attitudes of the institutional staff are thought to effect their behavior in such a way as to partially determine the atrophic behavioral outcomes of the resident elderly. For example, several researchers found that nursing personnel encouraged the development of atrophy by rewarding dependency behavior in elderly persons [12, 13, 24].

The second group of studies emphasizes that, while elderly persons are vulnerable to potential harmful effects of the institution, the atrophic process could be minimized or even prevented. It has been noted that skilled, purposeful nursing intervention increases both the psychosocial and physical functioning of institutionalized elderly persons [25–27]. To this end these writers stress the need for creating a therapeutic psychosocial environment predicated on the staff's possessing therapeutic, interpersonal communication skills [28–31]. The psychosocial variable of empathy is indicated as the critical component of therapeutic communication [7–9]; however, the possession of empathy in and of itself does not signify positive or negative value [32]. Therefore, in order for empathy to be used for humanistic and constructive purposes, it needs to be combined with attitudes that are not negative; together these variables have beneficial value for the elderly institutionalized person by facilitating the staff's therapeutic orientation toward treatment.

In summary, the literature supports the premise that nursing home personnel either encourage or discourage the phenomenon of psychosocial atrophy or development, depending upon the nature of the human interactions between nursing personnel and institutionalized elderly persons. Furthermore, an analysis of existing literature suggests that a therapeutic relationship between staff and elderly patients has beneficial value for both. Since a therapeutic relationship between nursing home personnel and patients is a critical determinant of whether psychosocial development of the elderly person is enhanced, all three aforementioned qualities are necessary resources for the staff to possess in order to interact and intervene therapeutically with the aged patients.

METHOD

Respondents

Data were collected from nursing personnel in seven nursing homes located in Cleveland, Ohio, from January through April of 1981. Two of the nursing homes were proprietary, and five were philanthropic. The nursing homes ranged in size from 100 to 250 beds. Four homes were certified for Medicaid only, and three were both Medicare and Medicaid certified. No nursing home below 100 beds was accepted into the study because of possible dissimilar characteristics to the larger nursing homes.

The actual allotted length of time for data collection varied at each nursing home, depending upon a convenient time for the nursing home. All the nursing homes offered to volunteer time and space for data collection, which normally would be used for inservice class, head nurse meetings, or general staff meetings. This provided volunteer nursing personnel time to participate in the study with minimal inconvenience and distraction. It also provided a structured time for the investigator to be present to provide instruction and to answer questions.

The sample consisted of three subsamples of respondents: 1) sixty-two registered nurses, 2) sixty-two practical nurses, and 3) two hundred thirty-nine nursing aids. The only criterion required in this convenience sample was that respondents be employed by a participating nursing home. Part-time as well as full-time personnel were considered eligible for participation in the study.

Results from analysis of the demographic data from the 363 respondents are as follows: First, the mean age of the 338 individuals answering this question was 38.4 years. Second, the majority of nursing personnel (280/361) responding were employed full time; 54 percent of the registered nurses, 25 percent of the practical nurses, and 13 percent of the nursing aides were employed part time. Thus, the most highly educated nurse, the registered nurse, has the highest percentage of part-time employment. Conversely, the least educated nurse, the nursing aide, has the highest percentage of full-time employment. Third, the majority of nursing personnel who responded (345/357) attained high school or at least partial college-level education. Diploma nurses constitute 67 percent of the registered nurses employed, although only 11 percent of the registered nurses had a bachelor's degree. Fourth, 12.7 years was the average length of the nursing practice of those responding (195/363), but the average length of practice with elderly clients was 6.4 years.

Instruments

Respondents completed a written questionnaire consisting of: 1) a Personal Inventory for obtaining demographic characteristics, 2) the Kogan Old People Scale (KPS), 3) the Gilbert and Levinson Custodial Mental Illness Scale (CMI), and 4) the LaMonica Empathy Construct Rating Scale.

The Personal Inventory—is a self-administered, written tool for collection of demographic data such as education, length of nursing practice, and length of practice with elderly persons. These selected variables were included in the study because they have been found to correlate with empathy [33].

The Kogan Old People (OP) Scale—is a Likert scale that consists of thirty-four items for assessing attitudes toward the elderly [34]. Items are constructed in the form of positive-negative pairs, thus yielding two OP scales—the positive scale (KPS) and the negative scale (KNS)—that can be combined into one total scale. Six response categories are provided for all of the items. A higher score (summed scores of all positive items) on the positive scale designates a favorable disposition toward old people, and a higher score (summed scores of all negative items) on the negative scale denotes an unfavorable disposition. Odd-even reliability (corrected using Spearman-Brown) of the Kogan OP Scale was moderate at the time of its development (.73 to .83 for the negative scale and .66 to .77 for the positive scale). Content validity also was reported by Kogan. To minimize response bias, the positively and negatively worded statements were intermingled with each other and with the Custodial Mental Illness Scale.

The Gilbert and Levinson Custodial Mental Illness Scale (CMI)—is a paper-and-pencil, self-administered report designed to ascertain whether personnel have either a custodial or a therapeutic orientation toward treatment regarding mental illness. The instrument comprises seventeen items aimed at a custodial orientation and three geared for therapeutic orientation. Respondents were asked to indicate the degree of agreement or disagreement with each item on a six-category scale. Gilbert and Levinson reported that the instrument supported construct validity and had a reliability of .85 (split-half correlation, corrected by Spearman-Brown formula) [14].

The Empathy Construct Rating Scale (ECRS)—developed by La-

Monica, is another paper-and-pencil, self-administered report consisting of eighty-four items that describe the way one person may feel about, or act toward, another [35]. The individual items are stated either negatively (thirty-five items) or positively (forty-nine items) to decrease the likelihood of an acquiescent response set. Scores range from −252 (low empathy) to +252 (high empathy). LaMonica reported that the split-half method corrected by the Spearman-Brown formula resulted in $r = .89$ for high-empathy items and $r = .96$ for low-empathy items. The scale also was found to support both content and discriminant validity. Like the Kogan OP and CMI Scales, the Empathy Construct Scale is vulnerable to response sets; however, this part of the entire questionnaire was given as LaMonica presented it because she had already addressed such problems.

Because this study examines the interrelationships of findings disclosed by three disparate scales, further reliability testing for each was warranted. After the tests were administered, the Cronbach alpha reliability coefficient was calculated for each instrument: .960 for the ECRS, .834 for the CMI, .866 for KNS, and .651 for KPS.

Relationships among the Psychosocial Variables

Three major hypotheses were tested: 1) there is a negative relationship between empathy and ideologic orientation toward custodial treatment among nursing personnel in nursing homes; 2) there is a negative relationship between empathy and negative attitudes toward the elderly; and 3) there is a positive relationship between negative attitudes toward the elderly and custodial ideological orientation toward treatment. All three hypotheses were supported in this study. The relationships among the psychosocial variables (as determined by the Pearson product-moment correlation) are as follows: 1) the more negative a nursing personnel's attitude, the lower the level of empathy ($r = −.499$, $p < .001$); 2) the higher the ideologic orientation toward custodialism, the greater the negativism on the Kogan negative-attitude scale ($r = .799$, $p < .001$); 3) the higher the ideologic orientation toward custodialism, the lower the level of empathy ($r = −.452$, $p < .001$); 4) correlations for respondents within individual nursing homes were consistent with the above results; and 5) partial correlations controlling for age, length of nursing practice, length of practice with elderly, and year of graduation from nursing schools were consistent with the above results.

In addition, two other hypotheses were tested concerning positive attitudes: 1) there is a positive relationship between empathy and positive attitudes toward the elderly, and 2) there is a negative relationship between positive attitudes toward the elderly and custodial ideologic orientation toward treatment. Neither of these hypotheses were supported by the data. The correlation between empathy and KPS was .074 (not significant) and between CMI and KPS, .024 (not significant). Also, scatter graphs of empathy versus KPS and CMI versus KPS indicated no nonlinear relationships. Correlations of KNS with empathy and CMI within nursing homes were not significant. The partial correlations controlling for age, length of nursing practice with the elderly, and year of graduation from nursing schools were also not significant.

The results from this study indicate that KNS and KPS are not correlated in the total sample ($r = -.054$). Some partial correlations between KPS and KNS controlling for various combinations of age, length of nursing practice, length of nursing practice with elderly residents, and year of graduation were significant at the .05 level. However, the largest partial correlation was only $-.149$. This correlation was based on only 182 respondents since many respondents did not answer all of the demographic questionnaire. The correlations among all respondents within nursing homes ranged from $-.292$ to .287 with two significant correlations ($-.292$ and .287). Thus, there does not appear to be any stable, significant relationship between KPS and KNS in this sample.

Differences in Levels of Psychosocial Variables among the Groups of Nursing Personnel

Using the F test of means, there were significant differences ($p < .0001$) in means among registered nurses, practical nurses, and nursing aides in empathy, custodialism, and negative attitudes. However, there were no significant differences among nursing groups in the mean level of positive attitudes. Furthermore, individual Scheffé test of means indicated that: 1) registered nurses were significantly ($p < .001$) more empathic, less custodial, and less negative in attitudes toward elderly persons than were practical nurses or nursing aides; and 2) practical nurses were significantly ($p < .025$) less custodial and less negative in attitudes toward elderly persons than were nursing aides (Tables 9.1 and 9.2).

Difference in Levels of Psychosocial Variables among Nursing Homes

The mean scores for the entire sample for empathy, CMI, KNS, and KPS were significantly different among nursing homes ($p < .05$, using the F test of means); that is, there was wide variation in scores (regarding empathy, attitudes toward the elderly, and ideologic orientation toward treatment) obtained at the various nursing homes (Table 9.3). These differences are thought to relate to the individual psychosocial environments

TABLE 9.1

Means of Psychosocial Variables by Nursing Group in Nursing Sample

Nursing Groups	Number Responding	Mean Score			
		Empathy	CMI	KNS[a]	KPS[b]
Aides	239	146	38	3.4	4.6
LPNs	62	154	33	3.0	4.6
RNs	62	183	27	2.5	4.6
Total Responding	363	154	35	3.2	4.6

[a]KNS (Kogan Negative Scale)
[b]KPS (Kogan Positive Scale)

TABLE 9.2

Tests of Difference Between Means of Psychosocial Variables for the Study's Three Nursing Samples

Groups	Empathy	Difference Between Means		
		CMI	KNS	KPS
Aides vs. LPNs	− 7.8	4.8**	.38*	.07
Aides vs. RNs	−37.1**	10.5**	.87**	.03
LPNs vs. RNs	−29.3**	5.7**	.48**	−.03

Note: If the difference is positive (negative), then the mean of the first group is larger (smaller) than the mean of the second group.
  *p .025 by the Scheffe test
 **$p < .001$ by the Scheffé test

of the nursing homes in which the respondents worked. Analyses of these differences, however, were beyond the scope of this study.

DISCUSSION

A CMI scope of thirty-five out of seventy for high custodialism supports the contention of several recent writers that custodial care is the norm in institutions today [2, 19, 36]. Whether or not this direction toward custodialism is changed to a therapeutic direction remains a societal decision in terms of funding and policies.

The present study lends support to aspects of the Nurse-Patient Interaction Model [11] by documenting the directional interrelationships

TABLE 9.3

Institution Means of Psychosocial Variables
among Seven Homes Sampled

Nursing Home	Empathy	CMI	KNS	KPS
I	139	38	3.6	4.5
II	141	38	3.5	4.5
III	175	31	2.5	4.8
IV	149	36	3.3	4.6
V	159	35	3.0	4.7
VI	149	36	2.7	4.7
VII	172	32	2.7	4.7
Total	154	35	3.2	4.6
Significance level of F test for difference in means	.015	.0001	.0001	.034

of the psychosocial variables of empathy, attitudes toward the elderly, and ideological orientation toward treatment. The finding that a high level of empathy is positively correlated with a therapeutic orientation toward treatment ($p < .001$) supports the contentions of Layton [6], Ludemann [37], and Rothberg [38] that nurturant empathy is a skill nursing personnel must possess in order to interact therapeutically. Moreover, the significant, positive correlation between negative attitudes and custodial orientation toward treatment agrees with the conclusions of Dye [14] and Palmore [2] and underscores the importance of attitudes to the well-being of elderly institutionalized persons. Further study is needed to determine whether training nursing personnel in empathy, attitudes, and therapeutic orientation toward treatment will result in a higher quality of nursing care and will favorably affect patient outcomes.

The results from KPS suggest that either there is little variation in positive attitudes among nursing personnel in nursing homes or KPS does not have construct validity [39]. Further research is necessary to answer this question. One possibility is to test the KPS further with other nurses in nursing homes, nurses in short-stay hospitals, and nursing students.

Clearly, additional study is also warranted in order to explain the differences among various levels of nursing personnel, as well as the factors accounting for dissimilar outcomes among the staffs of different nursing homes. The reasons for significant differences among the nursing levels cannot be explained here because the present study was not designed to examine this phenomenon; however, differences among these groups could be attributed to such variables as education, status, salary, more or less contact with residents, part-time or full-time employment, or other factors. In all likelihood no one factor is the answer. Furthermore, although it is beyond the scope of this study to explain the differences among the seven nursing homes, these variations do suggest that a more therapeutic environment can be created.

REFERENCES

1. B. C. Vladeck, *Unloving Care: The Nursing Home Tragedy*, Basic Books, New York, 1980.
2. E. Palmore, The Social Factors in Aging, in *Handbook of Geriatric Psychiatry*, E. W. Busse and D. G. Blazer (eds.), Van Nostrand Reinhold Company, New York, 1975.
3. R. N. Butler, *Why Survive: Being Old in America*, Harper and Row, New York, 1975.
4. R. R. Carkhuff, *Helping and Human Relations, 1*, Holt, Rinehart, and Winston, Inc., New York, 1969.
5. A. Joyce and R. Krawczyk, Preventive Nursing Intervention with the Elderly, *Journal of Gerontological Nursing*, 4:5, pp. 28–34, 1978.
6. J. Layton, The Use of Modeling to Teach Empathy to Nursing Students, *Research in Nursing and Health, 2*, pp. 163–176, 1979.
7. C. R. Rogers, *The Therapeutic Relationship and Its Impact—A Study of Psychotherapy and Its Impact*, The University of Wisconsin Press, Madison, 1967.
8. ————, Empathic: An Unappreciated Way of Being, *Counseling Psychologist, 5*, pp. 1–10, 1975.
9. C. B. Truax and R. Carkhuff, *Toward Effective Counseling and Psychotherapy*, Aldine, Chicago, 1967.
10. H. A. Wilmer, Defining and Understanding the Therapeutic Community. *Hospital and Community, 32*:2, pp. 95–99, 1981.
11. J. Weiss, *Nurse, Patient, and Social Systems: The Effects of Skilled Nursing Intervention upon Institutionalized Older Patients*, University of Missouri Studies, *LXVI*, University of Missouri Press, Columbia, Missouri, pp. 1–5, 1968.
12. E. M. Barton, M. M. Baltes, and M. J. Orzech, Etiology of Dependence in Older Nursing Home Residents During Morning Care: The Role of Staff Behavior, *Journal of Personality and Social Psychology, 38*:3, pp. 423–430, 1980.
13. M. M. Baltes and S. L. Lascomb, Creating a Healthy Institutional Environment: The Nurse as a Change Agent, *International Journal of Nursing Studies, 12*, pp. 5–12, 1975.
14. D. C. Gilbert and D. J. Levinson, Ideology, Personality, and Institutional Policy in the Mental Hospital, *Journal of Abnormal and Social Psychology, 53*, pp. 263–271, 1956.
15. C. A. Dye, Attitude Change among Health Professionals: Implications for Gerontological Nursing, *Journal of Gerontological Nursing, 5*:5, pp. 31–35, 1979.
16. J. F. Miller and C. B. Oertel, Powerlessness in the Elderly: Preventing Hopelessness, in *Coping with Chronic Illness: Overcoming Powerlessness*, J. F. Miller (ed.), F. A. Davis Company, Philadelphia, pp. 109–131, 1983.

17. A. R. Tarbox, The Elderly in Nursing Homes: Psychological Aspects of Neglect, *Clinical Gerontologist*, 1:4, pp. 39–52, Summer, 1983.
18. A. D. Whanger, Treatment within the Institution, in *Handbook of Geriatric Psychiatry*, E. W. Busse and D. G. Blazer (eds.), Van Nostrand Reinhold and Company, New York, 1980.
19. R. N. Butler and M. I. Lewis, *Aging and Mental Health*, C. V. Mosby Co., St. Louis, 1982.
20. T. L. Brink, *Geriatric Psychotherapy*, Human Sciences Press, New York, 1979.
21. M. G. Kovar, Health of the Elderly and Use of Health Services, *Public Health Reports*, 92:1, pp. 9–19, 1977.
22. J. L. Fozard and J. C. Thomas, Psychology of Aging, in *Modern Perspectives in the Psychiatry of Old Age*, J. Howells (ed.), Brunner, Mazel, New York, 1975.
23. A. Comfort, *A Good Life*, Crown, New York, 1976.
24. J. E. Birren and J. Renner, Concepts and Issues of Mental Health and Aging, in *Handbook of Mental Health and Aging*, J. E. Birren and R. B. Sloan (eds.), Prentice-Hall, Englewood Cliffs, New Jersey, 1980.
25. M. M. Alvermann, Toward Improving Geriatric Care with Environmental Intervention Emphasizing a Homelike Atmosphere: An Environmental Experience, *Journal of Gerontological Nursing*, 5:3, pp. 13–17, 1979.
26. K. D. Robinson, Therapeutic Interaction: A Means of Crisis Intervention with Newly Institutionalized Elderly Persons, *Nursing Clinics of North America*, 9:1, pp. 89–97, 1974.
27. D. J. Sperbeck and S. K. Whitbourne, Dependency in the Institutional Setting: A Behavior Training Program for Geriatric Staff, *The Gerontologist*, 21:3, pp. 268–275, 1981.
28. D. E. Gregg, The Psychiatric Nurse's Role, in *Psychiatric Nursing—Developing Psychiatric Nursing Skills, 1*, D. Mereness (ed.), Wm. C. Brown Company Publishers, Dubuque, Iowa, 1966.
29. H. E. Peplau, *Interpersonal Relations in Nursing—A Conceptual Frame of Reference for Psychodynamic Nursing*, G. P. Putnam's Sons, New York, 1952.
30. L. F. Stevens, What Makes a Ward Climate Therapeutic? in *Psychiatric Nursing—Developing Psychiatric Skills, 1*, D. Mereness (ed.), Wm. C. Brown Company Publishers, Dubuque, Iowa, 1966.
31. H. S. Sullivan, *The Interpersonal Theory of Psychiatry*, W. W. Norton and Company, New York, 1953.
32. R. L. Katz, *Empathy: Its Nature and Uses* (1st edition), The Free Press of Glencoe, Collier-Macmillan Limited, London, 1963.
33. G. L. Forsyth, Exploration of Empathy in Nurse-Client Interaction, *Advances in Nursing Science*, 1:2, pp. 53–66, 1979.
34. N. Kogan, Attitudes Toward Old People: The Development of a Scale and an Examination of Correlates, *Journal of Abnormal and Social Psychology*, 62, pp. 44–54, 1961.
35. E. LaMonica, Construct Validity of an Empathy Instrument, paper presented at the American Psychological Association Annual Meeting, Montreal, September 1, 1980.
36. C. Eisdorfer, Aging and Mental Health: An Introduction, *Generations*, 8:4, pp. 4–5, 1979.
37. R. S. Ludemann, Empathy: A Component of Therapeutic Nursing, *Nursing Forum*, 7:3, pp. 275–288, 1968.

38. J. S. Rothberg, Nursing Assessment of the Aged Person, paper presented at the third A. Daniel Rubenstein Lectureship in Gerontology, Boston College, October 28, 1968.
39. D. Magnusson, *Test Theory* (2nd edition), Addison-Wesley Publication Company, Reading, Massachusetts, 1966.

10

The Doctor/Patient
Relationship in Geriatric Care

Dennis W. Jahnigen • Robert W. Schrier

MANY OF THE ETHICAL DILEMMAS that arise in the course of caring for elderly patients are no different from those that potentially exist for patients of any age, but the elderly have more needs for medical care at all levels. The dramatic rise in the number of elderly citizens in our country, particularly those above the age of 85, has been well documented.[4, 5] The majority of these people are independent; however, institutional care increases with age to the point that about 20 per cent of U.S. citizens over 80 years of age reside in such facilities.[2] On average, people above the age of 65 years suffer from between three and four chronic disorders.[3, 8] The likelihood of hospitalization in a given year for people above the age of 65 is 18 percent.[6]

Elderly individuals display wide variability in their expectations from these encounters. Whereas some individuals genuinely expect to be cured of their disability, many others have substantially different desires from the medical experience. These expectations range from simple relief of symptoms to the affirmation by the physician of their worth as a human being. It is the increased contact with medical services that may lead to conflict with differences among the goals of the elderly patient and to ethical dilemmas in geriatric care.

Numerous pressures on the patient/physician relationship arise in caring for the elderly individual. Family members, in the face of the progressive disability of a loved one, may assume responsibility for decision-making for the older patient. When opinions of family members are not

Reprinted from *Clinics in Geriatric Medicine* 2, no. 3 (August 1986): 257–264, with permission, W. B. Saunders Company.

in agreement with the desires of the patient, the physician may experience extreme pressure to circumvent the patient's wishes. Third-party payers, faced with what they view to be an intolerable increase in health care expenses, have increasingly entered into the patient/physician relationship. For example, they have determined which services and technologies are eligible for payment and how much copayment is required by the patient. A third factor that may alter the doctor/patient relationship may be pressures from hospitals, which are themselves driven to an increasing degree by a need to become more efficient.

Few medical training programs include formalized teaching experiences in understanding any of these issues, let alone the ethical conflicts they may cause in the doctor/patient relationship. Knowledge of reimbursement systems, prospective payment schemes, health maintenance organizations, cost effectiveness, and cost benefit are but a few of the numerous areas of importance to today's physician.

Even more serious is the lack of appreciation of how these forces will alter the way physicians may be able to care for their elderly patients. Most physicians have had no special training in developing a personal approach to resolving ethical conflicts that arise and often feel uncomfortable when faced with such circumstances. Some physicians have developed a means of dealing with such dilemmas, but others have ongoing difficulty.

A major source of difficulty arises from the application of the care strategy that has been developed for acute illness. In the setting of acute illness, decisions for medical treatment are made rapidly and with a minimum of discussion with the patient. This model works exceptionally well in true life-threatening emergencies. It also works with some modification for most younger patients who suffer acute but not life-threatening illness. This approach frequently fails, however, when applied to the very old patient. The foundation of the acute-illness approach rests on the assumption that all patients have similar expectations for treament outcomes. However, this may not be true for an elderly person, and many of the assumptions about the efficacy of various therapeutic interventions are not valid for the older patient. Although there are elderly who might benefit from this acute-care approach, often such therapeutic interventions can lead to dissatisfaction for the patient and physician alike.

There is evidence of some dissatisfaction with the way medicine is currently practiced with respect to the elderly. Older people commonly express fear about having medical care "imposed" on them when they lose the ability to speak for themselves. Many medical interventions are far less efficacious in older individuals than they are in younger populations. In addition, attempts at diagnosis and treatment often lead to serious adverse effects. Although medical intervention represents a risk most patients are willing to take, evidence supports the assertion that the elderly are far more likely to suffer iatrogenic events. Nearly 50 per cent of the elderly patients studied in one hospital had an infection or a fall, became confused, or had a drug reaction.[1] This statistic does not represent incompetence on the part of the health professional; rather, it reflects the difficulty in predicting the most appropriate interventions for the older individual.

Physicians also often express frustration in caring for older individuals. Many practitioners prefer not to work with elderly individuals. This attitude is attributable to a multitude of reasons, including the fact that cures are seldom possible and success must often be measured in slowing the rate of decline. In addition, elderly patients have more complex interactions of multiple diseases that diminish the likelihood of having a favorable outcome. Some physicians understandably prefer to utilize their time and expertise on younger patients, who may appear more likely to benefit. Even among physicians who treat large numbers of aged patients, attempts at providing high-quality care are often unsuccessful. This is because presenting symptoms of the aged are often vague and nonspecific. Diseases rarely appear in the "typical fashion," and serious conditions often occur without the signs that are quite reliable in younger patients. The available diagnostic interventions that might be utilized increase logarithmically as the differential diagnosis expands; thus the potential for misdiagnosis and mistreatment is increased.

Many traditional therapeutic approaches are under attack because although they are effective, they might be judged to "cost too much." There is increasing consideration of health care rationing, which would certainly affect the elderly to a greater degree than any other group. This, too, will alter the patient/physician relationship. The obvious dangers in this trend are addressed in the following three articles in this volume.

ETHICAL DILEMMAS IN THE PATIENT/ PHYSICIAN RELATIONSHIP

Problems such as those mentioned are not unique to old age; however, physicians who care for the very old find that they are forced on a regular basis to make decisions and recommendations with respect to many of these important issues. One of the most frequent situations is that of ascertaining the competence of the individual. Physicians who care for these older individuals are also regularly faced with decisions regarding resuscitation and application of advanced life-support procedures. The primary care physician is frequently caught between the conflicts of potential benefit to the individual patient and cost to society to provide that benefit. Practical issues arise surrounding the determination of brain death and, even more troublesome, the management of patients who remain in persistent vegetative states.

In few other areas of medicine is the physician so commonly confronted with patients who are dying as in the care of the very old. Patients in long-term care institutions now outnumber those in acute care hospitals. In such circumstances major conflicts arise between what "might be done" and "what is best done." Physicians in outpatient settings are often consulted about questions regarding living wills, assumption of guardianship, or whether an individual patient should continue to drive. All of these situations have potential for significant ethical difficulties. It is in the context of a primary care relationship between a physician and a patient that the best resolution of these dilemmas should occur.

THE PRIMARY CARE RELATIONSHIP WITH
THE GERIATRIC PATIENT

Most older individuals have regular encounters with physicians,[7] and this regularity offers an opportunity that is not present in episodic encounters. Older patients seek something different from a primary care physician than they do from subspecialists, who are oriented to organ systems, or from physicians who have procedure-based expertise. In both latter cases, competence is assumed, but the encounter with a primary care physician is expected to be of longer duration. An ongoing relationship, therefore, is one of the key differences in expectations. In addition, the physician typically takes a "functional" approach with the older individual. Briefly, this is to ask "what is the dysfunction" rather than "what is the disease?"

Because the primary care relationship with the elderly often spans several years, it offers an opportunity to avoid confusion and conflict about patients' wishes with respect to their care in the event of catastrophic events. Many possibilities can be discussed in advance and with appropriate sensitivity. This approach need not compromise care, nor convey potential abandonment of the patient in his or her time of greatest need. In addition, this relationship offers the best potential of matching the capabilities of medicine as a profession with the actual desires of the individual. It is in this setting that useless care or care of marginal efficacy is least likely to be offered. The added benefit is improvement in the way resources are currently utilized. The relationship retains a traditional paternalistic orientation but in a way that very much respects the individual's wishes.

To understand appropriately the modifications necessary in the traditional doctor/patient relationship with older patients, it is pertinent to review the traditional doctor/patient relationship in Western society. Our Western culture has defined both roles and rules to guide behavior of both parties. The physician legitimates the fact that the patient is ill. This legitimacy exempts individuals from normal responsibilities. The physician also assumes obligations to care for the patient and to use the best of his or her skill to help the patient. The patient assumes the characteristics of not wanting to be ill, being desirous of being healthy, and having a willingness to participate in the recommended course of therapy. These roles have been very functional in our society. They recognize the difference in being a "patient" and being a "client." A patient is ill and typically has impaired autonomy. The physician is expected to share some of the patient's concern and to care genuinely about his or her welfare. By contrast, a business client is merely a consumer of services. The provider must be competent, but need not have genuine concern for the client. The "caring" element distinguishes the medical relationship from many other moral contracts.

Some of the adjustments in this relationship that are needed for very old patients are apparent. Very old individuals have seldom not thought about their own mortality and the finite nature of their own existence. They typically desire to discuss issues surrounding their mortality, and it is often the health professional who is the reluctant party to these discussions. The settings in which such discussions might appropriately occur are numerous. They include the presence of terminal disease, the coexistence of multiple chronic progressive diseases, entrance into a long-term-care facility, or participation in elective surgery in which the risk of significant morbidity exists. Even the presence of advanced age alone justifies such discussions because of the growing certainty of some catastrophic event with each passing year.

Primary care physicians can utilize a five-step process in order to seek information regarding the patient's value system and wishes at a time that is free from the severe emotional stress surrounding catastrophic illness. The systematic use of this process offers an opportunity to individualize the medical care that a person receives while at the same time preserving the professional autonomy of medicine.

Step 1: Value Inventory

A value inventory represents information that the patient voluntarily reveals or the physician elicits with respect to the patient's personal value system. It includes the self-perception of the patient in the context of his own existence. Is the individual just beginning adulthood? Or does he see himself as coming to the end of his life? Different values will alter the way the individual uses medical care. What kind of personal relationships does the patient have? How does he or she define "quality of life"? What are the circumstances under which he or she might not want to live? How does the patient feel about advanced life support and living dependent on the use of such technology? Seeking explicit answers for every situation is not possible, but a general sense of a patient's personal value system can be obtained. Without such information, the physician is left with suppositions about what the patient might want in an emergency situation.

Step 2: Patient Expectations from the Medical Encounter

Patients enter into a medical relationship with different expectations. If the physician and patient are not in agreement about what that expectation is, significant erroneous communication and dissatisfaction can result. Among the many different outcomes a patient might seek are: cure of a disease, increased longevity, relief of discomforting symptoms, explanation of what is occurring, or help in coping with disability. For some patients, validation of their worth as a person by virtue of occupying a physician's attention is the primary objective sought, and the importance of the physician in this process should not be ignored. In a rare instance a patient will seek to utilize the medical relationship for secondary reasons such as being exempted from normal social responsibilities. Understanding which one or combination of these possibilities the patient is seeking will enable the physician to individualize his recommendations to the patient.

Step 3: Medical Facts

In this step, the physician engages in the traditional process of obtaining an accurate history and physical examination. Essentially, one asks "what are the symptoms," "what are the physical findings," "what objective data exist?" From the answers one derives both a working diagnosis and a more extensive intellectual differential diagnosis. One estimates the natural history of the disease as well as the treatment options. The judgment is then made as to how likely the particular patient is to benefit from any of the options and the physician proposes a course of action.

Step 4: Reconciliation

In this step of the medical encounter, the physician attempts to match what is medically advisable with what is desirable or acceptable from the patient's point of view. These opinions may be very different and require careful education of the patient as to the options as well as careful listening by the physician to the values and expectations of the patient.

Step 5: Develop a Plan

Several strategies may be involved in formulating a plan. The strategy may be preventive in order to maintain health; it may be diagnostic in order to obtain more information to determine more accurately the disease or dysfunction; it may be acute therapy that is accomplished in an emergency room or hospital; it may be rehabilitative and designed to restore function that has been lost through disuse or disease; it may be palliative to ease the suffering of an individual with an irreversible disease; and finally, it may be supportive in the case of a patient who is near death and wishes humane bedside nursing care. The importance of agreeing on a common strategy is that each approach is judged successful by different criteria. The removal of an indwelling bladder catheter from a patient who has fractured a hip would be a desirable goal in a rehabilitative strategy, whereas placing such a catheter in a dying patient might be a very appropriate measure in retaining dignity and reducing discomfort.

Such a process, while utilized by many physicians, is certainly not the standard approach to the elderly patient; nor is it commonly part of training programs for physicians. Variables expressed in individual patient values and expectations may lead to very different answers as to what is *right* in any specific situation. This is in distinction to the usual view, that is, what is *correct*, which is defined by the medical algorithm of evaluation and treatment of a particular condition. For example, the "right" evaluation of microscopic amounts of blood in the stool of a young individual may be very different from the "right" evaluation of the same condition in a 98-year-old patient. In the latter setting, frank discussion can be initiated about the likely conditions responsible, the discomfort and risk of more thorough evaluation, and the treatment options available. In view of the annual mortality of nearly 50 per cent for patients of this age, the "right" evaluation in the asymptomatic individual may simply be observation.

In the primary care relationship, advice can be given with respect to whether a living will or durable power of attorney should be drawn. In addition, in caring for terminally ill patients, advice can be given with respect to arranging final affairs. For caregivers of patients with progressive dementia, assistance in obtaining guardianship can be offered. These suggestions can all be made in a way that preserves the hope of the patient and may represent very significant contributions to the patient's well-being by the physician.

There are some circumstances in which it will not be possible to engage in this type of information gathering. There may have never been an opportunity to discuss the patient's desires. The patient may desire more than is medically advisable or possible to provide. The individual may be incompetent at the time of the initial encounter with a physician. One must then seek the best information available from family members or friends as to what the patient would have wanted in the particular circumstance. . . . When the patient is merely frail and not incompetent, it is important that his or her wishes take precedence over the wishes of family members. One needs to establish family agreement about the best course of action when possible, but in cases of conflict between the wishes of the competent patient and those of other members of the family, the physician's primary obligation is to the patient.

Other health professionals, such as fellow physicians or nursing personnel, may object to a course of action in the care of the elderly person. This is usually based on a lack of information by these individuals regarding the values and wishes of the older patient. Much conflict can be resolved if this information is documented and shared with others who are involved with the care of the older individual.

A physician may also come under pressure from institutions whose interests are different from those of the patient. Although concerns about the economic burden of health care of the elderly are legitimate and must be addressed, other forums are more appropriate than when the physician is at the bedside for making such determinations. The physician's primary obligations are to those interests that serve the patient, and a physician who attempts to serve the economic interests of society at the same time may end up in a hopeless conflict.

SUMMARY

Information derived from the relationship of the primary care physician with an older patient provides the best possible way to eliminate or minimize many ethical conflicts that arise in the care of the very old. The conscientious physician can seek information regarding the patient's personal value scheme and his or her expectations and utilize the breadth of available technology to best serve the patient. . . . There is legitimate reason for optimism that, with education and thoughtful review, physicians will be able to improve the manner in which we care for older individuals.

REFERENCES

1. Jahnigen, D., Hannon, C., Laxson, L., and LaForce, F. M: Iatrogenic disease in hospitalized elderly veterans. J. Am. Geriatr. Soc. *30*:387–390, 1982.
2. Kane, R. L., and Kane, R. A.: A guide through the maze of long-term care. West. J. Med. *135*:503–510, 1981.
3. Rosin, A. J.: How a geriatric outpatient clinic can assist the family physician. Geriatrics, *30*(11):67–70, 1975.
4. U.S. Bureau of the Census: Prospective trends in the size and structure of the elderly population, impact of mortality trends and some implications. Current Population Reports, Special Studies, Series P-23, No. 78. Washington, D.C., U.S. Government Printing Office, January 1979.
5. U.S. Bureau of the Census: Demographic aspects of aging and the older population in the United States. Current Population Reports, Series P-23, No. 59 (Rev.). Washington, D.C., U.S. Government Printing Office, May 1976.
6. United States Department of Health and Human Services, Office of Health Research, Statistics and Technology: Current estimates from the health interview survey: United States 1978. Vital and Health Statistics, Series 10, No. 130, U.S. DHHS Publication No. (PHS) 80-1551. Washington, D.C., U.S. Government Printing Office, November 1979.
7. U.S. Department of Health and Human Services, National Center for Health Statistics: Health, United States 1980. DHHS Publication No. (PHS) 81-1232. Washington, D.C., U.S. Government Printing Office, December 1980.
8. Williamson, J., Stokoe, I. H., Gray, S., et al: Old people at home: Their unreported needs. Lancet, *1*:1117–1120, 1964.

11

The Hospital Center and Aging: A Challenge for the Social Worker

Susan Blumenfield

DESPITE WHAT MAY SEEM like a paradox, no volume on geronotological social work in long-term care would be complete without a discussion of practice in the acute care hospital. By definition, hospitalization in the acute setting is not long term. However, it is necessary to conceptualize the acute hospital as part of any system of long-term care for older people.

However short in time, a hospitalization may be pivotal in the life of any individual. Illness or accident may lead to a change in functioning of the older person, a breakdown in supports the person has had, a change in the social support system he or she needs, a need for a changed living situation, or alterations in the feelings of vulnerability and self-esteem. The hospital is often the setting for fear, pain, even death. It may be the ray of hope for cure or palliation of discomfort. Whatever occurs, the hospital is not an insignificant experience for the people who are treated there and clearly plays a role in the long-term care of older people.

It is almost inevitable that older people will have to spend some time in the hospital. "Older people have high rates of illness and disability and a high demand for health services."[1] They make up a large proportion of people cared for in hospitals and need longer and costlier care than the under-65-year-old population. In 1973, the average length of hospital stay for those 65 and over was 12.1 days. For those 15–44, it was 5.7

Reprinted from *Journal of Gerontological Social Work* 5 (Fall/Winter 1982): 35–60, with permission, The Haworth Press, Inc. Copyright © 1983 by The Haworth Press, Inc., 12 West 32nd Street, New York, NY 10001.

days.[2] People 65 and over make up 11% of the population but accounted for 29% of the bill for personal health care.[3] Hospital care is a costly but ever present reality, particularly in late life.

Because chances of hospitalization at some point in late life are so high, the hospital may actually be the point of entry in the health care system for many older people. It is during an acute hospitalization that many older people not only develop specific needs for services, but many have had needs which only during a hospital stay are recognized and addressed. Hospital social workers provide the linkages necessary to obtain services both from within the institution and from outside the specific hospital. The fact that the hospital is often a point of access to other services makes it an important component of long-term care of the elderly and a major setting for geronotological social work practice.

A final rationale for the discussion of practice in the acute hospital in this volume is the fact that the hospital setting is a microcosm of society. Attitudes that people hold toward the elderly carry over into this setting. While the hospital is a discrete institution providing total care for a period of time, it also remains a part of the community where care of any patient is influenced by many outside forces. Of necessity social work practice with older people in this setting takes on a long-term care perspective.

Social work in the acute care hospital has a primary care focus. It is the social work discipline that takes on the coordinating function with the goal of preventing breakdown due to remediable social causes. Social work is also practiced with a population receiving outpatient medical care. Such work is part of the long-term care of older people. While there is not space in this chapter to go into this arena in detail, it is important to note that it is a major focus for primary care and that many of the principles and issues discussed here are applicable also to outpatient work.

THE NATURE OF THE HOSPITAL SETTING

Before we look further at the social work function, we must look more closely at the acute hospital itself. John Knowles, in writing about the climate of the hospital, has stated:

> Progress in medical science and in the specialized division of medical skills has changed medicine from an individual intuitive enterprise into a social service. The hospital is the institutional form of this special service. It has developed from a house of despair for the sick poor to a house of hope for all social and economic classes in just the past 60 years.[4]

The general hospital today is a highly technical, high cost, acute care institution. The subdivision of labor has increased with the rise in technological advances. This has contributed to a "fragmented machine approach to the patient and dehumanizes what should be an intensely personal and humane encounter."[5] The evolution of the hospital from a palliative house for the poor and weary, to a high-powered curative center for the ill has undoubtedly been advantageous for mankind. "It is the spin-offs from this evolution that stimulates some wish for just a piece of the palliative qualities that once existed, particularly in the care of the old and chronically ill."[6]

Medical sociologists have explored the patient perceptions of their place in the hospital structure.[7] They have verified the feelings of dependency engendered by hospital routines and the feeling of vulnerability experienced by people awaiting procedures or medications. The waiting and the shedding of possessions, clothing, and control upon admission begins the process of depersonalization and dependency. Staying in the hospital fosters dependency and generally leads the patient to try to maintain him/herself in good standing with those in charge.[8] The patient soon learns what behaviors are rewarded and often feels as though he or she must comply in order to get the care he or she needs.

The older person entering the acute hospital quickly becomes enmeshed in this culture and may even suffer more because he or she is old. Stereotypical responses to older people may exacerbate the indignities. Such patients are often perceived by staff as an unrewarding drain on their limited resources. Frequently, the older person is robbed of his/her decision-making role. Personnel may treat the older person as if he or she is too old to understand, to contribute to planning for his/her care, or unable to respond to his/her surroundings. The fact that confusion can be a temporary result of illness is often not acknowledged. Younger patients seem to engender more frequent and more interested contacts with health care personnel than older patients. Thus, the older person occupies a position of even greater disadvantages than a younger person within the acute care setting.

IMPACT OF THE HOSPITAL SETTING ON SOCIAL WORK PRACTICE

In the hospital, social work is one of many disciplines which are involved in caring for the patient. The fact that social work is practiced within a "host" institution effects how and what it can accomplish. The social worker will not be the only professional speaking with the patient, gathering information about the patient's functioning, and psychosocial concerns, but how the information is gathered, the assessment that is made, and the intervention of the social worker will be unique. Each discipline has its particular contribution to make toward the diagnosis and treatment of the patient. Social work practice in the hospital must be accomplished in collaboration with other hospital personnel.

While the biopsychosocial model of patient care is always relevant,[9] the hospital setting makes the recognition of this particularly important. The nature of the person's physical condition and its impact on his or her functioning must always be taken into account.

The hospital setting leads to the possibility of disequilibrium for older people in particular areas of which the social worker must be cognizant. Research has been done on the types of problems which social workers frequently work on with older hospital patients.[10] Such problems generally include those regarding adjustment to the hospital environment or change in functioning, as well as issues involved in planning for discharge and/or transitions in role relationships.

Social work practice with older people in the hospital not only involves the particular patient but includes the patient's family or significant others. The hospital social worker works with hospital personnel in a variety of ways but also works with personnel from community agencies, long-term care institutions, policy-making bodies, and advocacy groups. The social worker in the hospital must often coordinate services both within and outside the institution and must help to balance the needs of the numerous people involved with the patient.

To add to all of the foregoing areas in which the acute setting will have an impact on social work practice is the pervasive one that the work will generally occur in conditions of crisis and severe time limits. Short-term crisis intervention becomes the often used treatment modality. This is not only because illness is a crisis, but also because of the short lengths of stay and acute nature of the problems. Much needs to be accomplished in a short time.

THE OLDER HOSPITALIZED PATIENT AS PART OF A SPECIAL POPULATION GROUP

Aging is part of the life cycle. It is a stage of growth, as Erikson tells us, with its own developmental tasks of maintaining a "sense of integrity" rather than a "sense of despair."[11] Hospitalization has a major impact during this life stage. How it will affect any individual is of course idiosyncratic and personal depending upon health status, income, family circumstances, culture, and personality.

Yet, we can separate the aged as a special population group to be considered because of special common concerns and needs which have a particular impact on the health care system. Of major import is the increasing number of people 65 years and over, and even more significant is the increasing percentage of this group who are over 75 years.

Another reason to consider the aged as a special population group is the extent of disability this group suffers. While most old people function quite well, the elderly, as a group, constitute the most disabled and impaired segment of the total population. Compared to younger groups, the ailments of older people are less often acute and more often characterized by multidiseases, chronic ailments, and disabling conditions. About 80% of those 65 and over have at least one chronic condition, about half, two or more.[12] Chronic illness is often accompanied by some impairment in function, and increasing age generally leads to greater impairment. Sensory deficits which rise with age can further complicate the effects of illness. These characteristics contribute to producing incongruence between older patients and the acute hospital which is organized to provide diagnosis and cure as rapidly as possible.

The aged can be identified as a special group not only because of numbers, chronicity of medical problems, and disability, but also, because there are age-related changes which cause some diseases to present in ways atypical for younger populations, many drugs to be metabolized differently and an even greater interaction of physical and mental illnesses than occur with younger people.[13] The aged also suffer disproportionately with problems of confusion, incontinence, and immobility as accompaniments to illness. Etiologies of these disorders are frequently difficult to find and difficult to treat. All of these issues have a strong impact on how the older person will interface with the acute hospital system.

Attitudinal issues often set the elderly apart as a special group. As has been discussed, older people, more than those at any other life stage, have been viewed as a homogeneous group. Stereotypical notions often color the perceptions of health personnel and can determine how they intervene.[14] This element is an overriding concern when looking at gerontological social work practice in the acute hospital setting.

IMPACT OF GERONTOLOGICAL SOCIAL WORK IN THE HOSPITAL ON THE SOCIAL WORKER

Any setting and population group have an effect on the people providing service. Working with older people in the hospital has some striking dimensions which need to be explicated.

The social worker is confronted by older people who are often at major crisis points in their lives. For many, the hospital stay may mark a change in their functioning, even in their independence. It is an emotionally difficult task to help people at such transitions.

Geronotological social work in the hospital is, by definition, complex. There is much history, often a scattered, not easily identifiable support system, and a great number of variables to explore in the assessment process. Work with family members or supportive others is the rule, not an occasional change in role. Collaboration with other disciplines is a necessity.

The interplay of physical and emotional problems is striking in the older hospital patient, and the social worker is witness to the impact of social problems on the disease process and outcome for the older person. Working with a patient who dies is not an infrequent experience.

Social workers in the hospital are also not exempt from the therapeutic nihilism which can afflict other health care professionals with regard to the elderly.[15] They, too, may feel that time spent on the elderly is unrewarding or unwarranted because of the likelihood that the older person has little time left.[16] They, too, may feel that working with the elderly has less status than working with other age groups who have greater status in society. They, too, may have accepted the myths of aging that would have them believe that the elderly routinely suffer from psychological decline, social ineptitude, physical decay, and family abandonment. However, in the acute hospital setting, even though the social worker may not have chosen to work with the elderly, he or she cannot avoid the older patient. The patient will frequently have many needs for social service. Gerontological social work in the acute hospital setting therefore is practiced often with conflicted feelings about older people and a lack of previous interest in the area.

Hospital social workers are often much younger than the hospitalized elderly patient. They may have had much narrower real life experience with this age group than with any other. Thus, they may be influenced more by their own limited experience with grandparents or transferential feelings which arise in relation to this population.

In addition conflict is inherent in gerontological social work in the acute setting because of the complexity and time-consuming nature of such work in an environment that has heavy workloads, conflicting demands and limitations in time. One seldom works exclusively with older patients in the acute setting. Thus, balancing the needs of a variety of populations adds to the difficulties of providing optimal service for this particular group.

Always being confronted with illness and disability produces feelings of vulnerability in the worker. Frustration can be particularly high when dealing with a population where not all problems can be resolved or even alleviated. The realities of chronic illness, of fragmented and inadequate services for meeting needs, and of societal deficits have a major impact on work with older people in the acute setting. All of these make up the dilemmas and challenges of gerontological social work in the hospital.

PRACTICE IN THE ACUTE CARE HOSPITAL

Gerontological social work in the hospital setting involves four major components:

1. Aiding adjustment of patient/family to hospitalization and illness.
2. Providing assistance in discharge planning.
3. Educating other staff about needs of older patients as well as of the particular patient.
4. Providing support for other staff involved in caring for older patients.

Each of these elements involves particular knowledge of the setting and the specific population as well as the utilization of generic social work skills in assessment and intervention.

Assessment

Assessment information is that which helps us look at the impact of an illness on a patient/family, in order to provide service where it is needed. In any assessment, we are dealing with the characteristics of the person/family, the illness, the environment, the social system, the needs of the person/family, and the resources available. It is the interaction of these characteristics which will contribute to the ability of the patient to function.

The assessment will be derived from how the following questions can be answered.

1. What is the illness?
2. Who is the patient? Family?
3. What are the strengths of the patient/family?
4. What are the needs of the patient/family?
5. What kinds of problems does patient/family have?
6. What kinds of help does the patient/family need?
7. Who in the environment can provide help?
8. What formal services can be brought to bear on patient/family needs?

Answers to these questions will always have a dynamic quality if hospitalization is a crisis situation. Assessment needs to consider the past, the present, and the prognosis for the future. The social worker cannot hope to have total information about any patient at any particular time, but listed in Tables 11.1, 11.2 and 11.3 are suggestions for areas in which information is most relevant in making an assessment of the patient and family.

Interventions in regard to aiding the patient's adjustment and discharge planning, as well as where education and/or support of other staff is needed, can be planned from the results of the assessment.

TABLE 11.1

Patient Characteristics

1. Demographic Data
Age
Sex
Race
Religion
Socioeconomic status
Place of birth
Language most comfortable in
How supported financially
Receiving or eligible for
    entitlements

2. Illness Data
Diagnosis
Prognosis
Life-threatening?
Change in Functioning?

3. Functional Data
Ability in ADL
Mental Status
Previous Functioning
ADL
Home Management
Social Interactions
Financial Management

4. Living Arrangements
Where living
With whom
Type of environment
Who available there to help
Safety
Accessibility

5. Social World
Who makes up social world of patient
Number of friends
How often seen
How helpful
Activities shared
Groups to which patient belongs

6. History
Education
Work History
Marital (family) history
Relationships with other
Areas in which patient had
    interest and found pleasure

7. Personality Characteristics
Coping style
Motivation
Flexibility
Expectations of self
                    others
                    system
Ability to use services

TABLE 11.2

Informal Support System Characteristics

1. **Family**
   Who is in Family?
   > relationship
   > age
   > particular situation

   Where do family members live?
   Who is available to the patient and for what?
   How willing is family to give support to patient?
   What are difficulties family has in helping patient?
   Is family able to help patient?
   What would help family in giving support to patient?
   What is assessment of family interaction?
   Family history with patient.
   What would be appropriate roles for family members in helping patient?

2. **Neighbors/Friends**
   Who does patient count on for help in the neighborhood?
   What are capacities and limitations of these neighbors/friends for helping?
   What kinds of services do neighbors/friends provide?
   How can they be supported in giving help?

3. **Informal Groups—How can they be of help?**
   Church groups
   Volunteers

TABLE 11.3

Formal System

1. **Eligibility for Entitlements?**
   Medicare
   Medicaid
   S.S.I.
   Social Security

2. **What services might be needed for patient out-of-hospital**
   How to apply
   Time lapse
   Eligibility
   Family involvement
   How to facilitate application procedures

INTERVENTION STRATEGIES

1. Adjustment to Hospitalization and Illness

The Patient. When the social work assessment determines that the older person has particular problems adjusting to the hospital or illness, we need to work with the patient, family and the environment. The social worker provides a consistent and understanding relationship. The worker helps to individualize this patient through assessment and the interpretation to other staff of this particular patient's needs. The social worker increases the patient's understanding of the hospital environment and facilitates ways to meet the patient's idiosyncratic needs within the institution. Often social workers must slow the rapid-fire pace of activities in the hospital, for the patient, by interceding to be sure procedures and regimen are explained by the physicians and understood by the patient. We work to understand who the patient is and how he/she is reacting to the crisis of this hospitalization. The following example will illustrate some of these elements.

> Ms. P. was a 77-year-old, white single woman who was admitted to the hospital with cancer of a kidney, intractable back pain, and immobility. She was seen by medical staff as an angry, difficult woman and was referred to the social worker because she was refusing diagnostic tests and was difficult to deal with.
>
> When the social worker came to introduce herself to Ms. P. it was striking how the emaciated, pale Ms. P. almost blended in with the bedsheets that she was bundled up under. It was her clear mind, decisive speech, and angry flavor which made her noticeable. Ms. P.'s initial response to the social worker was that she needed no help from anyone who could not relieve her pain. The social worker acknowledged Ms. P.'s disappointment at not feeling helped, but persisted in her interest in Ms. P. It became evident that Ms. P. felt thwarted and out of control because of her illness and helplessness in the hospital. To return some measure of control to Ms. P., the social worker suggested making an appointment to return for a longer conversation at a time to be chosen by Ms. P. The patient reluctantly agreed, but still appeared angry and disinterested. When the social worker offered her hand in parting, Ms. P. took it and allowed a faint smile to mark the beginning of an important relationship.
>
> The social worker met with Ms. P. consistently for short periods almost everyday, during the patient's hospitalization. She was able to help Ms. P. regain some control in ways other then denying

permission for diagnostic tests. This was accomplished by inter-preting this need to staff who were able to create other areas of choice for Ms. P. They allowed Ms. P. to choose when she would sit up, when to have inbetween snacks, etc.

Ms. P. was understood as a woman who had been functioning independently all her life. She had worked as a bookkeeper until her retirement about 10 years earlier, and had lived with her sister in an apartment all her adult life. About 2 years prior to this hospital admission, Ms. P.'s sister had become ill with cancer. Ms. P. cared for this sister until the sister's death 4 months previously and had, herself, gone into a severe decline since then. Ms. P. expressed the theory that working so hard caring for her sister was actually the cause of her own present illness. Ms. P. needed to deal with the anger toward this deceased sister and that she, herself, was now ill with no one left to care for her.

Ms. P.'s fear of the dependency she felt led her to defend against such feelings by pushing people away who were trying to help. Ms. P. was helped by the social worker to understand some of these feelings. Simultaneously, the social worker met with staff to share her assessment of Ms. P.'s coping style and needs. This helped those working with Ms. P. to understand her anger and not to feel per-sonally attacked. Tension lessened within the environment for Ms. P. at the same time that she was using the caseworker relationship for support and understanding.

Adjustment to the hospital often depends on helping the patient with concerns about things outside of the hospital. The older person, admitted to the hospital on an emergency basis, for example, might be demanding to return home prematurely in order to get a check or pay the rent. If there is no immediately accessible "responsible other," the social worker must often take on this role or coordinate the services of others, which can contribute to the patient's peace of mind while in the hospital.

The Family. Often the social worker must work even more closely with a family member. While the older patient is ill and receiving treatment, it is sometimes a family member who has difficulty accepting the illness, the hospitalization or the treatment. The family member, by overt actions or covert sabotage, may interfere with the patient's care. The social work role is to understand the meaning of such behavior and work with family members and staff to resolve these problems.

Mrs. M. was an 87-year-old, Orthodox Jewish widow, admitted to the hospital for internal bleeding and anemia. Mrs. M. had been living at home, suffering from a variety of chronic conditions. She had been cared for by an 8 hour/day home attendant. Overseeing her care was her 57-year-old, married son, who lived nearby.

During the patient's hospitalization, her son stayed at the hospital all day, everyday. Mrs. M. suffered one medical crisis after another with the physician needing to do a variety of procedures and nursing staff being particularly attentive. The patient was quite ill and inaccessible to interview. Mr. M. spent most of the time reading religious books, but would jump up to meet any physician or nurse entering his mother's room to ask questions, suggest changes in procedures or discuss the merits of particular foods for his mother. Staff began to avoid entering Mrs. M.'s room, unless absolutely necessary. They also had problems restraining Mr. M. from feeding his mother. Staff had warned Mr. M. of risks in trying to give his mother food since she was restricted to a special diet. However, he persisted in trying to urge her to eat ice cream or soup brought from outside. Staff became frustrated and angry in trying to deal with the son both because of his behavior in the hospital and their belief that he was acting out of guilt for having let his mother become so ill before being brought to the hospital.

The unit social worker was asked to see Mr. M. to help staff deal with the problems. Mr. M. was difficult to get to know. His orthodoxy contributed to the discomfort he had speaking with women and the social worker needed to respect such feelings. He was eventually able to respond to discussion about his concerns and needs and explained how fearful he was of the discomfort his mother was having, and his anger that the doctors couldn't seem to do more for her. He felt that no one was talking to him and that he was helpless in the situation, for he never knew when the physician would be around or when something new would happen. Mr. M. was almost frantic in his need to do something. Praying in the hall outside his mother's room was one thing he felt he could do, as was trying to force her to eat in order to regain strength.

The social worker met with staff and was able to reframe Mr. M.'s behavior to the staff, from that of inscrutable, angry and ungrateful, to frightened, overwhelmed, and lacking direction. House staff and nurses were engaged in considering ways to help Mr. M. with his problems while attempting to do the most they could for the patient. It was agreed that the intern in charge of Mrs. M.'s care would schedule a specific time each day to meet with Mr. M. Setting limits on Mr. M's demands, yet attempting to give him information and support appropriately was suggested by the social worker as a way of providing structure that would help the patient's son.

The social worker also suggested that they attempt to find some roles for Mr. M. to fill his need to do something. It was suggested that Mr. M. read to his mother and help feed her the specific diet provided by the hospital.

By providing more understanding of the patient's son and how meeting his needs could help in caring for the patient, the social worker was able to engage the staff in thinking creatively together. Providing structure in which to work with this family member and some role for him to play helped him to cope with the hospitalization of his mother and be ready to actively help in planning for his mother's eventual discharge.

The acute care hospital often seems a forbidding place to the outsider. Activity appears fast-paced and intense, and patients and families are often intimidated and overwhelmed. The social worker needs to be aware of such feelings on the part of patients and families and be able to bridge the gap between outside world and the high-powered institution. The social worker must often help patients to communicate with other health care personnel. Unscrambling medical jargon can be a difficult task. The social worker can assist the patient and family by helping them to ask questions of the physician or to make lists of concerns so these can be addressed.

Seemingly simple tasks of orienting patients and families to routines and procedures, helping to direct them to facilities and personnel who could be of assistance within the hospital are often overlooked. The social worker must remain aware of how important these are in the hospital adjustment process.

The social worker in the acute care hospital often provides the linkage for the older patient and family with both the institution and the outside. There is always the need to balance the needs of patient and family with their own capacities and the resources available to them in the environment.

2. Discharge Planning

Discharge planning is a major role of the hospital social worker, particularly when working with older people. The hospital, though a temporary experience, is one with major consequences for future functioning.

In order to help patients in planning for discharge, the social worker must be aware of the previous functioning of the patient. The worker must understand the patient's physical condition and any changes in functioning that will occur because of it. Collaboration with medicine, nursing, physical therapy, etc., is essential in assessing the patient's medical condition, prognosis, ability to handle activities of daily living and to sustain care. It is important to share with other staff the social work assessment of the patient's mental status, emotional state, informal supports, and possible formal supports. It is the combined assessment by all the various professionals involved, together with the capacities and wishes of the patient and family, which lead, ultimately, to the plan for care following hospitalization.

When the social worker is involved with the hospital patient, he or she must balance conflicting demands and pressures around planning for discharge. The case of Mr. G. is an example of finding such a balance.

Mr. G. came to the hospital quite confused, weak, and unable to walk. He was a 72-year-old, Hispanic man whose wife had died 8 years before and who had been living since that time with one of his married daughters. Upon his admission to the hospital, the daughter spoke to the social worker and discussed her feelings of being overwhelmed with his care and her inability to go on providing such care. Her own children aged 4, 8, and 10 needed her attention, the space in her apartment was cramped and tensions had increased between her and her husband.

Throughout Mr. G.'s hospitalization, his daughter's plaintive cry ran in counterpoint to his continuing improvement. Mr. G. proved a rewarding patient for staff. With medication changes, and improvement in the heart problems, Mr. G.'s mental status improved. He remained with moderate disorientation and confusion, but was able to respond appropriately in general and evidenced an engaging personality. He was cheerful, optimistic and amusing. With a great deal of nursing input, Mr. G. started to walk and provide his self-care with minimal assistance.

With the dramatic improvement, everyone was hopeful that Mr. G. could return to live with his daughter. All staff, including the unit social worker, began to press for such a discharge plan. However, the daughter, while guilty and most unhappy, remained adamant that Mr. G. could not continue to live in her apartment. The social worker began to receive calls from another daughter and son of the patient and was able to arrange a meeting with all the patient's children who were clearly at odds around the planning.

Mr. G. expected to return to his daughter's, although he acknowledged that his grandchildren were sometimes loud and bothersome. He also thrived on the attention given him by staff and responded to the interchange with the other patients in his room.

The social worker needed to help the family sort out their conflicting needs in regard to the patient. All three adult children were unhappy about sending their father to a nursing home, yet the brother and single sister could not agree to provide either a home or more aid for their father. The daughter who had been caring for him was still viewed as the logical person to continue such care, but her plight became clearer as they met together. Finding Mr. G. an apartment of his own and providing help there was ruled out as something not only difficult to do but something he had been unable to adjust to even years earlier. The fact that now, although appealing, Mr. G. needed direction, assistance, and help in orientation 24 hours-a-day made such a plan quite unrealistic.

The family agreed to apply for admission to an HRF near them so they could visit frequently. They found it difficult to discuss these plans with Mr. G. and needed help in including him in the planning.

The social worker was pressured by the family to "go ahead and make the arrangements." She was also pressured by the staff who were invested in this patient and who felt nursing home placement was inappropriate. The patient, himself, while speaking of returning to his daughter's was also somewhat aware of his comfort in the hospital. The social worker, herself, was not without bias and wanted this patient, who had improved so much, to return to the community.

However, the role of the social worker in planning discharge is to help to effect what is possible once the needs of the patient and resources at his disposal are known. The social worker had to work with the family to help them come to a plan of action. At the same time she helped them discuss this plan directly with the patient. Mr. G. was initially unhappy with the thought of not returning to his daughter's home. Because of the chance she had had to work through some of her ambivalent feelings with the social worker, the daughter was able to cope with Mr. G.'s disappointment and to help him see some positives in the proposal. The possibility of this being a temporary plan was also discussed.

The social worker also had to work with staff who were angry at this plan, and therefore at her for "allowing" it. The fact that families cannot be "told" what to do, as well as the ramifications of this particular family's interactions, were shared with staff. The feelings of investment in this patient and the fears that his improvement was "wasted" had to be acknowledged and dealt with. The social worker had to help staff see that the ways in which the hospital experience had been so positive for Mr. G. were features that would continue in a long term institution.

Another major area of work with older patients in the hospital is helping them to obtain entitlements. The social worker must be familiar with programs of benefits for older people and ready to assist them. A person often enters the health care system through the hospital. Thus it is in this institution, that he or she may be linked to other services which can be helpful.

In discharge planning, a person's eligibility for governmental programs like Medicaid, S.S.I., rent subsidies, etc., need to be assessed. Depending upon the financial situation as well as health care need, services may or may not be available to the particular patient. Often the social worker must act as an advocate to help the patient obtain needed services. The following case will illustrate such a situation.

> Mrs. F., 73-year-old black widow, living alone, came to the hospital for rectal surgery. Mrs. F. had been managing alone with the help of a woman, sent by a local Title III agency, who helped with housework 4 hours a week. Mrs. F. while independent, had become increasingly limited in mobility due to arthritis, a hip problem, diabetes, and now bowel problems. Neighbors were helpful as was her married daughter. The latter, however, lived 3/4-hour away and had family responsibilities which included a 12-year-old, handicapped child.
>
> Even before the surgery, Mrs. F. clearly needed more help at home and she had been assisted by the social worker in applying for Medicaid and for home help. These applications were already completed and approval verbally given prior to her short hospitalization. Both patient and daughter had been involved in this planning. There had been set backs and difficulties which the hospital social worker had helped them through and all seemed to be in place when Mrs. F. was discharged from the hospital. Mrs. F. was planning to spend a few days recuperating at her daughter's apartment before returning to her own apartment.
>
> The day after discharge the social worker received a frantic phone call from the patient's daughter informing her that the Visiting Nurse Service that came would be unable to provide the health aide as expected because this could not be covered under Medicare. They needed the last three digits of the Medicaid number or could not process the billing. What followed this phone call was the bureaucratic nightmare that can discourage even the strongest of families and is all too often part of working with older people in the hospital.
>
> The social worker had to verify the fact that the service was being withheld and attempted to advocate for the patient. She tried to get the necessary information from the Department of Social Ser-

vices, but was unsuccessful. It seemed that there was no way to revive the original plan.

In order to provide Mrs. F. with interim help so that she could return home, a dozen agencies were contacted by the social worker and possibilities discussed for how a package of services could be created for Mrs. F. while she awaited receipt of her Medicaid card and placement of a DSS Home Attendant. Eventually, by combining limited services from a few separate agencies, on this short-term basis, Mrs. F. was able to return home. Through the major efforts of the hospital social worker, Mrs. F. regained her independence and her daughter respite which allowed her to continue to be available to provide support when needed.

This case illustrates one of the time-consuming, yet very important roles of the social worker regarding older people in hospitals; that of coordinating services and advocating for creativity in meeting a patient's needs.

The social worker in the hospital setting must be familiar with resources in the community and skilled at interpreting the needs of patients to outside agency personnel. Even with this knowledge and skill, all situations cannot be resolved as the one illustrated here. Often because of the various funding sources, vagaries of eligibility requirements or prohibitive costs, patients do not have access to services that they need. Working within this complex system is both challenging and frustrating.

Helping the patient/family become aware of and use resources that are available demands a special blend of knowledge and skill. Working on meeting a concrete need is often an important entre to the patient. Engaging on work together to obtain resources, the social worker can develop a relationship with the patient. The patient can experience the assistance of the social worker as helpful at the same time as it supports his or her autonomy and self-esteem. Such experience can lay the foundation for further work together in other areas of need.

The social worker in the acute hospital may have to deal with patients who evidence major symptoms of confusion and/or disorientation. Part of the social work role, initially, is to advocate for the examination of reversible causes of these symptoms. In those situations where it is determined that the patient has a chronic brain syndrome the social worker can be instrumental in helping to either support the family in caring for such a patient at home or where this is not possible, to assist in making arrangements for care in a skilled nursing facility.

Working with the patient and family to accept change in functioning, whether physical or mental, is important when planning for discharge. Another major part of discharge planning is helping to create alternatives for the older person and his or her family, as well as providing assistance in weighing the alternatives. The social worker must draw on the strengths available within the patient and family and attempt to create ways to provide supports for the deficits.

The family which will be caring for the demented individual at home following hospitalization may be helped by referral for the patient to day hospital programs where they exist, for extra help in the home to give the caregivers some respite, for participation in group programs for patients or families. The social worker may be able to help the family receive necessary information from their physician about the patient's condition. It is important not to allow hospital care to end with the diagnosis. Rather, assistance with further planning must be offered.

There are often situations in which the demented patient has no family or supportive network and the social worker may need to take an even more active role in planning for the patient.

Mrs. S., 77-years-old, was brought to the hospital because of confusion, disorientation, memory deficits, and inability to care for herself. She was admitted to the psychiatry unit of a general hospital.

Mrs. S. had intact social graces which initially made her appear quite able. However, extended conversation revealed major cognitive deficits. Her history was a mystery. No one came forward who had any knowledge of her outside the hospital. Her identification cards gave only her name and address.

While medical workup proceeded, the social worker tried to get information about how Mrs. S. had managed to cope until that point, given her very severe deficit. In hope of obtaining more information and because Mrs. S. had grave concerns about some money left at her home, the social worker arranged with the nurse to accompany Mrs. S. to her home on a pass.

While at the hospital Mrs. S. was unable to find her own room or to remember the person she had held a conversation with 5 minutes before. It was striking to see her pull herself together when they arrived at her apartment building. Mrs. S. greeted the doorman, held her head high and led the way around the corner to the elevators. She greeted a gentleman in the elevator appropriately, asked about his wife and found her own apartment at the end of the hall. She confided to the social worker that she was "fooling" the people she had seen. They did not seem to be aware of how forgetful she really was, or that she was in fact a patient in the hospital.

The ability to be socially appropriate had helped to maintain Mrs. S. even as her mental capacities were failing. The apartment showed signs of having been kept up by someone, just as Mrs. S.'s well-dyed hair and polished nails on admission had been evidence of her having recently been to a beautician. Mrs. S. began to look for money and checkbooks she had hidden and despite rummaging and some anguish, she found what she had been seeking. The nurse and social worker found papers for Mrs. S. and learned the name of a lawyer who was taking care of her affairs.

The enormous difficulty Mrs. S. had in functioning and her lack of sound judgment in many areas was only partially balanced by her social skills and the discovery of the lawyer-friend who had helped her periodically. Mrs. S. was a widow with no family and had apparently managed with very sporadic help from neighbors and weekly visits from the lawyer-friend.

Despite attempts at trying to create further community supports, Mrs. S. was too deteriorated to manage without constant supervision and eventually was transferred to a nursing home.

This example points up the necessity of flexibility in activities under the rubric of discharge in obtaining information and planning when the patient is confused and no ready relative stands by. Such are frequently concomitants of geronotological social work in the hospital.

Also inherent in working with older patients on discharge is the phenomenon of "paper work." In this setting the social worker frequently provides a major coordinating role. As a part of this endeavor written communications of various sorts are mandatory. Chart notes for formal communication with medical staff must be concise and informative. Letters to outside agencies or helpers need to spell out clearly what the needs of the patient are and the agreed service conditions.

Forms to be completed seem to accompany almost any request for service, benefit or change. It is nearly always part of the social worker's role to be responsible for the completion of such forms. This is frequently a time-consuming and frustrating task whether it involves checking off boxes which do not seem to fit what one really has to communicate, or tracking down other staff who must be asked to complete forms they are required to sign. In the latter situation, the social worker may often bear the brunt of others' frustrations about completing forms. The difficulties of this task, however, have not yet made it obsolete. Therefore, the responsibility for using the paper flow most advantageously for the patient remains an important function of the social worker.

No discussion of social work in discharge planning would be complete without some mention of the patient who in hospital jargon becomes a "disposition problem." Such a person is usually old, generally very disabled physically and/or mentally, and needing large amounts of nursing care. Compounding his/her difficulties may be his/her financial level which places him/her just above the Medicaid eligibility levels but is insufficient to meet the high cost of nursing home care. This person needs residence and care in a skilled nursing facility, but because of bed shortages Homes can choose other "easier to care for" patients before admitting him/her. What occurs is that the patient will remain hospitalized much beyond the time he/she is medically ready to leave.

Such overstays have consequences for the patient, family and staff. The social worker not only has a major role in trying to facilitate placement but must work with patient and family around the prolonged uncertainty. Staff will have many reactions to the patient who presents "disposition problems," from "adopting" and protecting that patient, to angrily ignoring him or her. The "problem" is often seen as a failure of the social worker to effect a transfer of the patient.

In such instances, the social worker, while proceeding with the mechanics of effecting the transfer, must be active with the patient and family and work at interpreting the real situation to other staff.

3. Educating Other Hospital Staff

The hospital social worker shares information with other professionals about patients to contribute to the understanding and care of each individual. When dealing with the older patient the worker also needs to be knowledgeable about and able to communicate information regarding psychosocial issues in late life.

Developmental tasks of late life need to be understood and how they impact on the hospitalized elderly discussed. Often hospital staff are reluctant to take time necessary to really understand the older patient. Often they fear they will be recipients of irrelevant tales of the past. Social workers are generally more experienced with the use of reminiscence as a therapeutic modality[17] but physicians and nurses can be helped to see the usefulness of reminiscence in their own work. They can be shown how they can understand a patient better and learn more about his or her prior health habits and coping styles. They can see how reminiscence about areas of interest to the patient can lead to establishing better rapport and that much history, important to diagnosis and treatment, can be elicited from the older patient. The social worker can also educate other staff regarding the therapeutic use of reminiscence in helping the older person gain strength from remembering "better days."

The social worker can be in the position of dispelling myths about the aged, both by referring to the literature in this area, and by pointing out the individuality of each patient.

The social worker can help staff balance a view of the acutely ill elderly patient they are seeing, with information on the heterogeneous nature of people within this population group. Often the social worker is able to use information about demographics, patterns, and trends to enrich the case by case experience of hospital staff.

While it is the social worker who is generally most active in helping older people obtain and manage their entitlements, information in this area must be shared with other staff. When physicians prescribe specific types of care, they need to know how the costs of these are covered. The social worker can provide education about the uses of Medicare, Medicaid, and can be instrumental in dispelling the myth that "older people have no financial worries in obtaining health care."

Most hospital staff have a need to learn the rationale behind the forms they are asked to help complete. The social worker must understand these forms and be able to explain their use to other staff. The worker's experience with how such forms are received and interpreted is gained through his or her contacts with personnel at outside agencies. Educating other staff around such issues can take place on a case by case basis, or even in small meetings held specifically for this purpose.

Another way to educate others is to be a role model. The way the social worker responds to the older patient and/or his family helps to set a tone for others. Social work values of autonomy and self-determination when applied to the older patient, are often a model for other staff to follow. Specific techniques for interviewing where there may be sensory impairment should be used. Some of these include attempting to cut out distractions when speaking to the older person. Another is having the worker face the older patient and take care that light is on his or her own face to aid the patient in comprehending. The social worker can demonstrate the use of touch where appropriate and should be skilled in assessing the mental status of any patient who may have some confusion. For the patient who does exhibit signs of dementia, the social worker must help staff see that the diagnosis alone, does not determine functioning, but that multiple variables exist and some of these may be amenable to change.

The social worker operates from the perspective of "person environment fit" as explicated by Coulton.[18] This refers to the "degree of congruence between an individual's needs, capacities and aspirations, and his environment's resource demands and opportunities." The worker is in the unique position of viewing the strengths and disabilities of the older person within the context of the environment in which he will need to function. This perspective can be shared with other staff and is helpful to each discipline involved in caring for the older patient.

4. Providing Support for Other Staff

Working with older people in the hospital can be a demanding task. It is emotionally draining to be faced with illness, frailty, and vulnerability, as well as to deal with people often in a precarious balance of interacting deficits. Older patients frequently present complex diagnostic problems and complicated social situations. In the acute hospital pressures are high, the pace rapid, but the older patient frequently needs more time and greater patience than younger patients.

Hospital staff need support in the giving of skilled, compassionate care to elderly patients. They need help in seeing the challenges of giving such care. The hospital system does not have built-in rewards for this. Social work is one discipline which can take on a supportive role in this area.

> Mrs. R., a quiet 69-year-old Hispanic woman, came to the hospital with shortness of breath, malnutrition, and some confusion. She had been living alone in a small apartment prior to admission. With treatment, she improved past her medical crisis and was gaining strength and stability. She asked for nothing, seemed appreciative of any attention shown her, but was content to lie in her bed and initiate no activity.

> Ms. S., the R.N. assigned to her care, realized that Mrs. R. needed more stimulation, encouragement, and assistance in walking and in making her wishes known. Ms. S. took extra time to talk to Mrs. R., to bring her the extra coffee she began to ask for, and to initiate a regimen of assisting her in walking more each day to regain the use of her limbs. The social worker was active with Mrs. R. in planning to have a home attendant help the patient when she returned home. The social worker also provided encouragement and support for Ms. S.'s efforts with the patient and gave the nurse direct recognition at staff meetings for her major role in motivating Mrs. R. During setbacks which occurred in the patient's progress, the social worker continued to be supportive to the nurse. All of this reinforced Ms. S.'s motivation and supported her work with the patient.

The social worker can help a staff member to understand his or her own reactions to a particular older patient, can listen to frustrations and misgivings, can encourage the giving of time and energy to older patients. All these activities enter into the support the social worker can provide to those who deal with older patients.

Social work as a profession brings to the hospital setting a respect for the need to collaborate, and skills in engaging various others to participate together. These are essential in working toward optimal care for the older patient. The expertise in human development, systems negotiation, and resource management that social workers have is helpful not only for the patients, but is supportive for other staff as well.

SUMMARY

Geronotological social work in the acute hospital is an amalgam of the best that is in us. We are dealing with a vulnerable group at point of crises, and are instrumental in providing understanding and services necessary to the continued functioning of that person.

In the acute care hospital, the social worker is engaged in direct service to the older patient and his or her family, in collaborative work with other professionals, in negotiating the hospital system and in bridging the gap between the outside community and the institution. In order to do all this effectively, the worker must have a secure sense of his or her own professional identity. He or she must be flexible, creative and strong in the face of numerous and often conflicting pressures.

Working with older people on an outpatient basis demands the same qualities and practices that have been discussed. The primary care role for such outpatients also demands the same comprehensive assessments and interventive strategies to support strengths, shore up deficits and prevent breakdown.

It is impossible to cover every function of social work with older people in the hospital, but it is important to realize the complexity and challenges involved. Above all the acute care hospital must be seen as part of the overall care available to older persons. It is a major function of social work to place the acute care hospital squarely within the continuum of long-term care.

REFERENCES

1. Shanas, Ethel & Maddox, George. "Aging, Health and Organization of Health Resources," *Handbook of Aging and the Social Sciences,* Ed. by Robert Binstock and Ethel Shanas. New York: Van Nostrand Reinhold & Co., 1976, p. 593.
2. U.S. Department of Health, *Health, U.S. 1975* Public Health Service, Health Research Administration Department of Health, Education & Welfare Publication Number (HRA) 76-1232, Washington, D.C.: Government Printing Office, p. 513, 573.
3. Pegels, C. Carl. *Health Care and the Elderly,* Rockville, MD: Aspen Systems Corporation, 1980, p. 5.
4. Knowles, John H. "The Hospital," *Scientific American,* 229, September, 1973 p. 128.
5. Ibid., p. 132.
6. Blumenfield, Susan. *Counselor-Assistants for a Geriatric Program in a Community Hospital,* City University of New York: unpublished doctoral thesis, 1977, p. 15.
7. Mauksch, Hans O. "The Organizational Context of Dying," *Death: The Final Stage of Growth,* Ed. by Elisabeth Kubler-Ross. Englewood Cliffs, NJ: Prentice-Hall, Inc., 1975, p. 15.
8. Ibid., p. 19.

9. Engel, George L. "The Clinical Application of the Biopsychosocial Model." *The American Journal of Psychiatry*, May 1980, pp. 535–543.
10. Berkman, B. & Rehr, H. "Social Needs of the Hospitalized Elderly: A Classification." *Social Work*, July 1972, pp. 80–88.
11. Erikson, Erik. *Childhood and Society.* New York: W. W. Norton & Company, Inc., 1963.
12. Butler, Robert. *Why Survive? Being Old in America.* New York, Harper & Row Publishers, 1975.
13. Libow, L. & Sherman, F. *The Core of Geriatric Medicine.* St. Louis: C. V. Mosby, Co., 1981.
14. Saul, Shura. *Aging: An Album of People Growing Old.* New York: John Wiley and Sons, Inc., 1974.
15. Monk, Abraham, "Social Work with the Aged: Principles of Practice." *Social Work,* January 1981, pp. 61–68.
16. Kastenbaum, Robert. "Reluctant Therapist." In *New Thoughts on Old Age,* Ed. Robert Kastenbaum, New York: Springer Publishing Co., 1964 pp. 139–145.
17. Pincus, Allen. "Reminiscence in Aging & Its Implications for Social Work Practice." *Social Work,* July 1970, Vol. 15, pp. 47–53.
18. Coulton, Claudia. "A Study of Person-Environment Fit Among the Chronically Ill." *Social Work in Health Care.* Vol. 5, No. 1. Fall 1979.

12

Interdisciplinary Health Care Teams: An Educational Approach to Improvement of Health Care for the Aged

Audrey Olsen Faulkner

THERE IS A COMPELLING NEED to redefine the goals of health care for older people, and to develop new strategies for approaching those goals. Much of the necessary redirection will require comprehensive changes in public policies and will have to be debated in the national political arena. There is, however, an opportunity for gerontological and geriatric educators to take a leadership role in altering the face of health care for the elderly by their training of health practitioners who deliver service to the nation's hospitals, nursing homes, sheltered care settings, and communities.

There is a continuing tension between the goal of education for disciplinary specialization in the health professions and the goal of considering the older recipient of health service in his/her total biological, psychological, social and cultural context (Engel, 1980; Schwab, 1975). While there is expressed concern about the effects of uni-disciplinary visions of aging and old age by physicians, nurses, social workers, psychologists, and other health-related professions, educators have been more active in getting basic gerontology and geriatrics curriculum into place in their own specializations than in taking an interdisciplinary view.

The barriers to interdisciplinary collaboration by health profession-

Reprinted from *Gerontology & Geriatrics Education* 5, no. 3 (Spring 1985): 29–39, with permission, The Haworth Press, Inc. Copyright © 1985 by The Haworth Press, Inc., 12 West 32nd Street, New York, NY 10001.

als are formidable. Some case studies on health team experience (Banta & Fox, 1972; Wise, 1974) suggest that what might be called disciplinary ethnocentrism is commonly encountered. This is the pervasive tendency to view the discipline in which one is trained as the superior and most relevant one. It can lead to intractable disputes over turf and authority which in turn prevent utilization of professional talent on behalf of the patient. It has been the author's observation that there are other obstacles that present almost as great a challenge to health team functioning. Among them are the lack of a common interdisciplinary vocabulary, value perceptions that lead to different outcome goals, and an emphasis upon collection and use of different data for problem solving. In addition, socialization to the norms of any given health profession help to support insularity, and recognition usually accrues to health professionals for their own disciplinary work, not for interdisciplinary ventures.

Educating health care professionals for interdisciplinary team practice offers one promising possibility for overcoming these disciplinary barriers and reducing the fragmentation of health care for older people (Crooks, Lee & Yoskikawa, 1982; Jelly & Hawkinson, 1980). Such an approach will require a considerable broadening of the gerontology and geriatrics curricula, as well as a reorientation to goals of care and appropriate expectations about health and illness among the old.

There are some reports of team activities in the gerontological and health care literature (Banta & Fox, 1972; Blumenfield, Morris & Sherman, 1982; Pomerantz, 1984; Spiegel & Spiegel, 1984; Terry, 1981; Wise, Beckhard, Rubin & Kyte, 1974). Debates about the value of teams appear to be based more on opinion than on careful review of empirical processes and outcomes, but existing reports suggest that success or failure can be related to team goals, team members' orientation to aging and the aged, composition and structure of the team, problem-solving and interpersonal dynamics of the team, and mutual professional support. This paper will discuss these issues in relation to education for membership on an interdisciplinary health care team serving aged clients.

GOALS

National consensus on the goals of care for the aged has not been reached (Benjamin & Estes, 1983). It is not surprising, then, if no agreement about goals exists among health care professionals. If health practitioners are to function as a team, however, they must address this lack of agreement, since shared goals for team work are a prerequisite to cohesive effort.

Silverstone and Burack-Weiss (1983) propose a goal of maximizing the self determination of the frail elder in the helping process. Their auxiliary function model proposes that the professional helper expedite a loan transaction in which the elder borrows what is needed for as long as it is needed to accomplish restitution, compensation or accommodation in relation to the biological and social losses of old age. The model assumes that the loan may need to be for the remainder of the elder's lifetime. Building on the Silverstone and Burack-Weiss model, which distinguishes between self determination and self reliance, this author suggests that the primary goal for the interdisciplinary health care team should be supported autonomy for the older person. While practitioners speak of "helping older people to live independently for as long as possible," it can be argued that almost no individual lives independently of others. If the team aims its intervention at making the older person independent it may, therefore, program the team and the elder for failure.

Orientation to the goal of supported autonomy would permit the health professionals and the older person to discriminate between self determination and self reliance, and make it possible for the team and its client to accept what have been called the normal dependencies of old age (Blenkner, 1969). Viewing these normal dependencies as the right of the old would prevent a tendency to compromise the elder's feelings of self worth when help must be requested and accepted. Blenkner outlines these normal dependencies as (1) economic, when the old one becomes a consumer rather than a producer; (2) physical, when in the process of aging the ordinary chores of daily living become difficult or impossible to perform without some assistance; (3) mental, when the older person must rely on the problem solving abilities of others; and (4) social, when there is a loss of persons, roles and contemporaneity, and dependence on the recognition of the older person's rights instead of his or her power. Emotional dependency could be added as the fifth of the appropriate dependencies of the old, since most humans depend upon others for love and nurture.

With supported autonomy as the goal, the health team could consider its interventions with the aged along a continuum from maximum health service support to minimum health service support, adapting and modifying its behavior to take account of the unique complex of biological, psychological, social, cultural and environmental factors that are affecting the elder's need for health care. The aged may be capable of complete autonomy; they may be partially autonomous but have their autonomy under assault—social pressure tends to be in the direction away from self government for older people—or they already may have had to surrender all autonomy when they reach the attention of the health team. Older persons living alone who are relatively healthy and agile, whose emotional and cognitive functioning is adequate, and who make decisions to use only such family, neighborhood and community supports as persons of any age group would use, can be considered to be fully autonomous. These same individuals, if deprived by over-protective children of the right to make personal life-style decisions, would have shifted to another point on the continuum. The comatose elder, with life sustained by heroic medical measures, could be said to have completely surrendered autonomy. This individual, if conscious with cognitive and affective functioning somewhat intact, could still be relatively autonomous. The right to make decisions about one's care should not be compromised by the act of receiving that care.

A second team goal relates to the outcome of health care. The prevailing emphasis of health care is on acute rather than chronic care, total recovery after crisis, and life rather than death. For the aged, this orientation needs to be modified in favor of goals of continuous treatment of long term illness, restoration after acute episodes to functioning that represents what is possible, with a view of death with dignity and free of pain as a morally acceptable outcome. Birenbaum (1979) suggests that we need to focus on maximizing identified adaptive capacities, and that what the elderly patient may require is "comprehensive management," based on a more socially oriented model of care. This objective can provide the *raison d'être* for the health professional, and is one which the interdisciplinary team could be equipped to achieve.

A third goal concerns personal emotional growth and social interaction. One of the assumptions that underlies some health professionals' approach to practice with the older adult is that since old age is a time of decline and decrement, it cannot be a time for personal emotional growth. Such professionals may view the older person as being in a growth limbo from age 65 until death, with no expectation that there will be the positive challenge and the positive response that marks the ongoing life involvement of other younger persons who are in good emotional health. At the other extreme, some health professionals may view the older person almost as an object, to be programmed into a frenetic daily round of organized activity in order to outwit decline. Neither of these positions is appropriate. The team's goal should be to provide opportunity, support and encouragement for as much personal emotional growth and social interaction as the older persons they work with desire, and to help them contribute to society in accord with their individual potential.

ORIENTATION TO AGING AND THE AGED

It is assumed that the team members are expected to be secure in their knowledge and proficient in the skills of their own disciplines. They will need, in addition, an orientation toward working with the old that will permit them to derive professional satisfaction from being helpers rather than persons dispensing "cure." The team needs to recognize the dangers of its members' possible ageism. Ageism has been defined as the tendency to see the aging process as a series of social and mental problems for the elderly, rather than as a maturation process of responsible individuals which includes both joy and sadness (Blank, 1979). To combat this, the team needs to develop empathy for the old, although the members of the team, if new to gerontology and geriatrics, may initially view old age as a socially undesirable status. Empathic projection into the life situation of the elder is an exercise in preparing for one's own aging. If the team members can make this projection, they can help the older person to achieve the ego integrity of the last stage of life, which Erikson (1963) defines as "the acceptance of one's one and only life cycle as something that had to be, and that, by necessity, permitted of no substitutions" (pp. 268–269).

The team needs to become familiar and comfortable with some unique aspects of dealing with the elderly to whom they provide health care; often the team will be presented with conflicts about the appropriateness of sustaining life under conditions of extreme deficit; the aged may not offer the team members the professional reward of having accomplished cure; optimism and hope may be difficult for the team members to sustain when they work with a population for whom the opportunity channels for self direction and change may be very limited, and who have less time left and fewer resources left to overcome obstacles; and since the aged have a declining rather than a growing support system, their need for support from the team may become an increasing rather than a decreasing one over the period of team-elder contact. The team needs to be aware of the special characteristics, pitfalls and opportunities that exist for health care in the major settings where multiple disciplines practice. To name a few of these settings: multi-purpose resource centers, nutrition programs, public housing social service departments, acute care hospitals, community mental health centers and family counseling agencies, nursing homes, sheltered boarding homes, and hospices.

COMPOSITION AND STRUCTURE OF THE TEAM

The nucleus of the health care team should be the elder. This is the person who has the greatest vested interest in the outcome. Professionals tend sometimes to forget this when referring to "our" cases. The patient has a control over the outcome at least equivalent to that of the professionals. Lack of will, withholding of information, inadequate skill, or failure to observe prescribed treatment can prevent correct diagnosis and sabotage even the most tested treatment plan. The patient is the person with the most accurate information about response to treatment. As the only person on the team who is experiencing the total interaction of health problem, health care, and social environment, the patient may not feel the way a patient is "supposed" to feel. The rest of the team needs this information for corrective feedback.

The first addition to the nucleus should be the primary care designee. This may be a physician, if the patient is hospitalized; the institutional nurse if the older person is in a non-hospital health care setting; or a community nurse or social worker if the older person is in a private residence or congregate living facility. A family member may also serve when he or she is involved in health care delivery. As psychologists become more oriented to health care, they may be included. This discipline has traditionally functioned as primary care givers in settings more concerned with mental health than physical health care. However, the special skills of this discipline make the psychologist a likely candidate for addition to the team, either as a primary treatment professional or a consulting member for diagnosis and treatment design (Surwit, Feinglos & Scovern, 1983).

The physician brings to the team the skilled medical knowledge that is the basis for the ultimate medical responsibility for the outcome of the curative, palliative or preventive effort. The nurse's expertise is directed toward assisting older persons to cope with the effects of disability and disease, and to keep people well, especially people at high risk such as the ambulatory elderly. The social worker brings an orientation to the person-in-environment, working to enhance the problem-solving, coping and developmental capacities of older people, and to link them with the social institutions providing resources, services and opportunities. The family member, if on the team, can provide support for the older person and assistance with a health regimen.

The next module should include the clinical pharmacist and the nutritionist. The clinical pharmacist is a specialist in drugs and drug interaction, and can be expected to have highly specialized training in the differential rates of utilization, retention and excretion of drugs by the older body. Drugs figure centrally in the treatment and management of the chronic diseases of old age. Issues of drug compliance are critical to good health care (Besdine, 1979); possible drug interactions need careful review (Kayne, 1978) and the possibility of iatrogenic illnesses (Jick, 1977) is of serious concern. The nutritionist's skills are needed for health maintenance and disease treatment, since the older person's capacity for utilizing nutrients is reduced. Too, drugs and drug interactions, as well as the traumas of surgery and medical treatment, affect food intake. An adequate nutritional program is essential.

The team may also need a translator of language and culture where there are ethnic and racial populations with whom communication presents special problems.

The final member of the team may be the paraprofessional or aide. Too little use is made of this person when planning for health care. The aide may be the one whose daily or hourly interaction with the patient is greater than that of any other team member, and observations and insights resulting from her/his continuous contact can provide valuable data for decision making.

Other professionals should be added according to the status of the patient and the patient's environment, be it in a general hospital, an extended care facility, a congregate or independent living setting. The dentist, the rehabilitation, occupational, recreational or creative arts therapist, the adult educator, and the clergy all bring special skills, special views of ability and disability, and unique information about health maintenance and strategies for the amelioration of illness and its effects.

PROBLEM SOLVING AND INTERPERSONAL DYNAMICS

Valletutti and Christoplos (1977) describe two kinds of teams, those in which all of the members meet face to face and are directly responsible for prescribing a patient's treatment program, and those responsible for providing consultation to an intermediary who then provides direct treatment to the patient. Either definition would fall within the scope of the present approach to team care provided that certain conditions exist to make the team something more than a panel of experts consulting side by side, without synthesis and without pressure for producing an interdisciplinary study, assessment and intervention plan. Basic to team functioning should be multiple-way communication linkages between all members, a division of labor based on function instead of status, and shared responsibility for final decisions (Lowe & Herranen, 1981).

There are two tracks for team functioning: (1) the medical-health centered study, assessment and intervention, where interdisciplinary integration offers the possibility of high quality problem solving; and (2) the interpersonal dynamics by which the team can achieve its full potential for primary task accomplishment. The team requires a manager for both functions.

The medical-health function manager need not be the person with the highest level of medical expertise; in fact, automatic designation of the physician as the team manager may be counterproductive for interdisciplinary functioning, and may be cost ineffective as well. The person who is the primary care designee is the most likely candidate for this position. The manager for the interpersonal functioning of the team should be selected on the basis of temperament and skill in managing conflict, promoting synthesis, and facilitating problem solving (Kane, 1975; Nason, 1983).

Team members have to be considered as individuals trained, skilled and experienced in their own health areas, and as persons with insights and skills that can facilitate the care of the patient. All members must function as teacher-learners. They must be willing to teach their skills to the other members, and to take off disciplinary blinders and learn what other professionals know and do.

All members must be prepared to engage in advocacy for the older person and to support the elder's entitlement to knowledge about health conditions and decision making rights. The presence of the several disciplines, each with unique knowledge, should help to keep the team effective in this regard. The physician who commands the best of medical technology; the social worker who can help the patient deal with the interaction of the technology and the environment; the nurse who can educate the patient to what it means to care for oneself using the technology; the family member who knows the elder's life history; the pharmacist who may be a specialist in the hazards of the technology; the nutritionist who can provide education about maintaining health in the face of the effect of the technology; all have access to routes for advocacy and all have special knowledge to contribute to the patient's understanding of his or her situation.

INTERDISCIPLINARY DECISION MAKING

The team must operate in such a way that, with the data available, it will enumerate and consider the many alternatives and the consequences of the choices for action. It is in this process that the special disciplinary knowledge of the members is so critical, for single disciplines tend to be single alternative and single consequence oriented. At the same time that the team members engage in a disciplinary synthesis, they must maintain their own disciplinary integrity. If they fall prey to role yearning (Faulkner, 1975) or role identification with a professional of perceived higher status, they may nullify their own special expertise, and stifle their ability to contribute that special expertise, in favor of deference or novice-level copying of the role of another.

For the patient, assumption of responsibility for participation in the decision making should result in the alleviation of the anxiety of knowing one is the object of decisions, without being aware of the knowledge that guides them. Where the patient is unable to be fully involved in decision making, family or friends should serve in this capacity. There are, of course, some situations in which a single professional on the scene must make a decision without the team's particiption, such as when a crisis would make it unethical to do otherwise.

The interpersonal dynamics of the team, and its functioning as a social unit, are as important to success as the quality of the members' professional knowledge and skill. The principles of useful and productive interpersonal dynamics are well known; these include mutuality of goals, distributive leadership, full participation, conflict management and consensus formation (Johnson & Johnson, 1975). The team's process manager can be expected to be aware of them and experienced in putting them into practice. Effective interpersonal dynamics occur more easily when the team meets face to face as a group unit. However, the team cannot always gather at one place and at one time. Schedules vary, crises intervene, and people work at different locations. There are obvious problems in having the patient travel to conference sites. There is also resistance to the time that team meetings require. The word "team" sometimes conjures up the vision of endless hours of discussion about procedures while the patient's life quietly ebbs away. Alternatives to face to face problem solving are necessary.

Modular meetings, with proposed solutions conveyed to and discussed with other team members, written communications, and telephone consultations present possibilities that are in use. This is less than adequate for producing the group problem solving that is the team goal, but often must suffice. We may need a new professional, a group dynamics-communications facilitator, who can put the best of group dynamics theory and the best of communications technology at the service of the team. Closed circuit TV, computer terminals and teleconferencing all might be utilized to provide the opportunity for instantaneous visual and verbal communication, without a common location.

MUTUAL SUPPORT FOR THE TEAM

The focus of this paper is that the primary beneficiary of the team effort is the patient, not the professional. However, team support can contribute directly to the members' improved functioning, and hence to better outcomes for the patient under consideration, and for the patients of the same or similar teams as members interact in other areas. Teams provide for shared decision making around troublesome ethical issues so often present with the older patient; teams can help prevent "burn-out" by providing personal emotional support for the members; and shared accountability for outcome can remove the burden of any one professional's having to be the health care superstar.

ROLE MODELING AND REHEARSAL

Health care professionals receive their education and training through a combination of classroom, laboratory and clinical work. In all of these teaching-learning situations, students acquire attitudes, knowledge, skills and professional role behaviors through observing their teachers and mentors carrying out professional tasks. Students also have the opportunity in the clinical setting to rehearse their role behaviors in anticipation of their own professional careers. Role modeling and rehearsal are indigenous to the health professions' educational milieu.

Every student learning to deliver health care to the aged should have the opportunity to observe faculty role models engaged in interdisciplinary activity, and to rehearse their own future interdisciplinary role behaviors. Those who do the modeling will need to be secure in their own roles, their regard for each other's expertness, and their own place on the team. They must believe in the team concept, their profession's role in health care for older people, and the necessity for the unique contribution of other professions.

SUMMARY

This paper has called for education for interdisciplinary exchange and synthesis among the many professionals concerned with the health of older people. A focus on the interdisciplinary team approach has been proposed for gerontological curricula in the educational institutions that train health professionals. Education for teamwork is offered as one partial solution to the fragmentation of health care for older people, since the problems in the health care world of the elder American are too complex to be solved by a single discipline.

REFERENCES

Banta, H.D., & Fox, R.C. (1972). Role strains of a health care team in a poverty community: The Columbia Point experience. *Social Science and Medicine, 6,* 697–722.

Benjamin, A.E., & Estes, C. (1983). Social interventions with older adults. In E. Seidman (Ed.), *Handbook of Social Intervention,* (pp. 438–454). Beverly Hills, Calif.: Sage Publications.

Besdine, R.W. (1979). *Observations on Geriatric Medicine.* Washington, D.C., U.S. Department of Health, Education and Welfare. (DREW no. NIH 79–162).

Birenbaum, A., Aronson, M., & Seiffer, S. (1979). Training medical students to appreciate the special problems of the elderly. *The Gerontologist, 19,* 578.

Blank, M.L. (1979). Ageism in gerontologyland. *Journal of Gerontological Social Work, 2,* 5–9.

Blenkner, M. (1969). The normal dependencies of aging. In R.A. Kalish (Ed.), *The Dependencies of Old People* (pp. 27–28). Ann Arbor: Institute of Gerontology, The University of Michigan–Wayne State University.

Blumenfeld, S., Morris, J., & Sherman, F.T. (1982). The geriatric team in the acute care hospital: An educational and consultation modality. *Journal of the American Geriatrics Society, 30,* 660–664.

Crooks, V., Lee, P., & Yoskikawa, T. (1982). Geriatric medicine: A multi-disciplinary training and education model in an acute care medical center. *Journal of the American Geriatrics Society, 30,* 774–780.

Engel, G.L. (1980), Clinical application of the biopsycholosocial model. *The American Journal of Psychiatry, 137,* 535–544.

Erikson, E.H. (1963). *Childhood and Society* (2nd ed.). New York: Norton and Company, Inc.

Faulkner, A.O. (1975). The black aged as good neighbors: An experiment in volunteer service. *The Gerontologist, 15,* 554–559.

Janetakos, J., & Schissel, C. (1979). Partners: Nurse practitioner and social worker. *American Journal of Nursing, 79,* 1434–1435.

Jelly, E.C., & Hawkinson, W.P. (1980). Geriatric education in a family practice residence program: An interdisciplinary health-care team approach. *The Gerontologist, 20,* 168–172.

Jick, H. (1977). The discovery of drug-induced illness. *New England Journal of Medicine, 296,* 481–485.

Johnson, D.W., & Johnson, F.P. (1975). *Joining Together: Group Theory and Group Skills.* Englewood Cliffs, NJ: Prentice-Hall, Inc.

Kane, R.A. (1975). The interprofessional team as a small group. *Social Work in Health Care, 1,* 19–32.

Kayne, R.C. (Ed.). (1978). *Drugs and the Elderly.* Lexington, MA: Lexington Books.

Lowe, J.I., & Herranen, M. (1981). Understanding teamwork: Another look at the concepts. *Social Work in Health Care, 7,* 1–11.

Nason, F. (1983). Diagnosing the hospital team. *Social Work in Health Care, 9,* 25–45.

Pomerantz, B.R. (1984). Collaborative interviewing: A family centered approach to pediatric care. *Health and Social Work, 9,* 66–73.

Schwab, M. (1975). *Medicine and Aging: An Assessment of Opportunities and Neglect.* New York: Special Committee on Aging, United States Senate, page 31.

Silverstone, B. & Burack-Weiss, A. (1983). *Social Work Practice with the Frail Elderly and Their Families.* Springfield, IL: Charles C. Thomas.

Spiegel, J.S., & Speigel, T.M. (1984). An objective examination of multi-disciplinary patient conferences. *Journal of Medical Education, 59,* 436–438.

Surwit, R.S., Feinglos, M.N., & Scovern, A.W. (1983). Diabetes and behavior: A paradigm for health psychology. *American Psychologist, 38*(3), 255–262.

Terry, P.O. (1981). Clinical social work roles in an integrative, interdisciplinary team enhancing parental compliance. *Social Work in Health Care, 6,* 1–15.

Valletutti, P.J., & Christoplos, F. (1977). *Interdisciplinary Approaches to Human Services.* Baltimore: University Press.

Wise, H., Beckhard, R., Rubin, I., & Kyte, A. (1974). *Making Health Teams Work.* Cambridge, MA: Ballinger.

PART
VI

Humanistic Education

Introduction to Part VI

ONE OF THE MOST IMPORTANT GOALS of education is to influence a student's attitude and behavior. It is significant, therefore, that during the past decade the study of the human sciences—psychology, ethics—has achieved a place in the curricula of most health profession schools.

We must be realistic in our expectations, however. Even though we recognize the importance of integrating subjects that deal with human relationships into the curricula, we cannot overemphasize that the critical factor in imparting the importance of humane care is the example set by the instructors themselves. This is especially true in the health professions where so much training is carried out in patient settings and so many of the caregivers also serve as teachers. The manner in which the caregiver relates to the patient will not only have a great influence on the student but will also reinforce the content of the humanistic curriculum.

The first article in this section, "Evaluation of Humanistic Qualities in the Internist," outlines a landmark decision by the American Board of Internal Medicine in which the board extends its humanistic conviction beyond mere endorsement. In a careful delineation of its humanistic responsibilities, the board articulates guidelines for humanistic behavior, explores methods of assessing humanistic practice, and spells out the essential humanistic qualities required of candidates seeking certification. Recognizing that the principles enunciated by the board can be held in common by all health professions, this position paper represents a major development in the history of humanistic health care.

The article by Richard Gorlin and Howard Zucker, "Physicians' Reactions to Patients: A Key to Teaching Humanistic Medicine," discusses an innovative educational program that focuses on the caregiver's emotional and behavioral response to patients. The authors emphasize that it is imperative that caregivers recognize the philosophical and emotional context of their own interactions with patients in order to make those interactions more effective. The article describes the rationale, objectives, and specific elements of this educational focus.

Jurrit Bergsma and David Thomasma's article, "The Contribution of Ethics and Psychology to Medicine," addresses the humanistic medical curricula and examines the significant role that the disciplines of ethics and psychology can play when presented and taught together in an interrelated way. Bergsma and Thomasma suggest that the integration of ethics and psychology in the curriculum will give the student a structure in which to relate values, attitudes, and behaviors realistically. Bergsma and Thomasma's ideas complement the position of the American Board of Internal Medicine and Gorlin and Zucker's program for medical education by suggesting the combination of ethics and psychology as an essential component of the education of all health care professionals.

13

Evaluation of Humanistic Qualities in the Internist

Subcommittee on Evaluation of Humanistic Qualities in the Internist,* American Board of Internal Medicine

IN AN IMPORTANT DECISION on 6 June 1983 the American Board of Internal Medicine accepted the following report of its Subcommittee on Evaluation of Humanistic Qualities in the Internist. In adopting the four principles, the Board is committed to requiring high standards of humanistic behavior in the professional lives of every candidate. The Board has long insisted on acceptable moral and ethical standing in the care of patients by candidates. Through accepting this report the Board extends its conviction beyond the mere endorsement of humanism.

The Board also voted to initiate several actions recommended by the subcommittee. As a beginning, the Board will develop a process to assess (not measure) humanistic qualities in professional behavior during residency training. It will therefore rely heavily on colleagues in the certification process— residency program directors and their faculties and attending physicians.

The subcommittee consisted of five physicians from the Board and four non-physicians. This latter group provided philosophical, ethical, and sociological perspectives as well as the patient's point of view. The Board is indebted to them for their honesty and intellect, and rewarded once again by its reliance on experts from other disciplines.

The Board accepts the responsibility for establishing and maintaining its

*John A. Benson, Jr., Linda L. Blank, Eugene P. Frenkel, Edward W. Hook, Albert R. Jonsen, Julius R. Krevans, Chairman, Lynn O. Langdon, Lawrence Scherr, and Neil J. Smelser.

Reprinted from *Annals of Internal Medicine* 99, no. 5 (November 1983): 720–724, with permission, The American College of Physicians.

standards. Peers recognizing peers must set fair standards and apply them objectively. Assessment of this essential component of overall clinical competence will challenge its expertness and sense of equity. The public has a right to expect humanistic behavior in its physicians. We have every confidence that the Board and its colleagues will meet the challenge. The Board must do nothing less. (Julius R. Krevans and John A. Benson, Jr.)

BACKGROUND

In December 1981 the American Board of Internal Medicine appointed the Subcommittee on Evaluation of Humanistic Qualities in the Internist. The decision to establish this subcommittee resulted from the Board's longstanding desire to better define and assess these essential qualities. Several years before, a task force that addressed evaluation in general internal medicine had encouraged the Board to assure that candidates have satisfactory interpersonal and communicative skills, among other essential components of overall clinical competence. In early 1981 another task force charged to define clinical competence included humanistic qualities as essential skills every internist must have to be certified. It also recommended that a subcommittee be formed to assess the state-of-the-art of the evaluation of humanistic qualities and advise the Board of potentially useful evaluation strategies. Subsequently, the Subcommittee on Evaluation of Humanistic Qualities in the Internist was charged to:

1. Define further the humanistic qualities desirable in the internist by identifying the attitudes, habits, and behavior needed.
2. Identify the humanistic qualities a person brings to the educational process, and the qualities acquired in the educational setting that are important to the practice of internal medicine.
3. Explore methods of assessing humanistic behavior in any profession.
4. Assess the applicability of any of these methods to the education of internists, setting requirements for admission to the certifying examination and use in the examination.
5. Prepare a statement on humanistic qualities of the internist to show the Board's concern and to dispel the notion that noncognitive skills cannot be taught or tested.

Thus, the subcommittee was asked to go beyond the mere endorsement of humanistic qualities in the internist by advancing the evaluation of these attributes in candidates.

In many respects, concern over the humanistic qualities of physicians and medical ethics is timeless. Physicians and others have reflected on and debated about the proper conduct of medical practitioners for centuries. On the other hand, the subcommittee is aware that important changes occur in the scientific, economic, and social environments of medical practice, and that these changes affect physicians' commitment to the humanistic dimensions of medical care. Although some changes have enhanced the humanistic dimensions of medical care, some recent changes in medical practice have threatened and possibly eroded this commitment. The subcommittee considered the following developments:

The medical profession has been influenced by societal changes such as greater expectations for satisfactory clinical outcomes, disenchantment with the spiraling costs of medical care, and the concomitant desires for personalized care and for the advantages attributed to the type of care provided by a large medical center.

Patients are now more involved in clinical decisions regarding their health care and are more likely to fault physicians, particularly those who are perceived as unfeeling or authoritarian.

The high technology of medical care may contribute to costly, impersonal management. Some practitioners may have become preoccupied with quantitative and technologic approaches to diagnosis, leading to a deemphasis on personal interaction with patients in clinical settings.

Medical faculties have grown larger and training programs more complex, leading to less personalized faculty contact with residents, difficulty in identification of role models, and a loss of feeling of "family" within a residency program.

Faculty involved in graduate medical education may have distracting objectives and may slight personal interactions with residents and insistence on humanistic behavior toward patients.

Team care may diffuse the sense of responsibility and commitment on the part of individual physicians.

Subspecialization may detract from continuity of care.

Some physicians may be inclined to act excessively as entrepreneurs.

Reimbursement regulations shift responsibility for patients from residents to attending physicians and other faculty physicians. Although this shift may create better role models in faculties, residents may lose a sense of accountability.

Highly competitive attitudes have become pervasive in medical education—in the struggle for admission to medical school, in the demand for high performance during medical school, and in the competition for "good" residency programs. This competition may foster excessive concern with personal career success and overshadow commitments to the humanistic dimensions of medical practice.

These influences jeopardize several of the essential humanistic qualities of the internist. The abilities to engage in compassionate human relationships with patients and in cooperative relationships with colleagues may be damaged. The ability to engage in clear, mutually satisfactory communication may be stifled. Concentration on self may have diminished readiness to act altruistically. The humanistic qualities of the internist must be nurtured and sustained in medical education and practice.

WORK OF THE SUBCOMMITTEE

The subcommittee undertook its task with the conviction that medicine has the moral significance of a calling. It agrees that humanism is an essential part of internal medicine. Internists must function as personal physicians. The subcommittee recognizes that the Board has a unique opportunity and obligation to promote this viewpoint through its certification process. It supports the task force's statement that the qualities a physician should have if he or she is pursuing a career in internal medicine must include integrity, respect, compassion, honesty, trustworthiness, commitment, and humility.

Although the subcommittee is skeptical that humanistic qualities can be reliably measured by test instruments, abundant opportunities exist during residency training for assessing and reinforcing these qualities.

Even though it may not be possible to change character in a radical way, established personality traits and behavior can be modified and influenced by experiences.

The subcommittee would not dictate moral orthodoxy on the part of residents, but it recommends that the Board insist on principled behavior in clinical care.

The discipline of clinical ethics in its cognitive dimensions can be taught by experienced practitioners and scholars. The attitudinal (noncognitive) aspects of clinical ethics can be reinforced through acceptance of obligations in caring for the patient and to other professionals in engaging in cooperative care.

House officers can be taught that the humanistic qualities desirable in an internist may not be fulfilled merely by observing legal standards of behavior.

Residents can be sensitized to examine the relationship of their values to those of the patient.

In particular, residents can be informed that the American Board of Internal Medicine considers humanistic, moral, and ethical behavior to be an essential quality in the certifiable internist and subspecialist.

The subcommittee consulted clinical psychologists, investigators in health education, residents in training, and several residency program directors to explore available methods of assessing humanistic qualities. Educational techniques being used to teach and in some situations evaluate medical students and housestaff were observed and may warrant further attention. The subcommittee was not surprised to learn that validated, objective tests of humanistic qualities are not available for standardized use by any profession.

Another position reaffirmed by the subcommittee is that the Board has the discretion to set its standards, providing they have merit and are applied with due process. It uses such judgment in all of its standard-setting processes. On the other hand, where patients and values are concerned, the subcommittee recognizes that different standards and cultures breed different value systems and norms among diverse trainees and residencies. Therefore, although equity is sought, identical standards and processes may not be achieved.

PRINCIPLES

Principle 1: The essential humanistic qualities required of candidates seeking certification by the American Board of Internal Medicine are integrity, respect, and compassion.

Integrity is the personal commitment to be honest and trustworthy in evaluating and demonstrating one's own skills and abilities.

Respect is the personal commitment to honor others' choices and rights regarding themselves and their medical care.

Compassion is an appreciation that suffering and illness engender special needs for comfort and help without evoking excessive emotional involvement that could undermine professional responsibility for the patient.

Principle 2: Candidates for certification must meet high standards of humanistic behavior in their professional lives. The Board should not accept anything less. Moral behavior is an overriding professional consideration in caring for patients.

Principle 3: A major responsibility of those training residents in internal medicine is to stress the importance of the humanistic qualities in the patient/

physician relationship throughout the residency. The certification process must assure that this responsibility has been undertaken.

Recognition of positive and negative influences on the humanistic qualities of physicians during residency training is important. Awareness of both exhilarating, rewarding encounters and unintentional harmful factors in training or its environment can assist faculties and residents in a better understanding of patients' feelings and needs. The subcommittee collected from residents a list of training experiences that may affect their humanistic qualities (see Appendix 1).

Principle 4: The ability to affect attitudes, behavior patterns, and moral conduct in medical care should be recognized and utilized during the residency training period—a unique experience that is not available at other times in medical education.

The residency training period marks the beginning of the physician's total responsibility for patients and their care. Residents encounter the limitations of therapeutic responses and the patients' expectations of the physician. Interactions and relationships with patients, their families, attending physicians, nurses, and others create new demands, challenges, and opportunities. The resident must care for patients in terms of the patient's values, which often differ from the resident's personal values. Residents must deal with death and the personal acceptance of failure. The reality of acknowledging a commitment to responsibility for patients, family interactions, and teaching may bring to the surface fears of inadequacy. Residencies should offer a supervised opportunity to learn how to handle such doubts and fears.

The realities of institutional operations—administrative policies, limited resources, and conflicting priorities between administration and housestaff—require sensitive, adaptive and decisive behavior on the part of residents. They should establish and maintain honest and respectful relationships with supervisory faculty, consultants, peers, nurses, laboratory technicians, and other health care personnel.

Residents may need to be reminded that patients and families deserve honesty, information, respect for the wishes of the patient, and fidelity to promises and commitments.

Repeated experiences with acutely, critically, or terminally ill patients and hopelessly impaired patients may have a profound effect on the humanistic qualities of residents, and opportunities should be taken to cultivate positive, caring approaches.

Experiences offering continuity of care can provide a realistic setting for residents to demonstrate humanism in their care of patients.

The availability and emotional support of respected role models during residency training is critical. Their presence should be a requisite to accreditation of the residency program.

Because residents have repeated contacts, often of long duration, with medical students, recognition by the housestaff of the need to demonstrate humanism as an essential part of patient care should impart a positive effect on these undergraduates.

ASSESSING AND INFLUENCING HUMANISTIC QUALITIES IN RESIDENTS

The many new, unique, and dramatic experiences that occur during residency training provide an opportunity to influence the ideas and behaviors of residents. Program directors should recognize that the resident's lack of knowledge and experience can contribute to or create stressful or threatening encounters. Emotional support and exemplary leadership are essential.

Scenarios of common stressful demands on internists (informing relatives of the loss of a loved one, seeking permission for autopsies or studies associated with risk, relating personally to the critically ill, dealing with self-abusive patients) should be studied with careful attention to teaching and reinforcing high standards in the humanistic qualities of the internist.

The commitment of the program director to the importance of humanism as an aspect of residency training is critical. The program director should serve as a role model to residents.

Systematic observation of humanistic behavior in housestaff during patient care should be incorporated in the evaluation of residents by attending faculty, chief residents, and peers.

Regularly scheduled conferences addressing issues of humanism should be included in major educational sessions of the training program.

The cognitive dimensions of clinical ethics can be discussed and tested locally to assure that residents, regardless of their personal opinions, have a clear understanding of the ethical and legal aspects of medical care.

Structured activities to review patient care should emphasize the accountability of the resident for the overall care of the patient.

Comments from patients, families, nurses, and others regarding the humanistic qualities and behavior of residents should be considered.

Careful review of the schedules, workload, and support system of housestaff should be undertaken with consideration of their impact on humanistic behavior.

Supervisory faculty should be particularly sensitive to the need for support and sympathetic counseling of houseofficers who have experienced the inevitable "tragic mistake" in the care of a patient.

Other techniques that can be useful in fostering and monitoring humanistic qualities in residents include advisors, preceptors, role models, videotapes of physician/patient encounters, and patient simulations.

ACTIONS TO BE UNDERTAKEN BY THE BOARD

Expression of the Board's determination in emphasizing the humanistic qualities of the internist will have a powerful influence. The Board's conviction will undergird the efforts of program directors to demand a high standard of moral and ethical behavior in medical care. Publication of a strong standard provides notice that can serve in prevention and as legal notification. The subcommittee proposed seven actions that were approved by the Board of Governors on 6 June 1983:

1. Accept as policy the four principles contained in this document.

2. Continue to include questions that address the cognitive aspects of medical ethics on the Board's written examinations to signal their importance in the curriculum of internal medicine training programs.

3. Since humanistic qualities cannot be tested on written examination, the Board's principal opportunity to include their assessment in the certifying process must be extended through program directors and faculties in residency programs. Guidelines for standards and recommended methods for assessment of these qualities should be provided by the Board to program directors. The American Board of Internal Medicine annual memoranda to training program directors is an opportunity to convey such information and already incorporates some of the concepts and language contained in this report. The pamphlet describing the clinical evaluation program to residents also addresses standards of humanistic behavior. The Board's well-established Hospital Visit Program offers a forum for clarification and emphasis of the Board's standards. It also provides the opportunities to document

evaluation of humanistic qualities and to discuss ideas and methods of assessment with the program director, evaluation committee, and selected attending staff and residents.

4. Candidates, as evaluated by residency programs, whose humanistic qualities fail to meet the Board's standards will be excluded from admission to a Certifying Examination. An appeals process will be established.

5. Diplomates who fail to meet these standards of professional behavior in practice will be excluded from admission to subsequent certifying processes.

6. Cheating and other forms of dishonest behavior by candidates are unacceptable. A 3- to 5-year sanction will be imposed on those candidates who are documented to have cheated on examinations. They will be required to petition the Board for readmission to examination after showing that they have been rehabilitated and have performed in practice at a high level of integrity.

7. Continued research and development of better methods for reliable, objective assessment of humanistic qualities in the internist should be encouraged by the Board through its Committee on Research.

CONCLUSION

The Board acknowledges that it has only made a beginning. There is a danger that the self-evidence of the conclusion—that is, the desirability of affirming humanistic qualities in the practice of internal medicine—will mask the difficulties of building an assessment of these qualities into the certification process. The subcommittee spent its first two meetings discovering the complexity of moving from affirmation to assessment. The uncertainties of objective assessment of humanistic attributes make casual or dogmatic applications of the recommended actions unwise.

APPENDIX 1: EXPERIENCES DURING TRAINING THAT AFFECT THE HUMANISTIC QUALITIES OF RESIDENTS

A sampling of residents from diverse programs identified the following experiences during training as either reinforcing or interfering with the demonstration of humanistic qualities in the patient/physician relationship. Both positive and negative experiences are categorized into four groups relating to self, attendings/colleagues/peers, structured educational experiences, and facilities and administration.

Positive Experiences
1. Self
     Illness in self or family
     Reasonable on-call schedule
2. Attendings/Colleagues/Peers
     Role models
         Strong chief residents
         Attendings who have the competence and willingness to assume responsiblity for the total care of patients
         Attendings who seek rapport with patients
     Interactions with caring nurses
     Peer criticism and support
     Concern for impact of diagnostic tests and therapy on care of the patient
3. Structured Educational Experiences
     Experience with continuity of care
     Structured mechanism for dealing with death
     Emphasis on talking with patients
     Emphasis on management and management plans versus diagnoses
     Attention to the quality of life for chronically ill patients
     Curriculum or conferences on behavior and ethics in the clinical setting
     Experience with home care
4. Facilities and Administration
     Good physical plant and modern center facilities

Negative Experiences
1. Self
     Death and failed expectations
     Unrealistic expectations—yearning to do better, curing
     Overwork (perceived and actual)
         Heavy admission load
         Specter of the unknown workload in the hours ahead
         No certain end to the day's responsibilities
     No rewards for humanism—no change in "outcome"
     Difficult patients and the perceived futility of caring for such
         Patients with degenerative, complex, malignant, multisystem diseases
         Self-abusive patients
         Patients who are welfare abusers, unkempt, repeated admissions, malingerers
     Excessive fatigue
     Use of impersonal jargon
2. Attendings/Colleagues/Peers
     Role models
         Lack of "responsible physician"
         Unavailable faculty
         Preoccupied faculty (research, travel)
         Attendings who make rounds away from the patient's bedside
         Attendings and housestaff oriented toward excessive use of procedures

3. Structured Educational Experiences
   Team rounds
   Intensive care technology which promotes loss of patient's individuality
   Emphasis on diagnosis rather than management
   Little exposure to courses in sociology, psychology, ethics and liberal arts during premed or medical school
   Use of protective (medicolegal) diagnostic testing of patients
   Over-emphasis on health care costs and related business analogies (consumer-provider-system terminology)
4. Facilities and Administration
   Administrative hypocrisy: the dilemma of keeping the wards full versus emptying beds and discharging inpatients
   Scut work: laboratory, intravenous lines, venepunctures
   Unpleasant, archaic physical plant of the medical institution
   Hospital bureaucracy

14

Physicians' Reactions to Patients: A Key to Teaching Humanistic Medicine

Richard Gorlin • *Howard D. Zucker*

SOMETHING HAS GONE WRONG in the practice of medicine, and we all know it. It is ironic that in this era, dominated by technical prowess and rapid biomedical advances, patient and physician each feel increasingly rejected by the other. Clearly, one root of the problem lies in the patient-doctor relationship. High technology tends to dehumanize care, and third-party regulations, paperwork, and malpractice threats distract the doctor. Nevertheless, the responsibility for dissatisfaction with modern medical care lies not only with the patient and the system but also with the physician.[1]

We shall discuss below how some of the typical difficulties that arise in the doctor-patient relationship are linked to physicians' emotional responses and then describe a program of humanistic medicine that was initiated by the Mount Sinai School of Medicine's Department of Medicine in July 1979.

DEFINING THE PROBLEM

The need to improve the physician-patient relationship has been recognized for over 50 years.[2] Despite the advent of liaison psychiatry, general hospital psychiatry,[3-5] and increased teaching of behavioral sci-

Reprinted from *The New England Journal of Medicine* 308, no. 18 (1983): 1059–1063, with permission, Massachusetts Medical Society.

ence in medical school, the integration of psychological and social understanding and skill in medical practice remains fragmentary. The conceptual tendency to isolate the person and his or her social life from the body—a problem addressed by Engel through his biopsychosocial model[6]—is still pervasive.

Teaching together over the past five years, we have become increasingly convinced that medical educational programs concerned with patient care are incomplete if they emphasize only the patient's feelings and behavior. In defining the character of the doctor-patient relationship, physicians' feelings and the way they respond to them are of equal importance. Feelings about the patient, the illness, the role of the sick person and the doctor's own role all influence diagnostic accuracy and treatment decisions[7] as well as the doctor's style of communicating with the patient. At times they determine the outcome.[8]

Teaching centered entirely on the patient's medical and psychological problems covertly suggests that the doctor's own reactions are trivial or that they should be suppressed or simply mastered. At best, the trainee with strong reactions feels lonely; at worst, he or she may feel guilt, shame, and resentment. When it is made clear that all doctors, however humane, will at times have negative or positive feelings and impulses that can interfere with optimal professional action or judgment, the student is freed to consider whether a reaction is shared with others or is a highly personal reaction to a particular patient or a particular disease. Each of us, after all, has special vulnerabilities, usually with unconscious roots. By acknowledging his or her own emotional position, the doctor is able to consider the relationship with the patient more objectively.

Table 14.1 lists some of the common situations and types of patient that are likely to produce counterproductive behavior in health-care professionals, along with the emotions and kinds of behavior likely to be generated. Instead of a psychiatric classification, such as those listed in the *Diagnostic and Statistical Manual*,[17] we have chosen a typology that highlights the distortions of the ideal patient role, for it is these distortions that particularly endanger the doctor's response to the patient. Having identified the emotional components of the field, the doctor is in a position to develop coping strategies specific to the given situation. Practical and concrete objectives can be defined and integrated into the overall treatment program in a way that takes the patient's and physician's needs and expectations, as well as the capabilities and limitations of each into account. Table 14.2 lists some of the coping strategies that can be mobilized when the physician identifies feelings in himself or herself that are likely to interfere with effective professional judgment and behavior. Both tables offer broadly drawn examples of situations and feelings that physicians face regularly.

TABLE 14.1

Frequent Physician Responses to Commonly Encountered Situations and Patient Types

Situation	Physician's Emotional Response	Physician's Behavioral Response
Terminal illness/chronic incurable disease[9-11]	Sympathetic identification; feelings of inadequacy, impotence, lowered self-esteem, frustration	Denial, reluctance to discuss illness with patient, avoidance of patient and family
Patient in emotional crisis: physician lacks time or skill to treat emotional aspects	Feelings of helplessness, loss of control, inadequacy	Failure to obtain consultation or refer patient
Institutionally determined termination of relationship (rotation or completion of residency)[12]	Guilt, sadness	Procrastination or failure to inform patient
Patient Type		
Organic brain syndrome/dementia; language/cultural differences; inability to understand explanations of disease or treatment	Impatience, frustration	Hostility, rejection (abruptness, avoidance, minimizing seriousness of symptoms)
Hostile patient/borderline personality[13-14]	Taking patient hostility personally; hatred; feeling authority threatened	Reciprocal hostility, rejection (power struggle, derision, forced discharge)
Overly dependent patient[15]	Initial gratification, followed by resentment, anger, impatience, guilt	Hostility, abrupt distancing, coldness
Hypochondriacal patient[16]	Impatience, frustration, anger	Rejection (derision, avoidance, prescription given out of exasperation)
Antisocial/self-destructive patient	Disapproval, anger	Punitive hostility; rejection (neglect or overtreatment)
Noncompliant patient	Sense of loss of control, threatened authority; frustration; anger	Hostility, rejection, denial (power struggle, loss of interest)

One question that arises in connection with coping alternatives deserves special attention: how and when to consult or refer when there is a behavioral problem or excessive tension between patient and doctor. Most doctors prefer to believe they are assuming total care of the patient and are reluctant to delegate psychosocial responsibilities to others, particularly if they fear exposure of their feelings. Frequently, the result is a tendency to trivialize the psychosocial issues or defer their consideration. Conversely, there may be an anxious riddance reaction, in which the doctor delegates too much psychosocial responsibility too soon. The self-attuned, realistic physician knows when he or she is not equipped, whatever the reasons, to manage the psychosocial aspect of the patient's care

TABLE 14.2

Strategies for Physicians to Cope with Negative Emotional Responses

Physician's Emotional or Behavioral Reaction	Coping Strategies
Avoidance	Analyze why; attempt to understand and master feelings that lead to avoidance; stay with the patient; discuss with colleagues
Identification with patient	Recognize; avoid tendency to deny seriousness of disease or to give way to despair; stay with the patient
Hostility/rejection	Acknowledge and analyze; don't attempt to like the unlikable patient; use behavioral approaches; if situation is intolerable, transfer patient to another physician
Feelings of impotence, inadequacy (e.g., in caring for dying patient)	Discover areas in which help and comfort can be rendered physical and emotional; be realistic about limitations of medicine; give the patient time to go through the stages of bereavement
Feelings of loss of control or threatened authority	Acknowledge and analyze; be realistic about personal limitations and actual range of influence and authority; be aware that patient's need for control over his own body may conflict with physician's urge to control the situation
Frustration, confusion, uncertainty about dealing with the patient; coping strategies not effective	Request psychiatric consultation/referral
Anxiety, guilt, frustration about meeting patient's recognized emotional needs	Allocate time realistically according to need; request consultation/referral

and is not embarrassed about obtaining a formal psychiatric or social-work consultation.

The incorporation of humanistic factors, such as those we have outlined, in the treatment program can make outcomes more satisfying, with practical gains for both patient and doctor. For the patient such gains include better compliance, with improved efficacy of treatment, and more effective rehabilitation. For the physician they include an increased sense of security and fulfillment; a decreased risk of drug abuse, suicide, and family disruption; and probably, an enhanced practice with fewer mal-practice actions.

THE HUMANISTIC-MEDICINE PROGRAM

Rationale, Objective, and Methods

The impetus for establishing our humanistic-medicine programs derived from three primary sources: agreement that in our era the doctor-patient relationship is seriously stressed, recognition that there is no out-let in most teaching systems for the intense reaction of medical students and residents to their education and to their patients, and our sense that previously established programs were incomplete because they omitted or underplayed the role of physicians' feelings and consideration of strat-egies for coping with them.

The goal of the program is broad. Stated simply, it is to help the medical student and resident understand how his or her feelings affect the treatment of the patient. Once developed, this understanding becomes a professional skill that encompasses all aspects of medical practice: ap-proaching and taking leave of the patient; interviewing, including having the capacity to listen; conducting oneself constructively at the bedside; discussing such difficult topics as sex, death, and the patient's rejection of important examinations or treatments; and using consultations and referrals appropriately, be they psychological, social, or medical.

Our teaching methods comprise four basic approaches. The first is to expose students and residents to concepts of humanistic medicine in every year of their training, with increasing emphasis during their clinical experiences. The second is to design the program so that humanistic ele-ments are intrinsic to the educational experience and not separate exer-cises isolated from the main theme. The third approach is to provide sophisticated and sensitive role models for medical students and house staff. The fourth is to integrate into the skilled faculty liaison psychiatrists who are comfortable with and interested in the complexities of biomedical care.

THE PROGRAM

The specific elements of the program are outlined below.

Undergraduate Program

In the first-year course, Introduction to Medicine, the broad scope of medicine is covered in a variety of forms. Recurrently, attention is focused on the physician's feelings as they relate to the patient's illness and to the physician's self-image.

The second-year course, Clinical Examination of the Patient, has conventionally emphasized the techniques of physical diagnosis, the scientific needs of history taking and recording, and the methods of diagnostic thinking. The emotional and behavioral interplay between doctor and patient, overshadowed by these other important elements, has often been minimized. In our course the department chairman introduces this topic, senior faculty members conduct demonstration interviews, and the course preceptors are actively encouraged to model the humanistic approach.

During the third-year clerkship, students weekly present a case to the department chairman and a liaison psychiatrist. Such tandem teaching is designed to highlight the importance of balancing biomedical capabilities with psychosocial sensitivity and skill in effective and humane medical care. Our technique includes conscious role reversal. Students learn that, regardless of specialty, the doctor's aim is to establish a relationship with the patient that facilitates diagnosis, treatment, and mutual comfort.

Since awareness of one's own feelings and the ability to cope with them constructively is an essential aspect of humanistic medical teaching, one of us confronts the students by asking how the presenter or the others feel about the particular patient, or illness, or situation under discussion. When the students hesitate to discuss their feelings, one of us may volunteer his own reaction and thus legitimize the discussion. This type of discussion is also facilitated by showing a documentary film that presents some real-life interactions of students, house staff, and patients. (*A Complicating Factor: Doctor's feelings as a factor in medical care*, 1982, Humanistic Medicine Program, Department of Medicine, Mount Sinai Medical Center, 16 mm, color, 46 minutes.)

The ambulatory-care training of the third-year clerks takes place for the most part in the offices of the faculty members, both voluntary and full time. Here role models demonstrate the realities of practice and the nuances of doctor-patient relationships.

The fourth-year medical clerks, as subinterns, have exposure to most of the program that is designed for the interns.

Graduate Program

The interns are recurrently exposed to the validity and utility of the biopsychosocial concept. During both the periodic rounds of the department chairman and the unit's regular teaching rounds, liaison psychiatrists teach with internists. Case discussions after bedside visits focus on three elements: the patient's disease, the patient himself, and the intern's own response to patient, disease, and health-care system. This model is reinforced by the interns' interaction with liaison psychiatry residents in the daily work of the unit.

In 1981 we added to the program, for interns only, weekly group discussions led by a psychiatrist and an internist of the impact of the grueling first postgraduate year on the intern; all matters discussed are kept confidential.

The residents have ambulatory-care responsibilities during all three years of their residencies. The Department of Medicine has initiated a medical-practice plan under which our residents join a team that practices integrated biomedical and psychosocial care. The role models are young internists working collegially with other health-care providers. In contrast to the situation that prevails in the general medical clinics of most urban hospitals, the resident becomes the primary physician for a stable cohort of patients during a period of two to three years.

During their rotation as inpatient chief residents, our third-year residents are, with support from senior faculty members, expected to act as humanistic role models for medical students and interns while participating in the interactive exercises mentioned above or in dealing with day-to-day patient and staff stresses and relationships. These third-year residents also rotate through the medical consultation service. The rounds are led by a seasoned internist who is joined, twice weekly, by an experienced liaison psychiatrist. This coteaching endeavor not only reinforces previously acquired concepts of humanistic medicine, it also encourages consideration of the feelings, behavior, and interactions of the consultant and the person consulted.

DISCUSSION

A controversial issue that bears on the approach we have outlined is the question of the rigidity of the physician's character structure. Medical colleagues discussing our program often insist, "You can't teach caring," and many dynamic psychiatrists believe that the unconscious sources of anxiety and rage that may be mobilized in the encounter with patient and illness cannot be greatly modified outside psychoanalytic treatment, if then. Although we acknowledge that some physicians are psychologically inaccessible, it is our experience that the majority wish to be helped to develop more comfortable relationships with their patients.

The key to successful mastery of a professionally hazardous emotional response is first to acknowledge that it exists. The next step is acceptance of the response as justifiable and understandable, even though acting on it may be morally unacceptable and pragmatically ill advised. For example, it is natural to react with dislike and anger to an assaultive, noncompliant drug addict with infective endocarditis. The physician's task is not to try to like such a patient, but rather to recognize, accept, and then restrain his or her negative feelings so that medical judgment and professional decisions will not be unconsciously distorted by hostility (Table 14.1). Similarly, it is natural to feel uncomfortable with a dying patient, and avoidance of such a patient is easily rationalized. One must recognize why it is painful to be confronted with terminal or incurable illness. How and what does one say when the news is mostly bad? How does one deal with feelings of identification with the patient, impotence, frustration, and loss of self-esteem? It is critical to realize too that even when there is no further specific therapy available, there are constructive things that can and should be done to help the patient and the family endure the experience. By accepting his or her feelings and considering their roots, the physician can counteract the impulse to withdraw.

The changes that are induced in the humanistic program follow this two-stage concept. First, the doctors in training modify their attitudes toward their own feelings, positive and negative, about patients and illnesses. What they may have considered irrelevant to the "scientific" situation they now acknowledge as human, understandable, and relevant. Thus, in the second phase, they are freed to deal with their own feelings and to apply a variety of interpersonal techniques that are appropriate to the needs of patient, family, and their own lives.

The belief that role modeling is an effective tool in teaching interpersonal behavior, particularly complex behavior, is supported by the literature.[18,19] As we see it, role models in a case setting provide a dynamic learning experience that contrasts with the passivity of textbook and lecture-hall education; immediately relevant experiences are more readily remembered than vicarious ones.

Our method emphasizes coteaching by internists and liaison psychiatrists in the medical setting. This pattern is aimed at diminishing the tendency conceptually to split the body (the internist's province) from the mind (the psychiatrist's province) and from the environment (the social worker's province). Engel[20] had serious doubts about coteaching, leaving it all to the internist because the psychiatrist was doomed to be an outsider. Our own experience has convinced us that a shared vocabulary, the practice of role reversal, and the practical definition of goals can bring the two disciplines together. Strain and Hamerman's model[21] also reduces the alienation.

The importance attached to the humanistic elements of medical practice—in particular to physicians' emotional responses to patients—is established firmly at every level by the department head. There is no other way. The visibility of the interaction between a department chairman and a liaison psychiatrist, the inclusion of the psychiatric attending physician in teaching rounds, and the setting aside of time for the weekly interns' meeting leave no doubt about the status[22] of the humanistic-medicine component in the department's eyes. Thus, without separate seminars, faculty development is fostered as well as student and resident learning.

Beyond the effect of formal structures, the attitudes and behavior of their clinical teachers toward patients, family, nurses, social workers, and fellow physicians are silently observed by students and residents with great impact. Is the patient being treated as a person and brought into the bedside discussion? Any wide gap between humanistic pronouncements and dehumanizing behavior may embitter students—or worse, may be accepted as a model of the real world.

The internship year, and to some degree the subinternship year, are an intense period of transition. The stress and inevitable pain of this phase of professionalization include the conflict between learning critical biomedical skills and interacting with the human being who is the patient. Discussion of the physician's feelings on rounds and in the weekly interns' discussion groups helps diminish loneliness and assuage the conflict. Together, these programs provide an outlet for the frustrations, pressures, anxieties, and conflicts of those first critical medical years, as well as an educational vehicle for personal and professional growth.

The clinical milieu seems to have changed favorably during the life of the program. The faculty senses a different attitude in medical students and house staff toward patients and their life situations. There is increasing ease in discussing "how to cope."

Generally, the medical students appear to be pleased with and interested in the concepts we are presenting. House-staff members are more cautious in their acceptance, and some of them experience the humanistic aspect of their training as an intrusion; so do some of the teaching attending physicians. The third-year medical clerkships and the third year of medical residency seem to offer the most favorable climate for humanistic medical education. The third-year resident has mastered the fundamental elements of biomedical skill, freeing him or her to consider personal interactions more fully.

The ultimate measure of the effectiveness of this approach to teaching humanistic medicine, using the physician's feelings as the key, is to be found in the attitudes and behavior of third-year residents and graduates of our programs. The strength to feel one's own humanity and to deal with it makes the practice of humanistic medicine possible. So far, no objective assessment of the results of our program has been devised.

REFERENCES

1. Anstett R. The difficult patient and the physician-patient relationship. J Fam Pract 1980; 11:281–6.
2. Peabody FW. The care of the patient. JAMA 1927; 88:877–82.

3. Lipowski ZJ. Holistic-medical foundations of American psychiatry: a bicentennial. Am J Psychiatry. 1981; 138:888–95.
4. Bibring GL, ed. The teaching of dynamic psychiatry: a reappraisal of the goals and techniques in the teaching of psychoanalytic psychiatry. New York: International Universities Press, 1968.
5. Cope O, ed. Man, mind and medicine: the doctor's education. Philadelphia: JB Lippincott, 1968.
6. Engel GL. The need for a new medical model: a challenge for biomedicine. Science 1977; 196:129–36.
7. Spitz L, Bloch E. Denial and minimization in telephone contacts with patients. J Fam Pract 1981; 12:93–8.
8. Grant WB. The hated patient and his hating attendants. Med J Aust 1980; 2:727–9.
9. Adams GP, Cook M. The houseman and the dying patient. J Med Ethics 1981; 7:142–5.
10. Krueger DW. Patient suicide: model for medical student teaching and mourning. Gen Hosp Psychiatry 1979; 1:229–33.
11. Perry S, Viederman M. Adaptation of residents to consultation-liaison psychiatry. I. Working with the physically ill. Gen Hosp Psychiatry 1981; 3:141–7.
12. Lichstein PR. The resident leaves the patient: another look at the doctor-patient relationship. Ann Intern Med 1982; 96:762–5.
13. Stoudemire A, Thompson TL II. The borderline personality in the medical setting. Ann Intern Med 1982; 96:76–9.
14. Longhurst MF. Angry patient, angry doctor. Can Med Assoc J 1980; 123: 597–8.
15. Groves JE. Taking care of the hateful patient. N Engl J Med 1978; 298: 883–7.
16. Adler G. The physician and the hypochrondriacal patient. N Engl J Med 1981; 304:1394–6.
17. Diagnostic and statistical manual of mental disorders. 3d ed. Washington, D.C.: American Psychiatric Association, 1980.
18. Layton JM. The use of modeling to teach empathy to nursing students. Res Nurs Health 1979; 2:163–76.
19. Bandura A. Social learning theory. Englewood Cliffs, N.J.: Prentice-Hall, 1977.
20. Engel GL. The biopsychosocial model and medical education: who are to be the teachers? N Engl J Med 1982; 306:802–5.
21. Strain JJ, Hamerman D. Ombudsmen (medical-psychiatric) rounds: an approach to meeting patient-staff needs. Ann Intern Med 1978; 88:550–5.
22. Bosk CL. Occupational rituals in patient management. N Engl J Med 1980; 303:71–6.

15

The Contribution of Ethics and Psychology to Medicine

Jurrit Bergsma • David C. Thomasma

SEPARATE CONTRIBUTIONS of ethics and psychology to medicine have already been made. Among the contributions of ethics are establishing national guidelines for research, decisions made in clinical practices, contributing to policies on the distribution of health care, enriching legal theory and legislation, and developing more refined professional standards of medical conduct. Psychology's contribution to medicine lies primarily in its descriptive abilities with respect to behavior, personal attitudes and values. Secondarily, the discipline has developed a broad spectrum of methodological tools to evaluate aspects of human behavior. A third aspect is training methods in interpersonal skills. In general, the contribution of psychology to medicine seems to be underestimated in medical humanities programs, which nowadays concentrate more on ethics.

Instead of examining the separate contributions of ethics and psychology to medicine, however, we wish to concentrate on the more difficult task of articulating their interdisciplinary contribution. As far as we know this task has not been directly attempted. Medicinal educators, by introducing the behavioral sciences and subsequently the humanities into the curriculum, expected thereby an integrating influence which would resist the tendency towards fragmentation in medicine. Experience shows that medical education lacks a coherent framework for its curriculum that could be provided by an interdisciplinary effort.

Our aim is to offer a theory for educating humanistic physicians,

Reprinted from *Social Science and Medicine* 20, no. 7 (1985): 745–752, with permission, Pergamon Press Ltd.

not to describe conceptual ways in which psychology and ethics may complement one another. Some have suggested that our purpose is hopeless, given the totally separate objectives and methodology of the two disciplines. This would probably be so were we to focus on the two disciplines alone. But our challenge is different. It is to provide the framework for a holistic approach to medical education, within which both psychology and ethics function.

First, we discuss the problem of setting objectives for medical education with respect to 'humanistic' practice. Second, we discuss medicine as a social entity. Third, we defend the claim that an ethic of virtue or character best matches the ideals of physician education within this framework. Fourth, we show how psychology is an essential basis for a medical ethics of virtue. Our final section will contain a synthesis of our points, lest in spelling out the various ways contributions can be made, we create the impression that these are separate functions from an integrated humanist medical education itself. In so doing we will also provide some educational goals.

HUMANISTIC MEDICAL EDUCATION

There has been increasing interest in the development of programs at medical schools which aim to increase physician skills in practicing humanistic medicine. In the United States, out of approximately 120 medical schools, there are now 90 such programs [1]. While not as widespread, similar programs also exist in Western Europe. Demand and support for the programs often come from a recognition by health care educators that an increase in the technological capacities of modern medicine has created a lacuna. This gap appears in the abilities of its practitioners to treat the values traditionally associated with the healing task of medicine [2].

Despite the creation of such programs, however, some blurring of objectives can cause confusion or even failure. A careful examination of the programs reveals that some are dedicated to creating 'humanistic' physicians and other health care providers [3]. Most of these rely upon psychological skills rather than the humanities to obtain their object: interaction and listening skills are stressed and can be evaluated as such. Whether the goal of 'humanization' is attained is unclear. A few also approach the task of humanizing through courses in the humanities, especially in art, poetry, philosophy, ethics, religious studies and history. The theory is that to 'humanize' medicine is to reconstruct the humanities education lacking in students who concentrate on the physical sciences. Some of these programs stress the refreshment side of the humanities, with little or no effort to make the courses relevant to medical practice.

Other programs seeking to demonstrate that, in the words of Edmund Pellegrino, "medicine is the most humane of the sciences or the most scientific of the humanities" [4], try to relate the humanities to medical concerns. For example, one might explore the image of the physician in literature [5]. All the programs described, however, target the medical student for increased psychological skills or for general broadening and enrichment of *personal* resources.

In contrast, others employ the humanities, and most frequently, medical ethics, to increase intellectual performance. Some employ the humanities and social sciences to help students understand the complexities of modern medicine and patient values. Others directly influence the modalities by which physicians make medical and moral decisions [6]. Unlike the aims of those in the previous paragraph, these programs do not claim to 'humanize' medicine or even to make the students more 'sensitive'. Rather, the emphasis is on increasing intellectual sophistication about the plurality of values in medicine and society.

The problem with these approaches is that neither the humanistic nor the humanities approach can properly be said to contribute directly to an improvement in the quality of care. Increased interpersonal skills, unless clinically reinforced, cannot have any real impact on the humanistic dimension of care. On the other hand, knowledge of medical ethics issues, even improved skills in moral reasoning, without constant attention to clinical use, will wither before students reach their clinical clerkships [7]. Further, focusing on the student or clinician without attention either to clinical practice or the role of patients in medical decisions, and health care as a context of such decisions, will not improve the quality of care [8,9]. It is the quality of care that has caused public concern about modern medicine as a new social value [10].

Our first step, therefore, should be to provide a framework for a theory of medicine. We need an adequate conceptualization of medicine as a theoretical and clinical discipline. It will not do simply to plug holes within the ethics and psychology curriculum.

MEDICINE AS A SOCIAL ENTITY

To arrive at an appropriate educational program, it is important to outline our conception of medicine.

Being a healing science, medicine must address all aspects of the disruptions caused by accidents and by disease, not only the physical ones. To be sure, modern medicine possesses enormously successful physical interventions. But this success is precisely what has led it to ignore other aspects of human existence. The physical entity is an integrated part of a whole person who organizes the environment. But individuals are also psychological and social entities dealing with events and restrictions on the basis of values.

As an institution, medicine has always been a social force. But when it neglects the personal and social dimensions of its treatment of patients this social force becomes political and often negative. Thus by neglecting the personal and social dimensions of health care, medicine assumes an almost autocratic power. To focus on the organism and its physiological symptoms means that the organism cannot talk back; it only reveals a biological print-out gauged by various tests and procedures. Paternalism, acting for the good of another without their consent, is a direct result of this sort of positivistic thinking in medicine. The effect is that nothing less than a redefinition of medicine, and consequently the doctor-patient relationship, is needed.

A human being is in a state of constant flux. Because of continuous adjustments between people and their environment, medicine must become a science of processes. Change within relationships is a normal feature of being human. Each case, therefore, is like a film. There is no freeze-frame on the camera. Distinguished clinicians know that very well. The only stop-action is death itself. Thus each medical transaction includes a matrix of values. Values are brought to the transaction by the physician, the hospital, the health care system and society. To that same relation values are brought by the patient, his or her family, social network and religious faith. At the heart of the transaction is a loss-dependency dynamic which makes the patient vulnerable, destroying any chance for rebuilding self-sufficiency while simultaneously, given the miracles of modern medicine, recreating health.

As a result, students must be trained to deal with persons and their interactional patterns as a process. A patchwork approach to medical education will not work. It will not produce the kind of physician the public and the medical community demand [11]. Instead, a radical redefinition and reconstruction of medical education is required. There are signs of this shift everywhere. But so far it has been just turbulence—not 'The Day After' but 'The Day Before'.

Integrated medicine will reveal the processes of human life. These, in turn, will lead to disciplines united around a common terminus—the actual healing process itself. Naturally, there are many disciplines needed to reveal the richness of human life, but our focus is only on two: medical ethics and psychology. If a case can be made for the integration of these in a newly-conceived medical curriculum, then the arguments we employ may be extrapolated to other disciplines as well.

MEDICAL EDUCATION AND AN ETHIC OF VIRTUE

The task of a human values program in medicine is to provide an analysis of integrated human experiences which require improving cognitive skills. Through psychology, a mechanism is provided for translating these skills into clinical performance. Our focus now will be on the medical ethics aspects of this analytic task. Psychology is examined in the next section.

Note that no matter which ethical theory is adopted it will require some action to be performed or, at least, evaluate different actions to be performed. This applies to any ethical theory.

Ethics as Descriptive Value Clarification

First, we must examine some earlier proposals regarding the task of ethics in medical education. The 'softest' proposal is that ethics in a medical school should aim at helping to *clarify and rank* those *values* which arise in moral dilemmas. The strength of this position lies in emphasizing the careful analysis of all the values occurring in a medical transaction, without recommending specific action. K. Danner Clouser considers it an 'abuse' if medical ethics were to be seen as providing concrete recommendations to clinicians [12]. A similar concern is echoed by Arthur Caplan in his article against deductive forms of applied philosophy in the clinical setting [13].

The source of concern rests with an abhorrence of posturing as a moral expert [14]. On this view, moral experts are those ethicists who lack wariness about making concrete recommendations. They would do so by forgetting that they possess no particular claim to the truth, nor power to enforce this on others. To Singer's analysis is added the additional caution that recommendations by ethicists are in danger of being honored by some clinicians who might view them precisely as experts to be consulted. Thus their views rest on sand.

In its pristine form, this view of the task of ethics in medical education strikes us as being too limited, too circumscribed. First, clinical closure is an everyday fact of medicine. The very purpose of medical education is to help students gain greater confidence in their practical abilities to make the best decisions for patients. Judgment, including moral judgment, is the bedrock of such decisions. In order for it to be a right and good decision, it must respect the scientific, psychosocial [15] and ethical aspects of the patient's complaint and the cultural, institutional, and professional values brought to bear on the case. To sort through all these values and then stand back as a bystander appears to us to be a truncation of the proper educational role of ethics. To avoid being taken as a moral expert, one pays dearly—the ethical basis of the required decision, one which will be made come what may, drops from view. This process neglects both the ways in which ethics is part of critical thinking in general, and at the core of clinical decision making in particular [16].

Perhaps the most telling objection against the descriptive view of ethics in medical education is that the process of ranking values is accepted as a legitimate role. Nevertheless, to rank values is to give them 'weights' according to some criterion. Among the 'weights' offered by clinicians will be uniformed attitudes, dispositions and even moral training. Once such scrutiny is established one has entered the realm of offering recommendations because to critique values is to place some above others on rational grounds. If a decision is to be ethical it must follow the hierarchy of values so delineated.

Ethics as Normative

A more widely held opinion in medical ethics is that it can contribute norms for governing conduct in medicine. In general, this view holds that analysis alone is insufficient. One may, instead, refer to ethical principles to guide actions and policies. By definition, a normative discipline is one which contains prescripts for action.

There are basically two versions of a normative view of medical ethics. One, which is often called 'deductive', claims that to act ethically is to act on principle. Kant's famous categorical imperative (act always as if what you would do would become a universal law) is a good example of such a principle. Arguing from principle to conduct can be found in the work of Paul Ramsey. Ramsey argued that the principle of respect for persons means that one could never treat people as means but only as ends in themselves. For example, then, any attempt to use children in non-therapeutic research would be violation of this principle, because one would be using a person as a means (the good of future generations of children) rather than ends in themselves. A conclusion of this view is that a child cannot actually give consent to an experiment procedure. [17].

The strengths of the deductive, normative approach to ethics are almost immediately discernible. The main one is clarity; abstracting from the concrete dimensions of particular cases leads to a consistent and rational social policy which will not be subject to the whims of place or custom. Further, patients could clearly expect certain standards of behavior, easily taught to medical students. One could conceivably draw a portrait of a mortally educated physician, the way J. K. Roth has of morally educated persons [18]. This portrait would then lead directly to educational criteria in medical ethics.

But two main difficulties arise in this view. First, there is no unanimity about ethical principles, as exemplified by the constant dispute between teleologists and deontologists. Hence, to deduce a policy or a set of norms from a principle is only valid for those who accept the principle. The second more relevant difficulty is that deductive normative ethics neglects the role of fact in establishing and ranking values. Hence, there is too great a gulf, an unbridgeable gulf, between fact and value in this approach. The best way to understand this is to consider the widespread comments about the fine book by Thomas Beauchamp and James Childress on the *Principles of Biomedical Ethics* [19]. The authors did not agree on moral principles, yet they agreed on matters of policy. Thus, the objection arises: do principles make any difference at all in the resolution of moral difficulties?

A second view of normative medical ethics recognizes the role of principles, but not as single origins from which rules for actions can be derived. In this normative view, which can be a form of casuistry, of discretionary ethics, of experimental ethics or of professional ethics, one accepts a variety of principles. The methods differ with respect to the ways in which principles are adjusted to the case at hand. In the casuistic approach, these principles are fitted together for the best proportionate decision possible in a single case, often with the good of the patient prominently in mind [20]. Discretionary ethics is a term proposed by Stephen Toulmin. Ethical decisions are made as if among friends and intimates rather than among strangers [21]. Individual decisions are made on a case by case basis rather than on the basis of formal abstract principles. The values are changed because of social or emotional desirability.

Experimental ethics is advanced by Terrence Ackerman to argue that the object of medical ethics is to respect as many values as possible in the case. Openly pragmatic, this method would rely on psychological and other experiments to determine if the outcomes of decisions actually matched values and principles [22]. In the professional ethics approach the goal of the medical relationship is to heal. If a doctor violates this goal, by introducing another goal that is not in the healing relationship, the patient is harmed. Thus, 'Do not harm' becomes a nonnegotiable norm to affect healing [23]. Of course, patients may value other things more than healing, for example helping other people by agreeing to become an object of an experiment. In such a case, healing is no longer the object of the relationship. The patient has agreed to be an object instead of a subject within the doctor-patient relation.

Each of these methodologies, of course, possesses its own difficulties. Nonetheless, each can function within the medical educational context quite well. Each requires a bridge to the realm of facts and behavior.

Ethics as Virtue

Many physicians and even some moralists subscribe to the view that ethics is ultimately taught by prescript and example [24]. The character, the moral integrity, of the student will be based on his or her role model, or at least, upon the qualities reinforced by the clinical training environment.

This is especially true considering the publication of the commitment by the American Board of Internal Medicine to an evaluation of the humanistic qualities of an internist [25]. It is not hard to imagine other certifying bodies in the U.S. and elsewhere following suit. From our perspective, the subcommittee's report clearly defines three 'qualities' (or virtues) to be required of internists: integrity, respect (for the values and rights of patients) and compassion. Since no objective test is available to measure these qualities, the subcommittee insists on the role of attending physicians and scholars to teach the cognitive and attitudinal (noncognitive) dimensions of medical ethics and human values. In other words, the residency training director must be committed to the importance of humanism in the structure of the program so that he and all faculty sensitize, reinforce and assess humanistic qualities among residents. The importance of role model reinforcement cannot be understated, particularly since many studies have shown that there is no reliable prediction of behavior from attitudes [26-28].

As already mentioned, the problematic relation between fact and value lies at the heart of medical decision-making. If analytic ethics neglects the way values are part of this decision-making by arguing that recommendations cannot be made by ethicists, the 'harder', deductive view of ethics also neglects the fact-value nexus by too abstractly deriving recommendations for conduct and medical policy from principles alone. The former downgrades values in factual affairs, while the latter gives short shrift to factual affairs altogether. By contrast, the normative methodologies mentioned all require some theory of character or virtue in the sense that there is a reliance upon the practical wisdom of the one(s) making the decision.

The strengths of this positon are manifold. Some of them are:

(a) The position rightly considers moral activity flowing from internal convictions to be the essence of sound moral training;

(b) Recommendation and example are, in fact, the role model concept of medical education in the clinical setting;

(c) A moral character ethics avoids disputes over moral principles so characteristic of philosophical ethics since Kant;

(d) Character produces the 'right attitudes' that are the heart and soul of moral decisions.

The weaknesses of this position as an educational program for medical schools are difficult to surmount. One has no current control over the character of the role models, as moral integrity is not spelled out in behaviors for professors. Indeed, the student most often learns to imitate the attitudes and behavior of residents, perhaps the most busy, pressured, and therefore ethically unsophisticated of all health professionals. The American Board Subcommittee Report recognized this problem. In addition, current rights language governing patient relations to hospitals and doctors requires cognitive skills.

It is therefore possible to base an educational program on moral character, since it does recognize the importance of decisions and behavior, but this program would require articulation of appropriate behaviors to which psychology must contribute.

The cognitive aspects of medical ethics are: a skill in dialogue whereby one learns to identify values, sort them, rank them and critically reflect on the reasons for so doing. In addition one learns to defend them, discuss and modify the reasons for this defense in concert with peers and patients, and to take a course of action which respects as many values in the case as possible, while preserving certain norms of medicine, such as 'Do no harm' [29].

These skills can be analyzed and translated into clinical behaviors with the help of medical psychology. The behaviors, as suggested by studies, reportedly require higher levels of moral reasoning. These, then, can be the basis of course objectives. The skills to be evaluated would be those such as: Includes patients in decisions made; the student attempts to reconcile value conflicts, and so on.

While ethics does not directly aim at behavioral change, then, it does seek to influence action by cognitive dissonance, by dialectical juxtaposition of opinions, values and moral principles, with the general aim of making one more critical of one's decisions and freeing one from the tyranny of imitation. The *possibility* of moral integrity results, as does improved clinical decision making [30]. One does then improve the quality of care 'ethically' without guaranteeing that all students will be free of moral defects.

The review of methodologies in ethics demonstrates that medical education requires an ethic of virtue as its vehicle for translating values and attitudes into conduct. The quality of care will be truncated if it is not improved by translating the *possibility* of moral integrity into identifiable clinical skills such as those cited. This translation can be aided by medical psychology in its three forms to be adumbrated next.

MEDICAL PSYCHOLOGY AND MEDICAL TRAINING

Medical psychology can help in three ways: first, by the description and analysis of overt behavior, comparing it with certain standards; second, in developing educational and training programs; and third, by evaluating the results of those programs in order to determine whether the desired objectives have been reached.

Each physician's behavior is professional behavior. Consequently, it is interactional behavior because he or she must interact constantly with patients and their families. Many studies of this interactional behavior have been made and published [31]. Many analyses of physician-patient have been reported [32]. Often these analyses have been based on contrasting and even comparing theoretical assumptions. Therefore, they are difficult to compare. Examples are the ideas of Stack Sullivan, the kind of observations made by Foucault [33], followed later by Illich [34]. More recently, a strict systematic analysis by Duff and Ross has been developed [35]. Perhaps it is impossible to obtain a real value-free behavioral observation but is quite possible to make one's observational criteria explicit. There are, therefore, three criteria levels to which we must draw attention.

The first level is the most concrete. The doctor-patient interaction is measured in numbers of specific interactions, verbal, non-verbal movements, time spans, etc. In effect this method analyzes certain elements of behavior without attributing explicitly formulated values to that behavior.

The second level is the level of therapeutic success. Especially in the United States there are some good studies of physician and nursing behavior related to certain well formulated (medical) therapeutical outcomes. In this context we will only mention Wolfer, Tryon, Skipper and/or Leonard who conducted individual and cooperative research that may be called classical [36]. For example, these studies have shown that the greater the degree of information, and possibly personal engagement, between professionals, patients and their families prior to operations, the fewer the subsequent side-effects.

The third level is that of attitudes and values. Studies have been done on the way people compare their own illness with others, to make themselves more exceptional and unique.

The problem to be faced within the context of this article is that we have to deal with (1) elements of behavior, (2) therapeutic outcomes within the context of interactional behavior and (3) the motives of the person interacting. The heart of the problem occurs when psychologists, ethicists and physicians challenge each other with questions like: which behavioral elements are effective in a therapeutic sense but unjust in an ethical sense? Sometimes the problem arises in certain therapeutic activity. But it really comes to the fore in many palliative interventions. The physician is faced with the dilemma of acting to help the patient in the presence of an inability to cure. New values, and new roles, are forced on both patients and doctors. Uncertainty prevails.

The problem always arises, then, in readjusting a hierarchy of values. This is an ethical as well as a psychological problem. By contrast the purely psychological problem consists in a physician's dealing with the new ranking. He or she must make decisions which weigh values, often in an acute situation, sometimes without the patient's input, sometimes in conjunction with the patient.

It is not the psychologist's role to explain right or wrong, just or unjust. The psychologist's role is to help medical educators clarify the process of decision-making. In fact it may be preferable to speak of the process of (clinical) judgment. We will now explain it in more detail.

Observation. One of the most basic activities of psychologists is observing behavior. Landmarks would be Roger Barker's studies. In these studies he systematically described people's behavior within their environment and demonstrated the prevalence of patterns of interactional behavior [37]. Using comparable methods other researchers focused more specifically on medical practice. Without studies such as *Sickness and Society* it would be impossible to recognize the characteristics of medical behavior [38]. Recall our distinction of three levels of behavior. Barker's study is a typical level-one study. Duff and Hollingshead established the features of medical behavior on this level, thus making possible level-two discussions of therapeutic outcome and level-three of the motives behind therapeutic interventions.

Recently, one of us (Bergsma) did an observational study of General Practitioners with the idea of confronting them with their own behavior. Using studies like this it is possible to design educational activities in which physicians are confronted in graphs and tables by their own practices. For example, a physician with a 60% patient return might become unhappy with the medical visit, not knowing why and and not knowing how to handle it because he did not recognize what the problem was [39]. Even more effective perhaps would be to videotape physician-patient encounters. Psychologists could then comment on the tape, describing certain actions as effective (2nd level) or good (3rd level). Discussion could be focused on these behavioral judgments. The result of such discussion of physician behavior then would be part of the standards of physician conduct.

Translation. After this first step of making norms and values explicit in the observed clinical setting by discussing them on basis of measuring and recording the interactions, it is possible to translate those findings into educational goals. This may be easier said than done. Nevertheless, it is possible to succeed with this translation. For example, Bergsma reports an inventory of all those aspects in physician and nursing behavior that improved patients' well-being. This is a second level study.

An example of a 3rd level study would be an analysis of those philosophical and ethical values that may affect health care workers' behavior. Recently we have been working at Utrecht University on the construction of a new curriculum for medical students in which these goals are integrated. This program was started at Utrecht in 1984 so no general evaluations are yet available. Certain elements in the new curriculum were based on experience over a longer period reported by Gerritsma and Batenburg [40]. For over a decade programs in medical humanities have been offered in the United States, mainly focusing on the third level as we have described it. At Utrecht medical school, interactional analyses of student-patient relationships are in use, in which the patient-actors are trained to give feedback to the students. In some of the programs for continuing education the same plan occurs. In the United States the ethical work-up during patient grand rounds is becoming more and more familiar for students and physicians. All of these are examples of efforts to translate into educational goals a conception of good physician actions.

Goals and Means. Within medicine it is easier to discuss therapeutically effective behavior than the values and attitudes which lie in the background of that behavior. The former fits much more easily into the biological thinking pattern than the latter does. In addition it is much more difficult to translate values into terms of behavior.

A good example seems to be the difference found between two basic behavioral patterns in physicians: one we called 'autonomous', the other 'communicative'. The first pattern is strictly followed. Its rigidity is barely influenced by the patient whoever she or he may be, whatever the complaints may be. By contrast the second pattern is open and changing every time a new patient comes in for a visit. This second kind of pattern, client-oriented behavior, is the ideal in many educational and post-doctoral programs. It is more patient-friendly and gives the patient the opportunity to open the gates about his needs, complaints and problems. Consequently, it may be expected to be more effective. Indeed, research shows that this is true . . . in some cases. In observations this behavior is effective in some cases, but very ineffective in other cases. In the latter instances patients did not know how to cope with this open communication model. The same patients seem to cope quite well when face to face with physicians following a more rigid, clearly predictable behavior.

Another and special problem is the 'autonomous' physician who 'learned' communication skills and who behaves like an actor in an ill-fitting role. The ingenuinenousness is visible to patient and observer alike. It is quite clear what happens. The goal of improving communicative behavior has been a main topic of training and education for medical students, the result is a communicative doctor who changed behavior but not attitudes. In short, this is another example of the gulf between overt behavior and covert values which must be bridged in medical education.

It is important therefore to focus on the level of attitudes and values. Here we are concerned not with the problem of effectiveness but with the problem of a good and right decision. While it is impossible to determine the good and right decisions in each case ahead of time, since that decision varies from case to case, it is not impossible to provide the intellectual and behavioral environment in which such decisions can be formed. It is impossible, however, to predict how students will actually make their decisions. A thorough prospective study by Tazelaar demonstrates the difficulty of really influencing and changing attitudes [41]. On the other hand Gerritsma *et al.* proved that it is possible to clarify behavior for medical students and physicians in such a way that they become aware of the kind of behavior they use, and the effects this behavior has on their interactions with patients. When we speak about attitudes and values inspiring behavior, the goal should not be teaching right or wrong attitudes but an awareness among health professionals of their own attitudes and values. This makes it possible to use those aspects in their problem-solving and decision-making. Together with Duff, Bergsma created a model of value levels, useful for medical decision-making, which shows on which levels patients and physicians employ possibly conflicting value systems and how these, in turn, clash with those of the other party [42].

In continuing education for physicians and nurses this model has been especially helpful for the explicit demonstration of values which occur in observable clinical behavior. By using the model it is possible to make values and norms more explicit so professionals become aware of their attitudes and values. In this way a 'control mechanism' is developed that makes it possible to improve clinical judgment and the awareness of one's own attitudes and values in interactions. In future interactions, professionals become more self-critical about their conduct whenever the control mechanism issues its warning. A community of 'control-mechanisms' helps to create what we mean by an 'environment of care'. If in a clinical department physicians, nurses, physiotherapists, chaplains, are well aware of their own individual values guiding their interactions with each other and the patients, they also are able to discover collective values guiding their common conduct in relation to the patient. In such an environment, whether the accent is on care or training, the aim is not primarily to change behavior but to improve the characteristics of mutual control within behavioral interactions. Traditional methods included confronting students with taped interactions, their own role playing, and the use of simulated patients with whom a very direct confrontation is possible. In the latter method, teachers, but also the patient, can give feedback on the way the physician copes with decision-making and problem-solving.

It is important that psychologists as well as ethicists be involved in this teaching effort since there is a need for attention to the process itself as well as the content. For example, the danger of using only an ethical analysis in training situations lies in restricting the discussion to abstract, far-above-the-floor-ethics, resulting only in questions like 'who shall decide?' Including ethical issues in the clinical decision-making process will bring the values to the level where they belong: in the clinic. That is, the values will be part of the decision to be made, rather than only being an object for discussion. It makes no sense, therefore, to clarify values unless they can be used by physicians and patients in reaching a decision about their cases. Abstract analysis in medicine must translate into pragmatic utility. For example, after a thorough value discussion in which everyone involved understands the values at stake, patients still must determine their own priorities with their families and the doctor. Patients may choose a therapeutic course which will remove them from cherished values, e.g. a proscribed blood transfusion, or they may refuse pain medication in order to bear their sufferings as a religious challenge.

Evaluation. Among the techniques psychology offers to the scientific world is 'measurement of behavior'. Some people seem to think it is the only thing psychology has to offer! Although this is not true, there is a great deal of psychological expertise in evaluation techniques. It would be wrong to overestimate the value of those measurement techniques. It should, however, be recognized that in the evaluation of behavioral change, for instance in training or education, these techniques are helpful. With respect to our article we would only cite one evaluation of health care training in problem-solving [43]. After a 3½ year training project, patients were interviewed for their views on the behavior of medical and nursing staff comparing those who received special training with untrained control groups.

Results of evaluation mechanisms up to now seem to offer some hope that improving behavior is possible by clarifying the many considerations in decision-making. As a consequence of combining a more effective training in therapeutic behavior patterns and improved on-the-scene ethical deliberation, an interactional problem-solving method that is worthwhile for both physicians and patients can be created.

SYNTHESIS

We are now able to synthesize our arguments by proposing four goals for professional conduct and an integrated medical education. By combining ethics training with medical psychology, we can establish the objectives of a program seeking the improvement of quality of care and humanism in medicine.

Seen in the light of our perceptions, humanistic medical training may now be better defined. It is more than training to care for 'the whole person', a laudable but ill-defined object. It is also more than openness and awareness of the human individuality and self-worth of patients, as Ralph Crawshaw seems to argue [44]. Two editorials by Franz Ingelfinger quite properly question these abstract notions, first on the grounds that caring should not be substituted for technical expertise, and second on the grounds that humanism and the humanities have not demonstrated any clear, direct impact on improving the management of patients [45, 46]. Instead, humanism should be seen as the enemy of limited perspective. Medical models and professional habits of mind are unlocked to reveal new perspectives about values and patients as well as one's professional and personal task. This new perspective, what we called a 'control mechanism', enriches the life of the professional and enhances one's ability to respond to the elements of the human condition presented by the patient [47].

If one assumes that the goal of all the humanities and medicine programs is to improve professional behavior, and one recognizes that professional interventions in the lives of others take place within a value-determined situation, then the following goals of health professional education can be suggested:

(1) To improve insight into the rational and nonrational components of one's attitudes and conduct. This is a self-reflective goal embodied in Socrates' dictum that "the unexamined life is not worth living". However, it can be argued that such reflection is not only beneficial in reducing the chances of being chained to the thinking of others, but necessary for the professional who must be able to handle complex value interactions as part of his or her act of profession. At the very least a physician should be able to support his or her recommendations for treatment to patients and to peers on grounds of values shared with them. In this instance the recommendation should also rest on therapeutic effectiveness, an even stronger basis for a decision.

In fact, the determining behavior or appropriate conduct of the physician is related to people now impaired. These people, now patients, are dependent on the professional. They are, therefore, vulnerable to losing their human dignity and integrity simply because their bodies no longer function as they did. As a consequence, descriptive awareness of values and attitudes becomes an essential feature of professional responsibility. It is no longer optional. One cannot fault, demean, or diminish human beings by being unreflexive about one's own values and still be a health professional, much less a decent human being.

Both ethics and psychology support this step of professional responsibility: ethics by its arguments for such responsibility and psychology through the descriptive tools mentioned.

(2) To improve professional awareness, cognition of and respect for the patient's values. This goal is required by the professional commitment to act in the best interests of the patient; to be able to make evaluative judgments regarding health and disease; and to resolve moral dilemmas by suggesting a course of action [48].

The description of value systems and potential clashes among them and the tools for training, are contributions psychology can make to this objective. To these can be added training in a process of moral reasoning and a critique of reasons for acting in one way rather than another. Both of these are contributions of ethics. Without a descriptive base, ethics appears to be bald assertion untenable in a pluralistic age. But sorting through value clashes with the help of the descriptive discipline of psychology can aid in making better medical and better moral decisions precisely by determining whether the student has considered the patient's views in the decision to be made.

(3) To improve professional behavior by assessing the ways in which values are transcribed, made visible and concrete, in decisions made. The major problem in this sphere is the clash between the values of therapeutic interventions and the many other values patients, physicians and society bring to the clinical scene. Problems, therefore, arise whenever cases transcend the routine. But what is routine for physicians is often not routine for patients.

(4) To improve professional ability to enhance the self-determination of patients by helping them clarify their own values with respect to decisions about their own health. This is based on a conception about the ultimate goal of health care. The latter should be considered as some form of enhancing the autonomy of the person [49].

The focus on moral behavior and moral reasoning is the proper, and perhaps single most important locus for truly interdisciplinary cooperation between ethics, psychology and medicine. The intersection of behavior and values and the intersection of psychology and ethics, is determined by interactions occurring in the doctor-patient relation. It seems that we should reach for a more consistent pattern of relating values, attitudes and behaviors.

REFERENCES

1. McElhinney T. (Ed.) *Human Values Teaching Programs for Health Professionals.* Whitmore, Ardmore, PA, 1981.
2. Pellegrino E. D. and Thomasma D. C. *A Philosophical Basis of Medical Practice,* Chap. 5. Oxford University Press, New York, 1981.

3. Stoeckle J. D. The tasks of care: humanistic dimensions of medical education. In *Nourishing the Humanistic in Medicine* (Edited by Rogers W. R. and Barnard D.), pp. 263–276. University of Pittsburgh Press and the Society for Health and Human Values, Pittsburgh, 1974.
4. Pellegrino E. D. *Humanism and the Physician*, p. 16. University of Tennessee Press, Knoxville, 1978.
5. Trautman J. *Literature and Medicine*. Institute on Human Values in Medicine, Society for Health and Human Values, Philadelphia, 1975.
6. Thomasma D. C. Training in medical ethics: an ethical workup. *Forum Med.* 1, 30–33, 1978.
7. Carlton W. *In our Professional Opinion*. University of Notre Dame Press, Notre Dame, 1978.
8. Siegler M. A legacy of Osler: teaching clinical ethics at the bedside. *J. Am. med. Ass.* 239, 951–956, 1978.
9. Thomasma D. A philosophy of a clinically based medical ethics program. *J. med. Ethics* 6, 190–196, 1980.
10. Medicine as a social science. Entire Issue. *J. med. Phil.* 6(4), 1981.
11. Bergsma J. Op de plaats, rust. Promotion to Professor Address. Rijksuniversiteit Utrecht, Faculteit der Geneeskunde, 1981.
12. Clouse K. D. Medical ethics: some uses, abuses and limitations. *Ariz. med.* 33, 44–49, 1976.
13. Caplan A. Can applied ethics be effective in health care and should it strive to be? *Ethics* 93, 311–319, 1983.
14. Singer P. Moral experts. *Analysis* 32, 115–117, 1972.
15. Mechanic D. Psychosocial insights for everyday medical practice. *Art Medic.* 1, 15–20, 1980.
16. Pellegrino E. D. The liberal arts and the arts of the clinician. *Art Medic.* 1, 4–13, 1980.
17. Ramsey P. *The Patient as Person*. Yale University Press, New Haven, 1970.
18. Roth J. K. A portrait of a morally educated person: some sketchbook impressions. *Cousel. Values* 25, 29–39, 1980.
19. Beauchamp T. and Childress J. *Principles of Biomedical Ethics*. Oxford University Press, New York, 1979.
20. Jonsen A. On being a casuist. In *Clinical Medical Ethics: Exploration and Assessment* (Edited by Ackerman T., Graber G., Thomasma D. and Reynolds C.) [University Press of America, Lanham, MD, 1987].
21. Toulmin S. The tyranny of principles. *Hastings Ctr Rep.* 11, 31–39, 1981.
22. Ackerman T. What bioethics should be. *J. med. Phil.* 5, 260–275, 1980.
23. Thomasma D. C. and Pellegrino E. D. Philosophy of medicine as the source for medical ethics. *Metamedicine* 2, 5–11, 1981 (now *Theoretical Medicine*).
24. McKee F. W. Teaching medical ethics: Letter to the editor. *J. Am. med. Ass.* 241, 27, 1979.
25. Subcommittee on the Evaluation of the Humanistic Qualities of the Internist, ABIM. Evaluation of the humanistic qualities in the internist. *Ann. intern. Med.* 99, 720–724, 1983.
26. Blanchard C., Ruckdeschel J., Blanchard E., Arena J., Saunders N. and Malloy E. Interactions between oncologists and patients during rounds. *Ann. intern. Med.* 99, 694–699, 1983.
27. Ajzen I. and Fishbein M. Attitude-behavior relations: a theoretical analysis and review of empirical research. *Psychol. Bull.* 84, 889–918, 1977.
28. Bentler P. and Speclart I. Models of attitudes—behavior relations. *Psychol. Bull.* 86, 452–464, 1979.

29. Shelp E. (Ed.) *Beneficence in Health Care*. D. Reidel, Dordrecht, 1982.
30. Sheehan T. *et al.* Moral judgment as a predictor of Clinical performance. *Eval. Hlth Prof.* 3, 393–404, 1980.
31. Kertesz R. Research on doctor-patient relationship in a General Hospital setting. *Recent Research in Psychosomatics*. Karger, Basel, 1967.
32. Katon W. and Kleinman A. Doctor-patient negotiation and other social science strategies in patient care. In *The Relevance of Social Science for Medicine* (Edited by Eisenberg L. and Kleinman A.), pp. 253–283. Reidel, Dordrecht, 1981.
33. Foucault M. *The Birth of the Clinic*. Tavistock, New York, 1973.
34. Illich I. *Medical Nemesis*. Pantheon, New York, 1975.
35. Ross C. E. and Duff R. S. Returning to the doctor: the effect of client characteristics. Type of practice and experience with care. *J. Hlth soc. Behav.* 23, 119–131, 1982.
36. Skipper J. K. and Leonard R. C. *Social Interaction and Patient Care*. Lippincot, Philadelphia, 1965.
37. Barker R. *Ecological Psychology*. Stanford University Press, Stanford, 1968.
38. Duff R. S. and Hollingshead A. B. *Sickness and Society*. Harper & Row, New York, 1968.
39. Bergsma J. and Fieret G. *Naar de dokter en terug*. University of Tilburg. Tilburg 1980.
40. Batenburg V. and Gerritsma J. G. M. Medical interviewing: initial student problems. *Med. Educ.* 17, 235–239, 1983.
41. Tazelaar F. Mentale inconquenties—Sociale restrictiesgedrag Diss. Utrecht, 1980.
42. Bergsma J. and Duff R. S. A model for examining values and decision-making in the patient-doctor relationship. *Pharos* 43, 7–12, 1980.
43. Bergsma J. Evaluatie van een kommunikatieproject in een ailgemeen ziekenhuis. *Mens Ondern.* 76, 5–22, 1966.
44. Crawshaw R. Humanism in medicine—the rudimentary process. *New Eng. J. Med.* 293, 1320–1322, 1975.
45. Ingelfinger F. The physician's contribution to the health system. *New Eng. J. Med.* 295, 565, 1976.
46. Ingelfinger F. Specialty journals in philosophy and ethics. *New Engl. J. Med.* 295, 1317, 1976.
47. Veatch R. Professional medical ethics: the grounding of its principles. *J. med. Phil.* 4, 1–19, 1979.
48. Howard J. Humanization and de-humanization of health care: a conceptual view. In *Humanizing Health Care* (Edited by Howard J. and Strauss A.), p. 90. Wiley, New York, 1975.
49. Cassel E. Illness and disease. *Hasting Ctr Rep.* 6, 27–37, 1976.

PART
VII

The Bioethical Context

Introduction to Part VII

BIOETHICS is an integral component of humanistic care. Bioethics examines ways in which ethical decisions are made in the health care field and specifically deals with such fundamental human issues as rights of patients, quality of life, autonomy, confidentiality, and informed consent. It is vital that health professionals understand the role of bioethics so that they can appropriately identify and address ethical issues as part of humanistic patient care.

In today's highly technical, competitive environment, the number of choices facing caregivers and managers has grown dramatically. All health professionals face ethical dilemmas and decisions, regardless of their job description and practice setting. Bioethics does not provide easy answers; rather, it serves to structure the way in which health professionals deal with these issues.

Medical paternalism, the idea that the caregiver always knows what is best for the patient, lies at the heart of traditional medicine. In an effort to counteract the effects of this paternalism, medical ethicists have generated a model of patient autonomy for the physician-patient relationship. In "Beyond Medical Paternalism and Patient Autonomy: A Model of Physician Conscience for the Physician-Patient Relationship," David Thomasma concludes that neither paternalism nor autonomy is a unique characterization of the physician-patient relationship: the relationship necessarily must include both attributes. Paternalism by itself does not respect the rights of adults to self-determination, and autonomy alone does not respect the principle of beneficence that leads physicians to hold that acting on behalf of others is essential to their work. Instead, Thomasma proposes a model designed to meet the needs of patient and caregiver that combines for their mutual benefit aspects of both paternalism and autonomy.

In his article, "The Moral Responsibility of the Hospital," Richard De George distinguishes the moral responsibilities of the hospital as an institution, from the personal and professional morality of the people who work within it. He recites specific situations in which hospital, personal, and professional obligations interrelate. He suggests that the hospital's paramount moral responsibility and its primary moral obligation are to treat patients as persons worthy of respect while providing them with the best care possible with the resources available to the community. If the hospital is to fulfill this responsibility, he concludes, its procedures and practices must be so structured that patients receive quality care and receive it with dignity.

With De George's institutional analysis as a background, we present an article by Kurt Darr, Beaufort Longest, Jr., and Jonathon Rakich, "The Ethical Imperative in Health Services Governance and Management." These authors focus on applied ethics in relation to health services management, suggesting that the effective use of applied ethics enhances the patient-centered purpose for which health services organizations exist. The article discusses the ethical aspects of such issues as consent, confidential information, and resource allocation, and analyzes the significance of organizational philosophies, ethics committees, and ethicists.

16

Beyond Medical Paternalism and Patient Autonomy: A Model of Physician Conscience for the Physician-Patient Relationship

David C. Thomasma

THE DOCTOR-PATIENT RELATIONSHIP is a rich and varied partnership. No single characterization can properly do justice to this relationship, given the complexity of professional styles, patient expectations and values, and contexts in which the relationship is established. In this essay, I propose a model of the physician's conscience as a means for resolving the difficult problems that arise when a physician adopts either a model of medical paternalism or patient autonomy for the relationship. The core of traditional medicine has been paternalism; the purpose of offering a model of the physician's conscience is to modify this core.

My exploration of this topic is prompted by my dissatisfaction with other models as well: the legalistic model (physician-client); economic model (physician-consumer); contractual model (when the relationship is referred to as a contract between doctor and patient) (1); and religious model (when the relationship is defined as a covenant) (2, 3). The first three models pay insufficient attention to the human factor in the relationship by reducing it to a convenient mode. In fact, the relationship does embody legal, economic, and contractual characteristics, but it is

Reprinted from *Annals of Internal Medicine* 98, no. 2 (February 1983): 243–248, with permission, The American College of Physicians.

more than that. The religious model, although preserving some of the richness of the relationship, strikes me as too pious, bordering on the sacramental. Although I am in sympathy with religious dimensions that may occur in medicine, I am convinced that medicine is distinct from religion, and that the role of the medicine-man or priest is best left behind us (4).

There is another reason for my dissatisfaction with these four models. All four have been introduced to attack the traditional paternalistic model of medical practice but, in trying to root out the causes of excessive paternalism, the new models fail to provide a place for medicine's beneficence.

If the newer characterizations seem innocuous, it is important to realize that the mind catalogues reality according to certain visions, and then establishes expectations and roles that follow from these visions. Admittedly, a paternalistic view of medicine is antiquated and better fits the era of the gentleman generalist. But a model excessively focused on patient autonomy is equally absurd. People who are sick need help; their rights to autonomy should not get in the way of their physical needs.

REASSESSMENT

Reassessing the physician-patient relation has been going on since the Second World War. My contribution to this discussion is distinctive only because it is written by a philosopher with over 10 years' experience teaching in the clinical setting. As a result, my proposal is marked by a wariness about claims for patient autonomy not often found among philosophers.

The reassessment was occasioned by three factors. First, the medical profession had been very paternalistic. But the Second World War was the watershed of a rapid rise in higher education and a complex, technologic society. This rise led to a general mistrust of authority. Second, a combination of existentialist and personalist ethics, and a growing civil and individual rights movements undermined the one-sided code of professional standards. Existentialism was a post-war philosophical movement stressing personal development, individual ethical responsibility, and the importance of each gesture in day-to-day life, as opposed to community standards, political authority, and social obligation. Self-determination rather than acting from accepted practice was encouraged. Pellegrino (5) has written in this regard "Professional ethics derived from the existential situation of the patient are more authentic and more human than the traditional ethics derived from the self-declared duties of the profession."

The third factor is technology itself. Medical technology has its own economic and moral system, requiring more attention to the human values once taken for granted in the physician-patient relationship (6). Medical technology introduces a fourth party—the machine and its technician—into the physician-patient-insurance triangle. The patient often has more contact with the technician, especially in serious illnesses, than with the physician. Because of the pervasiveness of technology, many moral problems are resolved by technologic solutions, although we are not yet sure whether technology has a true, social good (7). In effect, we simply postpone the moral question until it becomes unavoidable—when, for example, we must propose criteria for selecting patients for exotic treatment. Finally, the unforeseen consequences of technology often leaves the feeling that the future of medicine will take rational control out of human decision making.

The problems associated with technology in medicine show the need to pay more attention to the human factor in the medical relationship. In my opinion, this factor is ignored in the models being proposed for modern medicine.

Before we turn to the proposal being made, there are certain terms that must be defined. The clash between paternalism and autonomy lies at the heart of many medical ethics problems. Questions about the roles of physicians and patients in difficult cases occupy much of our time. Should an aged patient's request to die be honored, or a teenager's refusal of life-saving therapy (8)? In the main, most moral thinkers would agree with Childress (9) that paternalism is wrong, justified only under the most stringent conditions. To understand this claim, it is necessary to agree on definitions of paternalism and autonomy.

Paternalism is an action taken by one person in the best interests of another without their consent (10). Paternalism is problematic precisely because it is difficult to defend the notion that the physician has better insight into the best interests of the patient than the patient. Paternalism comes in two forms. Strong paternalism is that exercised against the competent wishes of another. For example, the doctor in the Broadway play *Whose Life Is It, Anyway?* gives the main character, a quadriplegic, a sedative against his expressed wishes not to receive it. However, strong paternalism in modern medical practice is not as prevalent as weak paternalism.

Weak paternalism is an action taken by a physician in the best interests of a patient on presumed wishes or in the absence of consent for those who cannot give consent due to age or mental status. In some instances, weak paternalism is practiced when a physician ascertains the best course ahead of time and presents this option to the competent patient. Although the patient could refuse, other options are closed ahead of time in the hopes of persuading the patient to choose what is in his or her best interests. Ackerman (11) has argued that weak paternalism is justified in some instances of research on children. Few other defenses of weak paternalism are found in the literature.

On the other hand, patient autonomy has many champions. The term "autonomy" stems from the Greek for "self-law or rule." Kant made the concept the heart of his moral theory by proposing that the self, through duty, is the ultimate origin of law. Similarly, John Stuart Mill (12) proposed that a person cannot interfere in the freedom of others unless they may cause harm or cannot foresee the consequences of their action (for example, they are acting out of ignorance). In his classic exploration of the concept, Dworkin (13) argued that autonomy entailed authenticity and independence; that is, freedom of action (independence) and the assurance that motives for action were one's own motives (authenticity). These concepts were used by Cassell (14) to argue that the proper object of medicine is to reestablish autonomy.

I have kept my definitions as broad as possible and as close to their everyday understanding in order to encompass the greatest variety of opinions in examining this issue. To narrowly define the terms, as some ethicists have done, is the same as predetermining one's stance on the issue. For example, Culver and Gert (15) note that Childress' (10) definition of paternalism involves conflicting meanings, Buchanan's (16) is too narrow in the kinds of moral rules that are violated, and Dworkin's (13) is too dependent on legal cases and narrower still in its inclusion of coercion and interference with liberty.

Culver and Gert's definition includes the features of my own definition, but with the addition of two qualifiers: that a moral rule must be violated (and thus, paternalism must always be justified), and that the person towards whom one acts beneficially (by preventing an evil) is competent to give consent. I generally agree with the first qualifier, but prefer the distinction between strong and weak paternalism to the second qualifier.

For the purposes of this paper, paternalism should be broadly understood to mean: a medical action taken to benefit a patient; and an action done with full consent of the patient. Although full informed consent is a theoretical ideal, the amount of information patients receive needs to be reasonable, so that they can make a free choice about treatment. Most paternalistic acts violate the reasonableness of the information criterion for two reasons. First, an action may need justification if the patient is competent to give consent, because it violates a moral rule, such as truthtelling (strong paternalism). Or, second, an action may need no justification if the patient is not competent to give consent due to age or mental status (weak paternalism).

Traditional modes of paternalism clash with that autonomy we normally presume adults possess. However, there are two further considerations that cause some discomfort when concepts of paternalism and autonomy are applied to medicine. First, the moral principle of beneficence, acting for the good of others, is an inherent ethical foundation of medicine. Most often beneficence is expressed by the axiom of nonharm (4). It is important to preserve beneficence even if its paternalistic aspects are removed. Provider-client and provider-consumer models fail to show the ethics of medical practice in this regard. Second, the conscience of the physician, which I define as prudential judgment, not the superego, is not given sufficient place in the models supposed to correct paternalistic tendencies. Prudential judgment encompassing medical and value factors in the physician-patient relation is a hallmark of professional conduct. Because the model of physician's conscience is designed to correct deficiencies in both the patient autonomy and medical paternalism models, I examine the limitations of these models.

LIMITATIONS OF THE AUTONOMY MODEL

Stressing patient autonomy fails to properly respect the realities of medicine. Newton (17) writes that many proponents of patient autonomy assume that medical paternalism has been part of medical practice since Hippocratic times. As a result, the proposed cure tends to be more radical than may be needed if one properly understands the history of medicine with respect to the physician-patient relationship. Only in more recent times, as medicine became more scientific, and the gap in knowledge between the physician and unlettered patient enlarged out of proportion to the decline in numbers of the patient, did objectionable medical paternalism begin to appear (18). Care need not be thought of as paternalistic, but neither must patient advocacy be belittled.

Some philosophers who call for more patient autonomy on moral grounds forget that humans are not totally independent from one another. In other words, there is distinct neglect of human relatedness and, especially, the realities of the physician-patient relationship (4). The source of this atomistic individualism lies in the moral philosophies developed during and after the Enlightenment. One wonders whether these philosophies are valid in our complex, technologic age (19).

The patient autonomy model ignores the impact of disease on personal integrity (20). Although one may agree with Cassell (14) that medicine should restore patient autonomy, one cannot assume that autonomy is preserved in cases of serious illness. Bradley (21) formulates a telling objection to the position of Veatch (1), one of the most prominent philosophers arguing for the patient autonomy model. As Bradley says, "Veatch argues that the relationship between doctor and patient is an equal one, ignoring . . . the fact of illness which places the patient in a potentially vulnerable relationship with his physician . . . Based as it is on a wrong assumption, this model must be rejected when applied to the traditional doctor-patient relationship."

Even the briefest experience in the clinical setting shows that persons who are ill become angry or fearful, overriding judgments they would make in calmer times. A patient has a new relationship with their body, which is viewed as an object that failed the person. Patients become preoccupied with their disease and their body (22), and are forced to reassess their values and goals. These primary characteristics of disease (20) profoundly alter personal wholeness and should change our assumptions of personal autonomy as well.

The guilding principles of healing as moral components of the physician-patient relationship are not recognized in the autonomy model. At the heart of the physician's task is not just the prevention of harms or evils, the only paternalism Culver and Gert (15) feel is justifiable, but the reestablishment of full or partial biological function. Because this reestablishment is a primary need for patients with some degree of life-threatening disease, we can presume that health is of value to them. Acting for this interest without consent, even in the presence of resistance due to denial, fear, or other personal disruption, is acting altruistically and out of a high moral purpose. For this reason, I hold that weak paternalism, at least, does not need moral justification.

Nor does the patient autonomy model encompass the complicated role of context in medicine and in resolving the quandaries of medical ethics. Although general moral principles and our cherished values work for the most part, there are cases where these values are in conflict and priorities must be set. In such cases I find that thinkers like Childress (9), who recognizes the occurrence of such clashes, err on the side of autonomy rather than beneficence, for what I can only call an incorrect meta-ethical view—namely, that rights are always more important than goods. Unfortunately, insisting on rights can sometimes cause death, a presumption that cannot function as an absolute in medicine, which is dedicated to preserving life.

Philosophers often applaud one another for a distinguished tradition of political and ethical libertarianism inconsistent with the everyday realities of human relationships, the impact of disease on persons, and the overwhelming desire patients have for a cure at the expense of normal freedom and routine. Although it is true that occasionally a patient such as a quadriplegic in intensive care will demand rights and recognitions of autonomy over health care, these instances are rare. Most often the medical context permits assumptions of a desire for health as a more primary value to patients than their personal autonomy. Goods, like health, are judged more important than rights.

Finally, patient autonomy models of the physician-patient relationship have their roots in civil and personal rights movements rather than in an ontology of relations. Although no philosopher would disavow the gains made by emphasizing human dignity and rights, it is not surprising that the adversarial presumptions and tone of that movement often are carried over into debates about health care decisions. The vision of doctors as adversaries and the frequent assumptions by medically inexperienced ethicists of sinister practices are simply stereotypes imposed on medicine by the occasional dramatic case, television show, or the civil rights confrontation. In this regard, an ethics of charity, or a religious ethics of compassion for the needy, more closely approximates the ethical nature of medicine than enlightenment-based ethical theories.

LIMITATIONS OF THE PATERNALISM MODEL

Just as formidable objections to the patient autonomy model can be raised, so too can equally important objections to medical paternalism be enumerated. In general, paternalism seems to violate traditional values about persons and their dignity.

The foremost objection is that a physician often cannot heal a person just by curing a disease, especially if the physician systematically ignores or disregards the patient's views. Cassell's (14) argument that restoring function, or curing, should be a secondary aim of medicine, and that medicine's primary aim is to restore autonomy, is well taken. In this sense, healing involves restoring autonomy. For this reason, Culver and Gert (15) are correct, as are Buchanan (16) and Childress (10), to insist that strong paternalism always demands justification because it violates a moral rule. But Culver and Gert do not seem to plumb the depths of the morality of medicine itself. The reason strong paternalism is objectionable is not only that it violates moral rules but that it violates the aim of medicine itself, which is to heal.

Strong paternalism lacks respect for the civil rights of patients. When strong paternalism appears in medical practice, it violates those rights by assuming that a person cannot manage his or her own affairs. To overturn such rights demands justification.

Medical paternalism fails to capture an essential element of deontological ethics, which is also at the core of medicine. The element is respect for persons (23). Lack of respect for persons means that medicine does not attend to the needs of others, despite all protestations to the contrary. Acts of medical paternalism, such as failing to discuss all options with a potential bypass patient, can be a form of medical failure as well as ethical failure.

As with the patient autonomy model, medical paternalism also fails to distinguish contexts and their role in medical and ethical decision making. As a consequence, medical paternalism tends to become a stance or style, an authoritarian posture that may have been valid in one context (as in an intensive care unit) and extrapolated to others. Or it may have been suggested by a profound experience in which a physician saved a patient's life by adopting paternalism, and now applies it to all patients. The weakness in this approach lies in the invalid generalization of an experience with one patient or a number of patients into a moral posture.

Perhaps the biggest failure of the medical paternalism model is that it imposes relative values on patients as if these values were absolute. For example, a physician may decide with a surgeon that a bypass operation should be done to save a patient's life, but the patient may have already expressed fears and doubts about the operation, preferring to try calcium inhibitors instead. When the physician tries to talk the patient into having the operation "for his own good," the physician is acting paternalistically, although no coercion or interference in liberty of choice has occurred. The physician is acting as if the values implied or expressed in the discussion with the surgeon—the preservation of life by preventing a possible occlusion—should be taken as absolute and take precedence over the patient's wishes. The patient's wishes may be colored by fear but may also embody values regarding the body, family, and so on.

The values expressed by medical personnel are often accepted by patients. This does not mean that these values are absolute. When, from time to time, patients object to or reject those values, it does not mean that the physician's competence and dignity is automatically called into question. Instead it should remind us that the values of medicine are relative.

THE CONSCIENCE MODEL

Given the shortcomings of both the patient autonomy and medical paternalism models of medical practice, is there an alternate that is not reductionist or does not unduly stress one or the other model? I suggest there is. I call it the physician's conscience model. If space permitted, this model would be balanced with a comparable model of patient conscience as well; the complexity of the physician-patient relation can never be adequately described in a single model. The purpose of sketching the physician's conscience model is to circumvent the substantial problems with models I have already mentioned, although this is not to claim that the physician-patient relationship has been adequately defined by this model.

There are six major features of the model. First, the aim of medicine should be seen as a form of beneficence. Beneficence, acting for the benefit of another, responds to a plea for help. When medical help is requested, the appropriate response is to offer the best judgment of the patient's condition. There are three elements of medical beneficence. The first is the care of the patient. The patient's problems are the primary concern of the physician: all other concerns must be secondary. Second, do no harm. Beneficence requires the traditional ethical principle of medicine, because a physician cannot care for a patient while attempting to harm them (24). In other words, ethical judgment is an inherent part of every case in medicine, an essential component of medical judgment. Third, both autonomy and paternalism must take a secondary place to beneficence. That is to say, the choice of a style emphasizing autonomy or paternalism should be based on the needs of the patient rather than the intellectual convictions of the physician.

The second feature of this model is a focus on the existential condition of the patient, as Pellegrino (5) argued, rather than on traditional professional codes. A good example of this focus can be found in Siegler's (25) list of criteria used for deciding the limits of autonomy to be accepted by a physician treating a seriously ill patient. These criteria include the patient's ability to make rational choices about care; the nature and past values of the patient; the age of the patient; the nature of the illness; the values of the physician who must make choices in the care of the patient; and the clinical setting, especially the diffusion of care. Note that the first four items deal with the personal condition of the patient, and the last two only deal with the health care professional and environment.

Third, all elements of the physician-conscience model are recognized as having a value. This model requires the knowledge to identify, rank, and make decisions about values (26). One of the problems with the autonomy and paternalistic models was that both acquired an automatic quality through the process of extrapolation and generalization. In the physician's conscience model, each patient must be handled individually, not only for the medical but the moral implications as well. No ethical stance is chosen before hand. This is not to say, however, that ethical axioms applied to more than one patient cannot be used, as I will point out.

The fourth feature of the model is consensus. Because there is to be no imposition of values, or decisions made in the best interests of patients without their participation, a consensus with the patient and with other members of the health care team is needed. Admittedly, a consensus model takes time and energy but it also wards off many agonizing hours of conflict later in the course of a serious illness. In fact, one of the temptations of the autonomy and paternalism models derives from the comparative ease of decision making: either the physician makes all the decisions, or the patient is always thought to be right. Both models abandon the rewards and trials of a mutual exchange between doctor and patient.

Indeed, a consensus reached at the beginning of a patient's care should not be assumed to continue as new developments in the case occur. A mutual exchange of views must continue throughout the treatment. The consensus must be monitored for its continued validity.

The fifth feature is a pragmatic moral object, the resolving of difficult ethical quandaries in the treatment of patients by preserving as many values as possible in the case. Ackerman (27) has argued that this moral object should be the goal of bioethics. Whether or not one agrees, it certainly ought to be the goal of a consensus-driven, patient-oriented care approach in which prudential judgment is used to make decisions on a patient-by-patient basis.

Explicit axioms comprise the sixth and last major feature of the physician's conscience model. Just as the physician examines each patient in light of theories or categories of disease and health that span all persons, the prudential judgment used for each patient must adhere to a series of more general ethical axioms, or moral rules. These are necessary to avoid the moral pitfalls of the autonomy and paternalism models. These axioms also function as a summary of the paper.

Axioms of the Physician's Conscience Model

Both doctor and patient must be free to make informed decisions. Because of the necessity to reach a consensus, and to respect the values of both doctor and patient, both must feel free to express their values with sufficient information and freedom from coercion.

Physicians are morally required to pay increased attention to patient vulnerability (4). There is an imbalance of information due to the technical training of the physician which must be righted by conveying sufficient information to the patient who must make decisions (28). There is also an imbalance of power between persons who have the ability to care for their own needs and the patient who does not. Physicians must overcome this second imbalance through an almost excessive attention to the dignity and worth of each person, and by supplying what is needed through care of the patient.

Physicians must use their power responsibly to care for the patient. Because of patient vulnerability caused by the assault illness represents on personal integrity, the imbalance of power between patient and physician will always continue to some extent. The power the physician derives from the imbalance must be used to restore as much patient autonomy as is possible. The requirement of self-regulation in the medical profession as a whole is derived from the peculiarities of the physician-patient relationship, and not wholly from the self-professed aims of the profession or the expectations of society.

Physicians must have integrity. The primary quality of a physician must be the ability to make prudential judgments while considering the particulars of a case, the general features of the disease, and universal moral principles. It has become fashionable to downplay the importance of moral character in educating physicians in a pluralistic society, because no one wishes to impose values on others (29). However, educators may find that in a sea of relativism, there are characteristics of moral and medical judgment that must apply to all physicians. Exhorting physicians to follow this coherence will depend on training them in it as well. As Aristotle (30) noted, "It is impossible, or not easy, to do noble acts without the proper equipment." To avoid the autonomy-paternalism or the reductionistic models, the interplay between physician and patient in making medical judgments must also occur in making ethical judgments. This skill must be taught, and ought to be the basic objective of all medical ethics and medical humanities programs in medical schools (31).

The physician must have a healthy respect for moral ambiguity. Respect for ambiguity is difficult, especially when by training and disposition physicians aim for clinical closure and problem solving. But in the model of physician's conscience there is no single answer to the dilemmas a physician will face with patients. Respect for ambiguity would permit a physician to rationally discuss alternatives without the pitfalls so aptly described by Alastair MacIntyre (32): "It is a central feature of contemporary moral debates that they are unsettlable and interminable. . . . Because no argument can be carried through to victorious conclusion, argument characteristically gives way to the mere and increasingly shrill battle of assertion with counterassertion."

CONCLUSION

In proposing a model of physician's conscience for the physician-patient relationship, I have tried to show why the consumer, legal, and economic models, as well as the paternalistic and patient autonomy models, are inadequate visions of modern medicine. But I have also shown why each of the last two models has arisen, and why it is dangerous to medicine and its ethics to accept uncritically either model. In the end the danger lies not only in the models' unreality but also in the severe way that they truncate the moral decision-making responsibility of physicians acting in concert with their patients. The axioms I have proposed for the physician's conscience model are not exhaustive. The axioms are indicative, however, of the kind of education in ethical reasoning and its connections with medicine needed for modern practice if it is not to succumb to false arrangements of its present and future challenges.

REFERENCES

1. Veatch RM. Professional medical ethics: the grounding of its principles. *J Med Philos.* 1979;4:1–19.
2. Ramsey P. *The Patient as Person.* New Haven: Yale University Press; 1970: 5–32.
3. Veatch RM. *A Theory of Medical Ethics.* New York: Basic Books, 1981: 324–30.
4. Pellegrino ED, Thomasma DC. *A Philosophical Basis of Medical Practice.* New York: Oxford University Press: 1981:58–81, 77–8, 170–220.
5. Pellegrino ED. *Humanism and the Physician.* Knoxville, Tennessee: University of Tennessee Press; 1979:127.
6. Mamana JP. Ethics and medical technology—crossroads in decision making. *The Hospital Medical Staff.* 1981; November: 18–22.
7. Jonas H. Responsibility today: the ethics of an endangered future. *Soc Res.* 1975;42:77–97.
8. Thomasma DC, Mauer AM. Ethical complications of clinical therapeutic research on children. *Soc Sci Med.* 1982;16:13–9.
9. Childress JF. *Priorities in Biomedical Ethics.* Philadelphia: Westminster Press; 1981:14.
10. Childress JF. Paternalism and health care. In: Robison WL, Pritchard MS, eds. *Medical Responsibility.* Clifton, New Jersey: Humana Press; 1979:15–27.
11. Ackerman TF. Fooling ourselves with child autonomy and assent in non-therapeutic clinical research. *Clin Res.* 1979;27:345–8.
12. Mill JS. On liberty. In: Warnock M ed. *Utilitarianism on Liberty, and Essays on Bentham.* Cleveland: World Publishing Co.; 1962:256–78.
13. Dworkin G. Autonomy and behavior control. *Hastings Cent Rep.* 1976;6(1) 23–8.
14. Cassell E. The function of medicine. *Hastings Cent Rep.* 1977;7(6)16–9.
15. Culver CM, Gert B. *Philosophy in Medicine: Conceptual and Ethical Issues in Medicine and Psychiatry.* New York: Oxford University Press; 1982:126–35.
16. Buchanan A. Medical paternalism. *J Philos Public Affairs.* 1978;7:370–90.
17. Newton L. The patient as responsible adult: consequences of the revised perspective. *Proceedings of the Fifty–Fifth Annual Meeting of the American Catholic Philosophical Association.* Washington, D.C.: American Catholic Philosophical Association; 1982:240–9.
18. Lain Entralgo P. *Doctor and Patient.* New York: McGraw-Hill World University Library; 1969:101–47.
19. Thomasma D. The goals of medicine and society. In: Brock H, ed. *Studies in Science and Culture.* Newark, Delaware: University of Delaware Press. [1984].
20. Bergsma J. Thomasma DC. *Health Care: Its Psychosocial Dimensions.* Pittsburgh: Duquesne University Press; 1982: 81–9, 193–6.

21. Bradley P. A response to the March 1979 issue of the *Journal of Medicine and Philosophy*. *J Med Philos*. 1980;5:213–4.
22. Cassell E. Disease as an "it": concepts of disease revealed by patients' presentation of symptoms. *Soc Sci Med*. 1976;10:43–6.
23. Thomasma DC. The basis of medicine and religion: respect for persons. *Linacre Q*. 1980;47:142–50.
24. Thomasma DC, Pellegrino ED. Philosophy of medicine as the source for medical ethics. *Metamedicine*. 1981;2:5–11.
25. Siegler M. Critical illness: the limits of autonomy. *Hastings Cent Rep*. 1977;7:12–5.
26. Thomasma DC. Training in medical ethics: an ethical workup. *Forum on Medicine*. 1978;2:33–6.
27. Ackerman TF. What bioethics should be. *J Med Philos*. 1980;5:260–75.
28. Canterbury v. Spence. *Federal Reporter*, 2nd series: 1972; 772.
29. Bennett WJ. Getting ethics. *Commentary*. 1980;70:62–5.
30. Aristotle. *Nichomachean Ethics*. In: Melden AI, ed. *Ethical Theories: A Book of Readings*. 2nd ed. Englewood Cliffs, New Jersey: Prentice-Hall; 1967:96.
31. Thomasma DC. Report number 2. *Capstone Conference Workshops: Reflections on the State of the Art*. Washington, DC: Institute on Human Values in Medicine; 1982:66–79.
32. Mac Intyre A. Why is the search for the foundations of ethics so frustrating? *Hastings Cent Rep*. 1979;9:16–22.

17

The Moral Responsibility of the Hospital

Richard T. De George

LITIGATION has become a fact of medical life. Doctors, hospitals, and hospital administrators are frequently named in malpractice suits. In addition to legal liability, doctors and hospital administrators have moral responsibilities—characterized by some of the contributors to this issue as role responsibility. Does it make sense to say that the hospital also has moral responsibility? Is the hospital a moral agent, and if so, in what sense? The question is initially a conceptual one. But if we answer it affirmatively, as I propose we should, then we can appropriately ask what its moral responsibilities are.

I

Different societies have viewed hospitals and their functions differently. At one time hospitals were places where the sick poor were kept quarantined to prevent their infecting the general population. At other times hospitals were conceived of as places where the sick working poor were treated so they could return to work, just as army hospitals are sometimes considered as places where soldiers are treated to enable them to return to battle. A hospital may be run by a single doctor or it may be a vast complex. It may be a specialized (e.g., a maternity or a psychiatric hospital) or a general hospital. It may be private and run for profit, or public and a non-profit institution. It may be incorporated or not.

The Journal of Medicine and Philosophy 7 (1982) 87–100. Copyright © 1982 by D. Reidel Publishing Company. Reprinted by permission of Kluwer Academic Publishers.

Given the many different historical and cultural conceptions of hospitals[1] and the many different kinds of hospitals within our society, it is difficult to generalize about what a hospital is or must be. I shall therefore limit my discussion to one kind of hospital. Though I believe that some of the analysis will be applicable to other kinds of hospitals, I shall not argue that case. The kind of hospital I shall take as my model for analysis is the American general community hospital.

The American general community hospital is usually incorporated. It is supported in part by community funds and charitable contributions, and in part by the fees it charges those who use it. It is a voluntary hospital, rather than an involuntary one to which patients are committed without their consent. Its purpose is to provide medical and surgical treatment to patients admitted for care. It has a constant educative function, whether or not it is a teaching hospital connected with a medical school. It is typically governed by a board of trustees. The board hires a director or administrator or superintendent to run the physical plant and hire the non-medical staff. The board also hires a Chief of Staff responsible for the organization and administration of the medical staff.[2] Nurses form part of the regular staff, as do a wide variety of clerks (who handle records), technicians, dieticians, cooks, housekeeping personnel, and the like. Some doctors are part of the permanent staff. Of these, some doctors are interns finishing their medical training. Other doctors are not part of the staff but have the right to practice at the hospital and to have their patients admitted for treatment.

Though the physical plant is made up of the hospital building and its equipment, the building and its equipment by themselves do not constitute the hospital. The hospital is the complex structure that encompasses those involved in running the hospital, the patients cared for in it, and the physical facilities in which they operate. The hospital can be conceived of as an entity. As a complex organization, it is made up of its various parts. The individuals who make it up at any given time each fill a certain role or perform a certain function, the sum total of which adds up to the activities of the hospital. The hospital, therefore, as a structured organization, is differentiable from any and all of the people who fill its varied roles and functions at any given time. A given hospital may be several hundred years old though none of those who make up the hospital can be that old. A given hospital as an entity has continued existence not dependent on the individuals who make it up at any particular time. The hospital can develop and change. As incorporated, it is a legal being; but its unity does not derive from its incorporation. Except for legal purposes it could be the same entity with or without incorporation.

The claim that a hospital is an entity is one that coincides with ordinary usage and common sense. We correctly say that a hospital acts, that it has policies, that it owes debts, that it is efficient or inefficient, that it accepts patients freely or bills them quickly. Yet we also know that the hospital does not act unless those who fill positions within it act, either as agents for it or as participants in its structure. An administrator who orders supplies for the hospital commits the hospital to payment. A doctor who performs an operation in a hospital carries out one of the functions of the hospital.

In order for any being to have moral responsibility it must fulfill certain criteria. Only beings capable of action can do things, perform actions, for which they are responsible. Beings that act are morally responsible for their actions only if they act knowingly and deliberately, i.e., they are able consciously to choose between alternative ways of acting. Conditions that reduce a being's knowledge or that involve internal or external compulsion lessen that being's moral responsibility. Human beings acting under normal conditions fulfill the requirements necessary for moral responsibility. Such responsibility for their actions can appropriately, therefore, be ascribed to people (i.e., they can be held morally responsible). It is appropriately assumed by them.

Hospitals, we have seen, also act. The actions of hospitals affect people. The hospital can be held morally responsible for its actions because its actions are done with knowledge and deliberation in accordance with the rational decision procedure established by the hospital. Thus people can plausibly, intelligibly, and appropriately, ascribe moral responsibility to hospitals and judge the actions of hospitals from a moral point of view. Ascribing moral responsibility includes stating norms to which a hospital should conform, influencing hospitals to adopt these norms, and providing an appropriate basis for applying moral sanctions if the norms are violated.

Though hospitals are moral agents, they are not human beings. They act only insofar as those within them act. The moral responsibility of a hospital, therefore, can only be assumed and met by those within the hospital. The moral responsibility of a hospital may be centered in one person, it may be held jointly by several persons, or it may be distributed among many people.

The moral responsibility of the hospital straddles the distinction between individual and collective responsibility. Viewed as the responsibility of the hospital as an entity, it is individual responsibility. Viewed from within the entity, the responsibility of a one-doctor hospital will be individually assumed. But the moral responsibility of the American general community hospital is appropriately collectively assumed by and distributed to many individuals. Such responsibility is assumed and distributed within any given hospital in a variety of ways.

To gain clarity, we should distinguish between the moral responsibility of the hospital which can be assumed collectively or individually by people within the hospital, from the moral responsibility individuals within a hospital incur as part of their position, from the moral responsibility individual professionals may have in virtue of their role, from the moral responsibility each person has as a member of the human community. Each type of moral responsibility carries with it certain *prima facie* moral obligations. No type always overrides the responsibilities or obligations of another type.

We can distinguish the moral responsibility of a doctor in his role as doctor and a doctor in his role as member of a hospital. We can distinguish the individual responsibility of a doctor for his own actions, from the responsibility he has to help fulfill the general collective responsibility of doctors, from the responsibility he has to fulfill the general responsibility of the hospital. A doctor paid by a hospital and a doctor who simply brings patients to a hospital as a place where he cares for them are both doctors. Their obligations and moral responsibilities as doctors are the same. Their obligations and responsibilities vis-à-vis the hospital differ, and their obligation to assume the moral responsibility, or a portion of it, of the hospital may differ.

The Joint Commission on Accreditation of Hospitals in its 'Standards for Hospital Accreditation' states as its first principle, "The governing body must assume the legal and moral responsibility for the conduct of the hospital as an institution. It is responsible to the patient, the community, and the sponsoring organization" (1966, p. 499). The statement is unclear in several ways. As stated, it might mean that the responsibility for running the hospital falls on the governing body, or it might mean that all the legal and moral responsibilities of the hospital as an institution (unit, entity) should be assumed by the governing body (or must be so assumed if the hospital is to receive accreditation). Neither interpretation seems appropriate. The governing body can be morally responsible for seeing that the structures adopted in the hospital are morally justifiable, and responsible for promoting moral activity on the part of those within it. To some extent the governing body can assume some of the moral responsibilities of the hospital. But it can neither assume nor discharge them all. Though the governing body can see to it that the hospital has the personnel needed to fulfill its responsibilities and obligations, if the hospital does fulfill its obligations, many others within it must fulfill their obligations. The board does not and cannot bear full moral responsibility, if that means relieving all others of it, and it may be incapable of fulfilling some of the hospital's responsibilities at all. Moreover, if the hospital has moral responsibilities, it may be the obligation or duty of some others within the hospital to discharge those responsibilities, even if this requires acting contrary to the directions of the governing board.

Hence the moral responsibility of the hospital is distinguishable from the moral responsibility of the governing board, and fulfillment of the former may become the responsibility of others within the hospital if not fulfilled by the governing board.

The statement of the Joint Commission ascribes to the governing body moral responsibility for the conduct of the hospital. Most governing bodies are composed of a number of individuals. Is the body as such responsible but not the individuals who make it up? Are the body and the individuals who compose it both responsible? Is each individual who makes it up completely responsible for everything? Is each individual responsible only for certain designated areas? Is each individual only partially responsible, with the responsiblity of the body being the sum of each individual's partial responsibility? If a member of the governing body objects to some action as immoral but is outvoted, is he or she morally responsible for the action of the hospital resulting from the board's vote?

These questions form part of the problem of collective responsibility. The questions are the same as we can raise with respect to the hospital as a whole and all its members, agents, and participants insofar as they constitute part of the organization of the hospital. Some may be more responsible for certain actions of the hospital than others. But if the hospital becomes a place for eugenic experimentation or for racial extermination it may be the moral obligation of all of its employees to dissociate themselves from the hospital, even if they are not responsible for adopting the policies in question or are not directly involved in implementing them. For the hospital could not run without its various workers, each of whom contributes something, whether it be doing the laundry or preparing the meals or performing the operations.

Moral responsibility can be collectively held in many different ways. Sometimes it is shared; sometimes, as in a conspiracy, each person is totally responsible for anything done by any other member of the conspiracy; sometimes all share the same responsibility; sometimes each bears a different portion and kind of responsibility which together go to make up the moral responsibility of the hospital. Although there is no single correct way of ascribing or distributing a hospital's moral responsibility, there is frequently a correct way of assigning certain kinds of such responsibility.

The conclusion we can draw thus far is that the hospital can be considered a moral agent that acts, and its actions can be morally evaluated. As such an agent, the hospital can have moral responsibility. The responsibility to act in certain ways falls upon those who make up this hospital. Such responsibility may be collectively or individually assumed. It may be collectively distributed and assumed in many different ways, one of which may be appropriate for one moral responsibility and others of which may be appropriate for other moral responsibilities. These conclusions, however, are formal. We can understand them better by applying them with respect to specific instances of the moral responsibility of hospitals.

II

If we turn from the concept of the hospital as moral agent and the collective responsibility involved in such moral agency, to the content of the moral responsibility of the hospital, we turn to normative ethics. Since the hospital in any age or society is a creation of the society, its moral responsibility is a function of its mission in that society. The hospital, just as any other entity, be it a business corporation, a government, or an individual human being is bound by the general laws of morality. A hospital is morally bound not to cheat its patients, not to lie to them or misrepresent its services, and so on. But beyond that it is morally responsible to fulfill the specific goals for which it is established and supported by the community. Consequently, what may be right for one kind of hospital in a certain society at a certain time might be wrong for another hospital.

Once again I shall take as my model the voluntary American general community hospital. As a community hospital it represents community values and is established to achieve certain ends. These ends are no longer isolation of the poor with communicable diseases or the mending of the worker so he or she can return to work.

The American general community hospital has a variety of ends. Let me suggest, however, that its paramount moral responsibility and its primary moral obligation is to treat patients (and potential patients) as persons worthy of respect while providing them with the best care possible with the resources available to the community. This responsibility is consistent with the American Hospital Association's Statement on a Patient's Bill of Rights,[3] and makes it possible to derive those rights. If the hospital's paramount moral responsibility is to the patient, that responsibility takes precedence, at least in general, over the hospital's moral responsibility to the doctors, nurses, and non-medical staff. The implications of this are important.

The obligation to treat patients with respect can be viewed as a specific application of the Kantian formula that everyone should be treated as an end, not as a means only. But the statement of the paramount responsibility of the hospital goes beyond this. It specifies that the hospital is established primarily for the good of the patients and therefore gives them preference. The hospital may be viewed by some doctors as the place where they send their patients for the care the doctor wishes to provide or have provided. But if the hospital has moral responsibility for treating patients with respect, then the hospital, if it is to fulfill this responsibility, must be so structured that every patient is so treated. The hospital has this responsibility to every patient, whether cared for by a private physician or by a regular staff physician. The hospital is not simply a boarding house for patients or a way-station for doctors to send their patients.

When the hospital is responsible for providing the best care available to its patients within the resources available to it, if a particular doctor proves incompetent, the hospital should make good his failure, if possible. It should also insure the welfare of future patients by removing incompetent doctors, if necessary, or by denying them access to use of the hospital's facilities.

This responsibility of the hospital, as we noted earlier, just as every responsibility of the hospital, must be assumed by some person or group in the hospital. To see on whom this responsibility falls we must look at the structure of the hospital. Many community hospitals have an authoritative, hierarchical structure with respect to the administration of the hospital and a quasi-autonomous structure with respect to physicians. Each physician may be more or less independent, mapping out his or her own responsibilities. Where such autonomy reigns, there is a collective responsibility of all the doctors to establish standards for the protection of the good of patients. They are collectively responsible for establishing procedures to review each other's practice, to detect and punish, where necessary by expulsion, moral lapses and immoral treatment of patients. The collective responsibility in this case falls on all of them, though department heads and the Chief of Staff may have the additional responsibility to take the initiative in seeing that proper standards are adopted and procedures for enforcement established. The members of the governing board are also responsible to see that proper standards are adopted and procedures established.

If we take respect for the dignity of the patient as a human being as paramount, then patients are not simply specimens to be examined, interesting cases on which interns learn their art, or means to the ends of medicine. One consequence is that the decision about how patients are to be treated in hospitals is not simply a medical matter and hence not something to be decided only by physicians. A doctor in the practice of his profession may know better than the layman the newest surgical techniques, the latest drugs and procedures for treating certain ailments. But his expertise in this area does not entail his expertise in treating people as ends in themselves. If the paramount responsibility of a hospital is to its patients and not to its doctors, then the hospital should decide what is for the good of the patient—not in the sense of prescribing specific therapy—but in the sense of establishing procedures in which the rights of the patient are protected against possible encroachment by all, physicians included.

The dignity of human beings comes from the fact that as ends-in-themselves they are autonomous, can set their own ends within the broad range of what is rational and moral. They deserve, therefore, to have all the information necessary for them to make choices concerning their treatment and well-being. Just as there is danger in having doctors establish routines that suit doctors rather than routines that suit patients, so there is danger in having hospital administrators establish practices that suit the hospital and its staff rather than patients.

If the treatment of patients as ends-in-themselves worthy of respect really is a paramount moral injunction for a hospital, then it takes precedence over other moral injunctions. It means that the good of the patient should be considered first, and the rules and structures that are developed should be developed from a point of view that justifies consideration of the patient first. The convenience of the physicians, of the staff or of the administrator should all come after the good of the patient. Each hospital rule should be evaluated from this point of view. Is the practice, for instance, in some hospitals of awakening patients at dawn and feeding them early, for the benefit of the patient? If so, it is morally justifiable. If it is for the benefit of doctors who want early rounds so they can get to their offices for nine o'clock appointments, and if it is not beneficial for patients, then the practice is not morally justifiable.

The board of a hospital, charged with seeing that the hospital's paramount responsibility is met, should see to it that the rules and regulations, procedures and structures established by the Adminstrator and the Chief of Staff are justifiable in terms of the good of the patients. This covers everything from initial admittance to the hospital and the way potential patients are treated either at the reception area or in the emergency room to the way the final dismissal and billing take place. What happens in between these is of course crucial.

Patients frequently tend to be submissive. Submissive patients who do what they are told are usually considered good patients. Such submission makes many things easier for the staff. This attitude is, therefore, fostered by many hospitals. Is it in the best interest of the patient? Does it treat him as worthy of respect? Does it respect his autonomy? Does keeping information from him respect his autonomy? I shall not attempt to answer these questions in detail. But I suggest that if respect for patients is truly a paramount responsibility, then hospital procedures should be able to be defended in terms of this respect. It is the hospital's moral responsibility to have procedures that accord with this. It falls, consequently, on each member of the various parts of the hospital to think in those terms, to attempt to devise procedures that achieve them, to work to change procedures and practices that do not. Since the responsibility is a collective one, there should be procedures which enable anyone who sees anyone else failing in this duty to report such action without fear of reprimand or loss of job. If a nurse sees that a doctor is not scrubbing as he should before an operation, there should be a mechanism whereby she can let this be known. The collective responsibility of doctors in a hospital is to maintain standards of the practice of medicine and the treatment of patients. Each doctor has the responsibility to live up to the standards himself or herself. But the collective responsibility is to see that all the others do also, and jointly to set high standards with mechanisms for enforcing them.

The implications of the paramount moral responsibility of the hospital that I have touched on here can be drawn out at length. I should like, however, to turn to two specific cases and see how the moral responsibility of hospitals reflects or is connected with the community. The first deals with the amount of expensive modern equipment such a hospital should have. The second deals with policies, such as a Catholic hospital's refusal to give abortions.

If a general community hospital has the moral obligation to treat all its patients and potential patients with respect, then it needs the facilities and personnel necessary to make this possible. It can fulfill the moral charge made to it by the community only if it is supported by the community or if it has access to funds through its fee or through other means that make it possible for it to hire an adequate number of trained nurses, and other support staff, to have an adequate number of beds, and sufficiently modern equipment to handle the routine level of practice that every modern community expects. Respect for patients, however, does not mean that every hospital has to have the latest equipment available in all areas of medicine, no matter what the cost.

A community hospital that did not have provisions for obstetrical care would be failing its community. A hospital that did not provide for emergency care would be failing its community. For births and accidents are routine matters that occur frequently and are standard expectations of community hospitals. Not every general community hospital, however, need have dialysis machines or CAT scanners. These are expensive and specialized kinds of equipment. Whether a hospital needs such equipment and should have such equipment depends on the call for such equipment in the community, the availability of trained people to use the equipment, and the ability of the community to sustain the cost. There are some kinds of treatment and equipment that are simply too costly for some hospitals. The hospital does not act immorally in not having equipment it cannot afford. It must consider, moreover, whether if it does get such equipment the community can afford it. The decision, I suggest, is not one to be made by the medical staff or by the administrator. It might be made by the board if the board is truly representative of the community. But the board frequently is not truly representative. And if it acts out of the desire for prestige rather than the good of the community, it acts immorally.

Concern for the will of the community, for considering the effect of prices of hospital care on the members of the community, are real concerns with moral dimensions that a board of trustees should not overlook.

The second case concerns policies of a hospital. May a hospital adopt a moral stance on an issue and enforce that moral norm by refusing or mandating treatment?

No one can ever have the moral obligation to do what is immoral. Respect for persons also involves respecting their consciences and not forcing them to do what they believe is immoral. A hospital that wishes to be moral, therefore, should make it possible for those within it not to be required to do what they consider immoral. A standard case is the performance of or assisting at an abortion. If a hospital is to respect the conscience of its doctors and nurses, then it cannot force them to do what they consider immoral. If either doctors or nurses feel that an abortion is the killing of an innocent human life and so immoral, then the hospital should make it possible for them not to be required to perform or assist at abortions. In this case, what the doctor might be expected to do as a doctor in the hospital may conflict with what his conscience tells him he can morally do. He is morally required not to do what is immoral. Many hospitals make provisions for doctors and nurses to be excused in such cases. Those that do not, when it is possible to do so, fail to respect the conscience of its staff and so act immorally.

What, however, of a hospital that believes that abortion is immoral and refuses to allow such procedures to be done at the hospital? Suppose a woman has just been raped, is taken to the emergency room, and the community law requires that she be treated in such a way as to prevent possible pregnancy. Is the patient's right being violated by a refusal to provide such treatment and can a hospital go against what is required by law? Can it censure a doctor or nurse for performing such an abortion?

The hospital has the moral obligtion to respect the consciences of all involved. A Catholic hospital can be expected to follow Catholic moral doctrine. If this precludes abortion, then the hospital, just as individual moral agents, acts appropriately in refusing to peform a medical practice it considers immoral. What of doctors or nurses who work there? They are bound by the practice of the hospital. If they think it is immoral not to perform abortions in certain cases, and they feel morally impelled to perform them in those cases, then they should not accept employment in such hospitals. While a hospital can relieve someone from performing a procedure the person objects to on moral grounds, that is different from allowing someone to perform a procedure that the hospital believes is immoral. Allowing someone to opt out allows someone else to do the act instead. But if the act is believed to be wrong, the hospital cannot morally allow it to be done in its facility.

What, however, of the right of the woman and what of the law that protects her? The reply is that the law cannot change the morality of an act. The law cannot morally force a hospital to do what the hospital on defensible grounds believes to be immoral. The woman, however, has the right to know what is *not* being done to her that is standard procedure elsewhere in the community, as well as knowing what is being done to her. She should therefore be informed about the matter in detail. It should be up to her whether she wishes to go elsewhere to get done what the hospital in question will not do. Complete information is her right and only by giving her complete information can the hospital fulfill its moral obligation to treat her with respect. The hospital has no right to keep the information from her, and if a procedure is mandated by law she should be informed clearly and fully that it is not being carried out and why it is not being carried out.

This analysis is not the last word on what is a complex moral issue. But if this and the other normative analyses I have given in this paper are plausible and persuasive, then they add weight to the conceptual analysis of the hospital as moral agent with which I began. To the extent that the initial distinctions have been fruitful in handling moral issues that are otherwise intractable, the case for adopting the distinctions is bolstered. The normative analyses in this way lend support to the claim that hospitals are moral agents, morally responsible for their actions, their policies, and their structures. As organizations rather than human beings, however, they are not ends-in-themselves, and their concrete moral responsibilities can only be fully explicated in light of their multiple relations to those who act for them and to the community of which they are a part and which specifies their ends.

NOTES

1. For the history of the development of the modern hospital, see Bochmeyer and Hartman (1943), Churchill (1949), Poynter (1964), and MacEachern (1962).
2. On the organization of hospitals, see Freidson (1963), Freidson (1970), and Georgopoulous and Mann (1962).
3. The Bill of Rights concludes: "All these activities must be conducted with an overriding concern for the patient, and, above all, the recognition of his dignity as a human being. Success in achieving this recognition assures

success in the defense of the rights of the patient." (American Hospital Association, 1967).

REFERENCES

American Hospital Association: 1973, *Hospitals* 47, 41. Reprinted in *Ethics in Medicine: Historical Perspectives and Contemporary Concerns*, ed. by S. J. Riser, A. J. Dyck, and W. J. Curran, MIT Press, Cambridge, Mass., pp. 148–149.

Bochmeyer, A. C. and Hartman, G. (eds.): 1943, *The Hospital in Modern Society*, The Commonwealth Fund, New York.

Churchill, E. D.: 1949, 'The development of the hospital', *The Hospital in Contemporary Life*, ed. by N. W. Faxon, Harvard University Press, Cambridge.

Freidson, E. (ed.): 1963, *The Hospital in Modern Society*, The Free Press of Glencoe, New York.

Freidson, F.: 1970, *Profession of Medicine*, Dodd, Mead & Co., New York.

Georgopoulous, B. S. and Mann, F. C.: 1962, *The Community General Hospital*, Macmillan, New York.

Joint Commission on Accreditation of Hospitals: 1966, 'Standards for hospital accreditation', in *The Medical Staff in the Modern Hospital*, ed. by C. W. Eisele, McGraw-Hill, New York.

MacEachern, M. T.: 1962, *Hospital Organization and Management*, Physicians' Record Co., Berwyn, Ill.

18

The Ethical Imperative in Health Services Governance and Management

Kurt Darr • Beaufort B. Longest, Jr. •
Jonathon S. Rakich

INTRODUCTION

WHAT IS ETHICAL in this situation? Which interests should be considered? These questions increasingly affect those governing and managing health services organizations. This article suggests a construct in which to consider them.

Some may see a direct correspondence between law and ethics, that is to say, "Whatever is legal is also ethical, and vice versa." This need not be the case and isn't necessarily true for several reasons. The most important is that law provides only the minimum standard of performance, either positive or negative (but usually the latter), expected from members of society. Professions demand compliance with the law but add other duties and hold members to a higher standard. This means that even when the law does not require a certain activity of *any* citizen, including a specific group, a profession's code may. This makes an activity legal, but not necessarily ethical. A model showing the relationship of law to ethics has been developed by Verne Henderson.[1] Figure 18.1 presents a matrix of the possible combinations of legal, illegal, ethical, and unethical.

Reprinted from *Hospital & Health Services Administration* 31, no. 2 (March/April 1986): 53–66, with permission, The American College of Healthcare Executives.

FIGURE 18.1

A Conceptual Framework

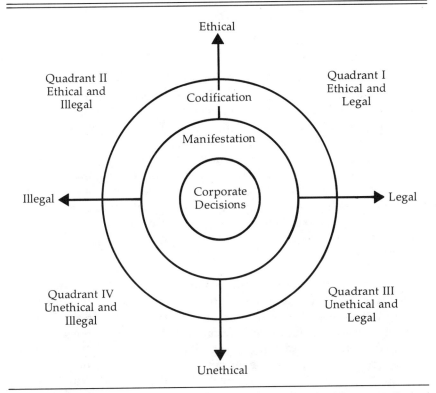

Source: Verne E. Henderson. "The Ethical Side of Enterprise," *Sloan Management Review.* Vol. 23, No. 3, Spring 1982, p. 42. [Reprinted by permission of the publisher, copyright © 1982 by Sloan Management Review Association.]

This article discusses the administrative ethical aspects of issues, all of which have biomedical components as well. Issues analyzed and for which preventive measures or solutions are suggested are fiduciary duty, conflicts of interest, confidential information, resource allocation, and consent. Primarily biomedical ethical issues such as medical experimentation, death and dying, and abortion are not considered.

The technical and complex nature of medical care severely compromises the patient's ability to judge it and effectively interact with care givers. This highlights the need for everyone in the organization to protect and further the patients' interests, whether affected by biomedical or administrative ethics. Since all are moral agents whose decisions and actions have moral implications, this is the ethical imperative for those who govern and manage health services organizations.

GUIDANCE FOR LEADERSHIP

Personal Ethic

Those in positions of leadership have already developed a personal morality—a *weltanschauung*—to guide their lives. This is their personal ethic, and those leading health services organizations consider this an important part of their professional lives. To effectively identify and understand, but most importantly to solve, ethical problems—whether biomedical or administrative—one must have a well-developed personal ethic. Leaders as well as followers in health services organizations apply this ethic in the context of their organization's philosophy—that statement of morality developed by the organization. A compatibility between the two is important to developing an affective corporate culture.

Principles

Implicit in any personal ethic adequate to effectively solve ethical problems will be the presence of four basic principles as they affect the patient: autonomy, beneficence, nonmaleficence, and justice.[2] It is patients the health services organization serves, and all actions must be measured against the goal of protecting them and furthering their interests.

Autonomy means that the wishes of self-legislating (competent) patients are followed, that they are involved in their own care to the extent they choose to be, and that when patients are not self-legislating because they are children or of diminished competence, the organization has special procedures for surrogate decision making or substituted judgments. Autonomous patients are treated with respect; it is unethical to lie to them. The principle of autonomy is especially important in terms of consent and use of confidential patient information.

Beneficence requires a positive duty to contribute to the patient's welfare. This principle has a long and noble tradition in the health professions and is equally applicable to the organization's governance and management. Tom Beauchamp and James Childress divide beneficence into two components: provision of benefit (including prevention and removal of harm) and balance benefits and harms. The latter can be used only to consider the costs and benefits of a treatment or action, not to override the other principles.[1]

The third principle to be included in a personal ethic is nonmaleficence, a duty that obliges us to refrain from inflicting harm. This harm can be mental as well as physical and is readily extended into an organizational setting to issues such as patient privacy. While beneficence is a positive duty, nonmaleficence is negative—refraining from doing something that harms. Beneficence and nonmaleficence affect governing body members and managers in issues such as fiduciary duty, use of confidential information, and conflicts of interest.

Justice is the final principle important to a personal ethic. A major problem is defining what is just or fair. Egalitarians say that it is just to provide like amounts of services to all with similar needs. Libertarians stress merit and achievement as measures of what is just. Aristotle asserted that "equals" should be treated equally, "unequals" unequally. An interpretation of Aristotle's view means that most medical care should go to those in greatest need, since in terms of health they are situated unequally. There is broad latitude in developing the specific content of the principle of justice, but there are limits, nonetheless. Considerations of justice have most apparent application in resource allocation.

These principles are found explicitly or implicitly in codes of ethics propounded by various professional groups. The American College of Healthcare Executives' Code of Ethics is among the most comprehensive, but even it is specific and precise *only* on conflicts of interest. Governing body members and managers should look to organizational philosophy and professional codes for assistance, but they can only be effective leaders if they have a well-developed personal ethic that includes attention to the principles of autonomy, beneficence, nonmaleficence, and justice.

ETHICAL ISSUES AFFECTING GOVERNANCE AND MANAGEMENT

Fiduciary Duty

Fiduciary is a concept that arose from Roman jurisprudence and means that certain obligations and duties are present in a relationship. A fiduciary is someone with superior knowledge or position, and neither may be used ethically for personal gain. This requires managers to act only in the organization's best interests, with the caveat that the independent duty of the moral agent toward the patient cannot be ignored.

Governing body members of both for-profit and not-for-profit corporations have a fiduciary duty. The legal standard for meeting this obligation is more demanding when governing body members are true trustees, i.e., they hold title to the assets and administer them to further the purposes of the trust.

> Loyalty means that the individuals must put the interest of the corporation above all self-interest, a principle based on the biblical doctrine that no man can serve two masters. Specifically, no trustee is permitted to gain any secret profits for himself, to accept bribes, or to compete with the corporation.
>
> The fiduciary duty of responsibility means that members of the governing board must exercise reasonable care, skill, and diligence proportionate to the circumstances in every activity of the board. In other words, the trustees can be held personally liable for negligence, which can be an affirmative act of commission, or omission.[4]

The legal standard sets the tone for ethical guidelines, but should be considered only a minimum. Managers are not fiduciaries in the same sense as are governing body members, but they have similar ethical responsibilities in the terms of loyalty and a duty to avoid conflicts of interest. The American College of Healthcare Executives' "Code" recognizes these duties.

Conflicts of Interest

Conflicts of interest are major sources of problems in health services organizations. They occur when someone has sets of obligations and duties that are inconsistent—they are in conflict—and meeting one set means abrogating another. Accepting extravagant gifts is an obvious example. Others are more subtle.

Has the manager acted ethically who uses a position of influence and power to gain personal aggrandizement of title, position, and salary at the expense of patient care or other organizational activities? Is the manager behaving ethically who is lax in implementing a more effective patient consent process? Is it ethical for a governing body member whose physical and mental capacities are diminished to remain on the board? Is the manager behaving ethically who insists that all reports to governance be prepared in a manner that inadequately shows negative results? Is it ethical for a governing body member or manager who suspects there are problems in the department of surgery to fail to prove or disprove this suspicion? While problems of these types *may* have legal implications, all raise ethical questions.

The difficulty with conflict of interest is that many types are very subtle and it takes continued questioning and self-analysis to identify them. They are likely to increase as competition intensifies. The College's "Code" and the American Hospital Association's statement on conflicts of interest suggest ways of reducing or eliminating the problem. They concentrate on disclosure of real or potential conflicts of interest, divestiture of outside interests that that might cause a conflict to arise, seeking guidance from the governing body when questions arise, and not participating in or attempting to influence any matter in which conflicts might exist.

Confidential Information

Any unauthorized use of confidential information about the patient or organization is unethical. The most common misuse occurs when employees and medical staff gossip about patients. Though this may seem innocent, it is not, and discussion of patients should be on a need-to-know basis only.

Careless internal use of patient information is the most common problem regarding confidential information, but misusing it in other ways receives more public attention. This latter abuse occurs when patient or organization confidential information is used to benefit an individual or other persons with whom that individual is associated or related. Examples include disclosing information about governing body decision making so associates can make advantageous sales or purchases; giving or selling patient medical information to the media or attorneys; and making marketing strategies available to competitors, whether for profit or revenge.

An example with potential for both conflicts of interest and misuse of confidential information is found when the health services manager serves on the governing body of another health services provider or planning agency. Allegiance to one's organization conflicts when another's certificate of need or marketing activity is considered. A more subtle problem arises when those in such a situation become privy to information important for business purposes or planning in their own organization. Regretfully, the importance of that type of confidential information in a competitive environment may necessitate that managers and governing body members avoid all involvement with any potentially competing organization.

The College's "Code" views misuse of confidential information broadly and prohibits all that are inappropriate. It is immaterial that the organization is unharmed.

Resource Allocation

The process of resource allocation has recently received more attention as an activity raising ethical issues. Whether macro or micro, it necessitates making decisions—literally who gets what, when and how. This means making judgments about importance, worth, usefulness, merit, need, societal value, and the like. Sometimes when the government is involved, decisions are also based on political motives and ideals.

Like governments, all health services organizations make macro allocation decisions. Micro allocation is usually a function of the physician's willingness to refer; the patient's access to services and technologies; and, sometimes, economic considerations. Often, micro decision making is guided (in a sense, prejudged) by policies and procedures of government as well as the organization.

Numerous theories have been developed about making macro allocation decisions. At one extreme are those who argue all technologies must be available to all persons; a corollary of this hyperegalitarian position is that if services or a technology are not available to all, none should receive them. This position is based on the concept that each human being has inherent dignity and thus a right to receive equal health services. Conversely, there are those for whom health services are not a right to be guaranteed by society; rather, they are an earned privilege. This hyperindividualistic position also holds that health services providers have no obligation to those who cannot pay, unless they choose of their own free will and humanitarian instinct to provide care. Between these extremes is a view that society is obligated to develop, encourage, and perhaps even provide health services in limited situations. Medicare and Medicaid are examples where such a position has been adopted.

Theories about allocating exotic life-saving treatments on a micro basis—i.e., to individual patients—have been developed by Childress and Nicholas Rescher. These theories aid decision making about which patients get what. Childress rejects subjective criteria such as future contributions and past record of performance saying that such comparisons demean and run counter to the inherent dignity of the human being. He argues that a system which views as equals all persons needing a certain treatment recognizes human worth, and once medical criteria are used to determine need, opportunities for a scarce treatment should be available first-come, first-served, or alternatively, on a random selection basis, such as a lottery.[5]

Rescher's schema is two-tiered: The first is basic screening and includes factors such as constituency served (service area), progress of science (benefit of advancing science), and prospect of success by type of treatment or recipient, e.g., denying renal dialysis to the very young or old. The second tier deals with individuals and uses biomedical factors (relative likelihood of success for that patient and life expectancy) and the social aspects such as family role, potential future contributions, and past services rendered. If all factors are equal, a random selection process is used for the final choice.[6] Social aspects are the most difficult. They are heavily dependent on value judgments and cause ethical dilemmas when true scarcity exists. For example, the shortage of donor kidneys raises questions about the appropriateness of foreign nationals on transplantation waiting lists.

Each micro allocation theory has advantages and disadvantages. Yet, it provides guidelines that permit the issues to be addressed in an organized and predictable fashion. This may not result in decisions which satisfy everyone, but it has the advantage of systematizing the frameworks for decision making. Public awareness of how choices are made is an important attribute in a democracy.

Consent

The concept of consent began at law as a recognition of one's right to be free from nonconsensual touching. The ethical relationship expands this right and includes the principle of autonomy: self-determination. It also reflects the special trust and confidence (a fiduciary relationship) between physician and patient, as well as that between those who govern and manage the organization and the patient. Inherent in consent is a view of the equality and dignity of human beings. Its emphasis on patients' rights or sovereignty is an idealized view and contravenes long traditions of medical paternalism which put the physician in the role of authoritarian figure who makes decisions in the patient's best interests.[7] Such a history suggests the difficulties inherent in perfecting the principle of autonomy.

The *legal* minimum requires full diclosure about the nature of the condition, all significant facts about it, and explanation of likely consequences that might result from treatment or nontreatment. Ethical guidelines build on this base. The principles described above suggest active patient participation. Guidelines developed by the President's Commission for the Study of Ethical Problems in Medicine and Biomedical and Behavioral Research state that patient sovereignty with complete participation is preferred.[8] The Commission recognized such participation as a goal to be sought rather than a readily achievable relationship.

Organizations generally apply a legally-oriented consent process that focuses on self-protection. There is relatively little emphasis on the ethical relationship with the patient. This is legally prudent, but ignores the separate, positive ethical obligation to maximize involvement of patients out of respect for them and recognition of their autonomy.

SOLVING ADMINISTRATIVE ETHICAL ISSUES

Organizational Philosophy

A crucial starting point for solving administrative ethical issues is that there be a specific statement of philosophy that defines the organization's reason for existence and the goals it seeks to achieve. Such a philosophy must be sufficiently precise and detailed so performance can be reviewed or, even more preferable, evaluated. Anecdotal information suggests that few health services organizations have an explicitly stated philosophy; fewer have philosophies with components specific enough to measure achievement of them. Nonetheless, an implicit philosophy is identifiable for all organizations.

Decisions and actions of governing body and management have a philosophical basis, even if vague or ill-defined. The lack of a stated philosophy providing a basic point of reference encourages inconsistency and a lack of continuity and may lead to contradictory policies and results. Furthermore, it diminishes the organization's ability to develop an effective corporate culture.

Responsible governing bodies will emphasize in their statements of philosophy and mission, as well as derivative policies, the importance of protecting patients and furthering their interests—an application of the principles of autonomy, beneficence, nonmaleficence, and justice. Accountability will be included as inherent in the independent relationship between organization and patient. This relationship results from the fiduciary duty owed the patient as well as the ethical responsibility to protect patients from harm.

This accountability is broad. Some argue it is sufficiently demanding that patients harmed through medical malpractice, but unaware of that harm, should be informed of it by representatives of the organization.[9] A radical view? Perhaps, but one consistent with the high degree of trust the public places in health services organizations and an appropriate measure of the duty that those who govern and manage them should execute in return.

The strategic planning process is also a function of the organization's philosophy, a primary manifestation of which is the mission statement. An organizational philosophy must be articulated before planning objectives can be established. The organization's mission statement reflects ideals—ends thought unattainable—but progress toward which is believed possible.[10] In this respect, perhaps the most difficult aspect is selection of an appropriate balance between social responsibility and economic performance.[11]

Governance and management are responsible for developing the organization's philosophy and deriving the mission and specific operational plans. In addition, management interprets and implements the plans. The dynamic is clear. The probability of an organization's moral survival is enhanced to the extent there is maximum congruity between its philosophy and expressions of the personal ethic of governance and management. This is not to say professional managers cannot work effectively in an organization where there are variances between personal and organizational ethic. But the duty of loyalty and allegiance to the organization requires governing body members and managers to uphold the organizational philosophy until it is at variance with their personal ethic.

None can disregard their role as moral agents whose actions have consequences for patients and others. If they act unethically even at the behest of organization or superior, it is no defense to argue they were only following orders.

Institutional Ethics Committees

As conceived, institutional ethics committees considered a terminally-ill patient's prognosis and assisted in answering the question about ending life support. This concern with biomedical ethical problems was reflected in their membership and purposes. Here, it is recommended they be used to assist in developing and implementing an organizational philosophy and to assist governance and management in identifying and solving administrative ethical problems.

Robert Veatch argues ethics committees can and should have various roles, many of them mutually exclusive.[12] Adopting this view, it is apparent that a committee most likely to be effective in administrative ethics will have fewer clinical personnel and more representatives from governance and management. Clinical personnel must be included because research suggesting organizations are most effective when they involve clinicians in management decision making is also likely to apply to solving problems of administrative ethics.

A national study conducted by the President's Commission about the structure, procedures, activities, and effectiveness of biomedical ethics committees in hospitals suggests some useful parallels as well as pitfalls to be avoided in establishing administrative ethics committees. The Commission reported biomedical ethics committees facilitated decision making when they clarified important issues, shaped consistent hospital policies with regard to life support, and provided opportunities for professionals to air disagreements.[13] The committees were not found particularly effective for educating professionals about issues relevant to life support decisions.

The study also found that only one percent of hospitals had committees; on average they reviewed only one case per year. Although specialized ethics committees, specifically infant care review committees, are rapidly growing in number, anecdotal information suggests there are fewer new biomedical ethics committees with general functions than had been predicted.

One President's Commission finding suggests there are problems with patient autonomy.

> The composition and function of committees identified . . . would not allay many of the concerns of patients' rights advocates about patient representation and control. Committees were clearly dominated by physicians and other health professionals. The majority of committees did not allow patients to attend or request meetings, although family members were more often permitted to do so.[14]

This is a matter affecting resource allocation and consent and should be of vital concern to governance and management.

There is evidence that biomedical ethics committees are most effective when they wait to be consulted rather than interposing themselves. A consultative role means committees make recommendations, not final decisions.[15]

Similar limitations may apply in administrative ethics—depending on the specific facts and issues under consideration. Generally, the committee should be proactive in developing and revising the organizational philosophy and in considering macro resource allocation questions. Similarly, it should take the initiative in reviewing and revising the consent process. However, it may choose a more passive role and wait to be consulted in specific instances of conflicts of interest and misuse of confidential information.

The President's Commission's finding as to the relative ineffectiveness of biomedical ethics committees in educational activities is puzzling and may be an aberration. The composition and experience of an administrative ethics committee will make it a reservoir of knowledge and expertise, and these resources should be made available to the staff. This will generally add sophistication and improve the quality of ethical decision making. Two recent books provide useful information about establishing institutional ethics committees.[16]

Ethicists

Many large teaching hospitals, typically those with university affiliations, include ethicists on their staff. Ethicists are usually doctorally-qualified philosophers who are teaching faculty at a university or medical school. Primarily, they participate in solving biomedical ethical issues. There is no reason, however, why their involvement should be limited in that fashion. Ethicists could aid governance and management as well.

Health services organizations interested in obtaining the assistance of an ethicist should not limit their search to medical schools, but should consider all persons with specialized preparation in ethics and its application in the health field. The literature reports that physicians are more likely to ask assistance of an ethicist than an ethics committee. One reason suggested for this is that committees are not seen as cost effective. Similarly, and beyond considerations of efficiency, it may be more palatable for the typical manager to consult with an ethicist to assist in identifying and analyzing the moral obligations and rights and responsibilities bearing on a case than to seek guidance from a committee.

SUMMARY

Organizational philosophies, ethics committees, and ethicists provide assistance to governance and management. But, as with all tools, those who use them must know when there is a problem and when assistance is needed. This requires governing body members and managers to be sophisticated about the presence of ethical problems. Such knowledge comes with education and experience. More importantly, those who would implement their personal ethic and meet their duties as moral agents must be willing to act. Lacking this, all else is futile.

CONCLUSION

All decision making and activities of health services organizations contain ethical dimensions, whether administrative or biomedical. In this regard, two problems confront managers and governing bodies. The first is to recognize the presence of administrative ethical issues. The second is to apply analytical and reasoning processes to address them, thereby enhancing the quality of decision making. Applied ethics is an emerging aspect of health services management. Its effective use enhances the purpose for which health services organizations exist.

Economic pressure from cost cutting by third-party payors and increased competitiveness affect all health services organizations, but especially hospitals. Governing bodies and managers may be tempted or feel compelled to take actions that negatively affect patients in terms of the principles of autonomy, beneficence, nonmaleficence, and justice. To do so puts them in derogation of their independent moral duty to protect the patient; and, in so doing, they fail to honor the ethical imperative. The potential conflict between economic interests and patient care considerations are not far below the surface in the patient relationship; for those who govern and manage health services organizations, the ethical implications are enormous.

REFERENCES

1. Verne E. Henderson, "The Ethical Side of Enterprise," *Sloan Management Review* Vol. 23, No. 3 (1982): 41–42.

2. Tom L. Beauchamp and James F. Childress, *Principles of Biomedical Ethics.* 2d (New York: Oxford University Press, 1983).
3. *Ibid.*, p. 149.
4. Arthur F. Southwick, *The Law of Hospital and Health Care Administration* (Ann Arbor, MI: Health Administration Press, 1978), p. 47 and 50.
5. James F. Childress, "Who Shall Live When Not All Can Live?" *Soundings, An Interdisciplinary Journal* Vol. 53, No. 4 (Winter 1970).
6. Nicholas Rescher, "The Allocation of Exotic Medical Lifesaving Therapy," *Ethics* Vol. 79 (April 1969).
7. *Making Health Care Decisions.* Vol. 1, President's Commission for the Study of Ethical Problems in Medicine and Biomedical and Behavioral Research. Washington, D.C., U.S. Government Printing Office, October 1982, pp. 2–6.
8. *Ibid.*
9. Kenneth Williams and Paul Donnelly, *Medical Care Quality and the Public Trust* (Chicago: Pluribus Press, 1982).
10. Russell L. Ackoff, *Creating the Corporate Future* (New York, John Wiley & Sons, 1981).
11. James B. Webber, "Planning," *Hospitals* Vol. 56, No. 7 (April 1, 1982): 69–70.
12. Robert M. Veatch, Ph.D., quoted in "Ethics Committees Proliferation in Hospitals Predicted," *Hospitals* (July 1, 1983): 48.
13. *Deciding to Forego Life-Sustaining Treatment,* President's Commission for the Study of Ethical Problems in Medicine and Biomedical and Behavioral Research, Washington, D.C., U.S. Govt. Printing Office, March, 1983, p. 447.
14. *Ibid.*, p. 448.
15. Benjamin Freedman, "One Philosopher's Experience on an Ethics Committee," *Hastings Center Report* Vol. 11 (April 1981): 20–22.
16. William Read, *Ethical Dilemmas in a Changing Health Care Environment: Hospital Ethics Committees* (Chicago: The Hospital Research and Educational Trust, 1983).
Ronald E. Cranford and A. Edward Doudera, eds. *Institutional Ethics Committees and Health Care Decision Making* (Ann Arbor, MI: Health Administration Press, 1984).

Epilogue

" 'Tis remarkable, that nothing touches a man of humanity more than any instance of extraordinary love or friendship, where a person is attentive to the smallest concerns of his friend and is willing to sacrifice to them the most considerable interest of his own. . . . They are the more engaging, the more minute the concern is, and are a proof of the highest merit in any one who is capable of them."

David Hume, *A Treatise of Human Nature*

IN RECENT YEARS, there has been a resurgence of interest in humanistic care. Much of the debate has centered around how the "corporatization" and "technological transformation" of the American health care system has effected its historic altruistic mission. The significance of this debate, in which all health constituencies are participating, lies in the fact that health professionals recognize the positive benefits of humane care and remain concerned about its potential erosion.

For this reason, it is essential to retain—indeed to expand—the focus on humane health care. To that end, we have attempted to assemble outstanding articles in one book so that key issues and perspectives can be accessed, considered, and addressed. As would be expected in the examination of so complex a topic, more questions are raised than are answered.

While there is a committed core of scholars and researchers studying humanism, their numbers are still small when one considers that the mission of those persons, disciplines, and organizations who provide health services is to render personal, compassionate care. The reality is that humanism remains an unfocused and understudied component of professional health services. It is our hope that this book will stimulate further study in this area and support humane practice by all health care professionals.

About the Editors

GERALD P. TURNER, FACHE, FCCHSE, is President and Chief Executive Officer of Mount Sinai Hospital in Toronto, Ontario. He is also an Associate Professor of the Department of Health Administration, University of Toronto, and Immediate Past Chairman of the Ontario Hospital Association. Mr. Turner is the author of numerous articles and has received prestigious awards such as the President's Achievement Award from the Society of Graduates in Health Administration, University of Toronto, and the Extendicare Award from the Canadian College of Health Service Executives for his distinguished contribution to the improvement of Canadian health service management. He is a graduate of Hospital Administration from the University of Toronto.

JOSEPH MAPA, FACHE, CHE, is Vice President of Mount Sinai Hospital and former President of the Association of Young Health Executives, Toronto. Mr. Mapa has received many awards for his articles on health care management. He was a recipient of the Bugbee-Falk Book Award given by the Association of University Programs in Health Administration, Washington, D.C. Mr. Mapa is a graduate of Hospital Administration from the University of Toronto.

Messrs. Turner and Mapa were coeditors of a previous collection of readings on humane medical and institutional care, *Humanizing Hospital Care* (Toronto: McGraw-Hill Ryerson, 1979). In addition, they were coauthors of the consumer guide, *The Choice is Yours: Making Canada's Medical System Work for You* (Toronto: McGraw-Hill Ryerson, 1981).